DOES FEMINISM
DISCRIMINATE
AGAINST MEN?

POINT/COUNTERPOINT SERIES

Series Editor

James P. Sterba, University of Notre Dame

AFFIRMATIVE ACTION AND RACIAL PREFERENCE

Carl Cohen and James P. Sterba

GOD? A DEBATE BETWEEN A CHRISTIAN AND AN ATHEIST

William Lane Craig and Walter Sinnott-Armstrong

DOES FEMINISM DISCRIMINATE AGAINST MEN?

Warren Farrell and James P. Sterba

DOES FEMINISM DISCRIMINATE AGAINST MEN?

A DEBATE

Warren Farrell
with Steven Svoboda

James P. Sterba

OXFORD
UNIVERSITY PRESS
2008

Oxford University Press, Inc., publishes works that further Oxford University's
objective of excellence in research, scholarship, and education.

Oxford   New York
Auckland   Cape Town   Dar es Salaam   Hong Kong   Karachi
Kuala Lumpur   Madrid   Melbourne   Mexico City   Nairobi
New Delhi   Shanghai   Taipei   Toronto

With offices in
Argentina   Austria   Brazil   Chile   Czech Republic   France   Greece
Guatemala   Hungary   Italy   Japan   Poland   Portugal   Singapore
South Korea   Switzerland   Thailand   Turkey   Ukraine   Vietnam

Copyright © 2008 by Oxford University Press, Inc.

Published by Oxford University Press, Inc.
198 Madison Avenue, New York, New York 10016
http://www.oup.com

Library of Congress Cataloging-in-Publication Data

Farrell, Warren.
    Does feminism discriminate against men? : a debate / Warren Farrell,
with Steven Svoboda, and James P. Sterba.
        p. cm. — (Point/counterpoint series)
    Includes bibliographical references.
    ISBN 978-0-19-531282-9 (cloth)—ISBN 978-0-19-531283-6 (pbk.)
    1. Feminism—United States. 2. Sex discrimination against men—
United States. I. Svoboda, Steven. II. Sterba, James P. III. Title.
HQ1421.F38 2007
305.32—dc22   2007005494

Printing number: 9 8 7 6 5 4 3 2 1

Printed in the United States of America
on acid-free paper

Dedicated to Dad, Gail, Liz, and the Memory of Mom and Lee—W. F.

Dedicated to Janet and Sonya, a feminist's feminists—J. P. S.

CONTENTS

PREFACE

If we are to have justified views on any topic, we must take into account important criticisms of our views with respect to that topic. And this is just as true concerning our views about feminism and its relationship to men as it is with anything else. Unfortunately, it has not been easy to bring about respectful exchanges between defenders of feminism and their critics. With this book, we hope to help correct for this deficiency.

We have taken up the question of whether feminism has discriminated against men with respect to military service, healthcare, domestic violence, rape, the criminal justice system, the workplace, divorce, child custody, the media, and public education. One of us, Warren Farrell, argues that feminism has discriminated against men in each of these areas, while the other, James Sterba, argues that feminism has not discriminated against men in each of these areas. It is important to recognize that we regard our exchange as the beginning of a discussion and not its end. Accordingly, we have taken steps to continue our discussion with a public debate at the University of Notre Dame; an Authors Meet Critics Session at the American Philosophical Association Eastern Division Meeting sponsored by the Committee on the Status of Women in Washington, DC; and another Authors Meet Critics Session at the American Philosophical Association Pacific Division Meeting in San Francisco. We truly believe that such open, respectful exchanges, as represented by our book and the events organized around it, are the only way to achieve truly justified views on feminism and its relationship to men—or, for that matter, on any other topic.

Warren Farrell
www.warrenfarrell.com
James P. Sterba
sterba.1@nd.edu

ACKNOWLEDGMENTS

From the day James Sterba asked me to write this book with him to the present, two things have evolved: a book and a friendship. In an era when ideological differences beget war, it is a pleasure to see our differences create only the pleasures of intellectual stimulation and the friendship that emanates from a respect for each other's underlying integrity.

As I updated data I had gathered and written about in *The Myth of Male Power* and my other books, Steven Svoboda was helpful enough to award him with credit on the book's cover. I am very appreciative of the computer support of Tynan Burke, Erik Gordon Bainbridge, and Darius Parsia, the emotional support my beloved wife, Liz Dowling, and the joys of supporting our daughters, Alex and Erin, as they morph into adults.

Warren Farrell

A friendship between Warren Farrell and myself might be thought to be an unexpected consequence of writing a debate book where each of us defends opposing views on a wide range of gender issues. As I see it, a major reason why this occurred in our case is that we are both strongly committed to bridging the gap that currently exists between feminists and their opponents.

You really don't want to know what my contribution to this volume would have looked like without all the help I received. In particular, I want to thank William Bolton, Harry Brod, Cheshire Calhorn, Claudia Card, Victoria Davion, Judith De Cew, Tom Digby, Lin Doversberger, William Edelglass, Donna Engelmann, Leslie Francis, Ann Garry, Jill Gordon, Gillian Havey, Lorraine Juliano, Michael Kimmel,

Dwight King, Kenneth Kinslow, Eva Kittay, Ellen Klein, Janet Kourany, Jane Lyman, Joan McGregor, Amy Mullin, Patti Ogden, Diana Raymond, Alison Reiheld, Claire Rensetti, John Robinson, Sally Scholz, Nancy Snow, Christina Sommers, Rosemarie Tong, Karen Wallace, and Jackie Warrilow. At Oxford University Press, special thanks also go to Sarah Calabi, John Challice, Robert Miller, and Emily Voigt, who went the extra hundred miles it took to make this book possible.

James P. Sterba

DOES FEMINISM DISCRIMINATE AGAINST MEN?

PART 1

Does Feminism
Discriminate Against Men?

Warren Farrell

Introduction

Worldwide, I am unaware of more than a few classes in the social sciences (such as gender studies) that require even one text that offers a male-positive perspective of men. If you've been assigned this book for such a class, you have an exceptional professor. I say this because when I critique feminism's analysis and attitude toward men, I am critiquing the 99 percent of classes and teachers who would not assign this book as a required text. Your professor is obviously an exception.

Everyone's life experiences create biases to which they are usually blind (they see them only as their life experience). I would like to share mine up front.

Although I am critiquing the feminist analysis of men and what I perceive to be feminist dependency on "victim power," my background is as a feminist, and I support the portions of feminism that strive to create new options for women. Because I feel the underlying biology of men and women is to adapt, I see the future as an opportunity to develop more flexible roles than the past allowed. **I feel that the male–female roles that were functional for the species for millions of years have become dysfunctional in an evolutionary instant.** I feel that traditional men and women are incomplete psychologically. In these respects, I differ from most conservatives.

Without feminism, fewer companies would have experimented with part-time workers, flexible schedules, childcare options, and improved safety standards. Without women in police work, few police forces would have discovered that 95 percent of conflicts are not resolved by physical strength; without women doctors, few hospitals would be cutting back ninety-hour work weeks for doctors; without women therapists, short-term counseling and couple counseling would be much less available. The feminist movement has allowed thousands of workplace assumptions to be reexamined; feminism brought into the workplace not only females, but female energy.

When I see girls playing baseball, my eyes well up with tears of happiness (Farrell is Irish!) for what I know they are learning about teamwork. Without the feminist movement, those girls would be on the sidelines. Without the feminist movement, millions of girls would see only one dimension of their mothers and, therefore, of themselves. They would have to marry more for money than for love. They would be even more fearful of aging.

My background as a feminist includes serving three years on the board of the National Organization for Women (NOW) in New York City, starting hundreds of men's and women's groups, and speaking around the world from this perspective during the 1970s and 1980s. In the process, I put tens of thousands of men through "men's beauty contests" to give them an emotional experience of what it was like to be viewed as a "sex object."

Let me share with you first some of the personal reasons I was so receptive to feminism, and then some of what led me to balancing that with equal empathy for men.

Growing up (in the 1950s and 1960s), I had seen my mother move in and out of depression—into depression when she was not working, out of depression when she was working. The jobs were just tempo-rary, but, she would tell me, "I don't have to ask Dad for every penny when I'm working." At forty-eight her depression and a dizzy spell led to a fall that led to her death.

My mother died before the current feminist movement was born, but she would often say, "I'm your mother, not your slave." I can recall coming home after being elected seventh-grade class president, proudly announcing it to her, and saying, "Our class meetings are on Fridays....Could I have an ironed shirt when I have to preside in front of the class?" She said "sure," and without missing a beat, took out the ironing board and showed me how to iron my shirts.

Whether for these reasons or others, when the women's movement surfaced, it made sense to me in an instant. I found myself at the homes of emerging feminist friends in Manhattan, plopped in front of their husbands with instructions to "tell him what you told me." Soon I was involved with NOW, formed men's groups, gave up my position as an assistant to the president of NYU, wrote a book called *The Liberated Man* on the value of women's independence to men, and began speaking around the world on these issues.

Some years later, though, another family experience was to open my eyes differently. My brother Wayne, twelve years my junior, and his woman friend went cross-country skiing in the Grand Tetons. They came to a dangerous pass. It was April, and they both feared the avalanches. Two of them going forward would put them both in danger, yet would give each the opportunity to save the other. Wayne went forward alone. The snow slipped from the mountain, gathered momentum, and tumbled its thousands of frozen pounds over my brother, burying him forty feet under. He would have been twenty-one.

Wayne and his woman friend had unconsciously agreed that it was *his* life that would be risked—and in this case sacrificed—as he and she both played out their roles. I would soon see much more evidence of how deeply ingrained it is both for women to unconsciously expect men's protection (even when it means the man sacrificing his life) and for men to compete to give it in exchange for approval, respect, and love.

The experience with Wayne catalyzed my thinking about male vulnerability. In my presentations, rather than just having men walk a mile "in the beauty contest of everyday life" that women experience, I asked women to experience male vulnerability by asking men out on a "role reversal date" and risking just a few of the 150 or so risks of rejection that men might experience between eye contact and intercourse.

Risking rejection male-style opened up women's eyes to male vulnerability and opened up men's mouths about their feelings, especially feelings of powerlessness that evolve from men's sexual desire—whether they're in college or "single again" after a divorce. For example, a man who talks about the compulsive sexual feelings he has is being vulnerable exactly because he is revealing his compulsiveness. This makes the woman he'd like to feel closer to feel less special, and more distant from him—and therefore makes him vulnerable to losing her love.

I began to see men's vulnerability in other ways. **After divorce, a man is ten times as likely to commit suicide as is a woman.**[1] Why? Because women are more likely to have custody of the children—someone to love them and need them. People who feel loved and needed rarely commit suicide.

And women develop support systems. **Women's traditional support systems support women to be vulnerable; men's traditional support systems support men to be *in*vulnerable.**

This creates a paradox: The support men get to be invulnerable makes them more vulnerable; the support women get to be vulnerable makes them less vulnerable. It is just one example of how women's strength is their façade of weakness and men's weakness is their façade of strength.

Take, for example, the most archetypal of men's support systems—the cheerleader, his football team, and his family. When a cheerleader says, "First and ten, do it again!" she isn't saying "First get in touch with your feelings again." Nor is his coach. Nor are his parents cheering in the stands. All of us are unwittingly supporting him to "risk a concussion again." His motto is, "When the going gets tough, the tough get going" (they don't cry to the school therapist). If, instead of getting a touchdown, he gets in touch with his feelings and quits his position on the team to avoid the concussion, the cheerleader doesn't say, "Next week I'm going to cheer for you—I noticed how open and vulnerable you were when you were playing football." Yes, next week she does cheer. But she cheers for his *replaceable* part.

Expressing feelings of vulnerability brings women affection and men rejection.

For years, as I explained women's perspectives to men, I often noticed a woman "elbow" the man she was with, as if to say, "See, even an expert says what a jerk you are." I slowly became good at saying what women wanted to hear. I enjoyed the standing ovations that followed.

The fact that my audiences were about 90 percent women and 10 percent men (most of whom had been dragged there by the women) only reinforced my assumption that women were enlightened and men were "Neanderthals." Then one day (in one of those rare moments of internal security), I wondered if the reason so many more women than men listened to me was because I had been listening to women but not listening to men.

I decided to experiment with other ways of getting men to express feelings. I noticed men were often most open about their feelings on the first date. On the first date, the woman often used what I came to call "awe training"—those looks of "Wow, that's fascinating" in her eyes (if not in her words). The men felt secure and opened up.

So when men in my men's groups spoke, I exercised some "awe training." It worked. I heard things I had never heard before. Now when women asked, "Why are men afraid of commitment?" or feminists said, "Men have the power," my answers incorporated both sexes' perspectives.

Almost overnight my standing ovations disintegrated. After each speaking engagement, I was no longer receiving three or four new requests to speak. My financial security was drying up.

I would not be honest if I denied that this tempted me to return to being a spokesperson only for women's perspectives. I liked writing, speaking, and doing television shows. Now it seemed like all three were in jeopardy. **I quickly discovered it took far more internal security to speak on behalf of men than to speak on behalf of women**—or, more accurately, to speak on behalf of both sexes rather than on behalf of only women.

I was learning that we live in a world that is gifted of the mouth and retarded of the ear. The real job of this "debate" book, then, is not to teach debate, but to teach listening. Debate training is divorce training. Training to listen is training to love, especially if that listening is with empathy. I've never heard someone say to me, "Warren, I want a divorce; my partner understands me."

Listening Matrix

Female experience of powerlessness	Male experience of powerlessness
Female experience power	Male experience power

I began to visualize a "listening matrix" as a framework within which we could hear these different experiences. It looked like this:

During the past thirty-five years we have taken a magnifying glass to the first of these four quadrants, the female experience of powerlessness. I saw I was subconsciously making a false assumption: **The more deeply I understood women's experience of powerlessness, the more I assumed men had the power women did not have.** In fact, what I understood was the female experience of male power. When a woman is divorced and has two children, no alimony, no child support, and no job experience, that is her experience of powerlessness; when a man is in the hospital with a coronary bypass operation caused by the stress of working two jobs to support two children his former wife won't let him see and feels that no other woman will get involved with him because of those very circumstances, that is his experience of powerlessness. Both feel loneliness. The flip sides of the same role make both sexes feel powerless.

In visual form, the magnifying glass we have taken over the past thirty-five years to the first quadrant—the female experience of powerlessness—gave us the following view of the world.

Instead of understanding male powerlessness, we had come to understand only the female experience of male power. In fact, the greater a woman's expertise on the issue of female powerlessness, the less she tended to understand the male experience of powerlessness. Why? She assumed that female powerlessness meant male power. The imbalance will not be corrected until we hold the same magnifying glass to the second quadrant, giving us the following picture.

The more I immerse myself in life—whether in the life of my wife, Liz; or in the lives of our two daughters, Erin and Alex; or in the world of Israelis and Arabs; or in the world of the United States versus most of the rest of the world—I realize that the development of ideologies is part of the problem. Our compassionate immersion in each other's stories comes closer to the solution.

As I apply this to men and women, I find myself conducting more and more couples' communication retreats (as the schedule on my website, www.warrenfarrell.com, reveals). And so my wish for this book is not that it creates two sides to debate, but two opportunities to listen.

1. DO WE NEED MEN'S STUDIES? HISTORY IS MEN'S STUDIES, RIGHT?

"Feminists call it sexism to refer to God as He; they don't call it sexism to refer to the Devil as He."

Women's studies help us create heroes and role models out of women who deviated from their traditional role (Madame Curie, Susan B. Anthony, Harriet Tubman, Marion Evans [a.k.a. George Eliot]), women whom society did not highlight, but made invisible. As such, it offers women options in place of invisibility, inspiration in place of ridicule. That's one of many reasons women's studies exists and one of many reasons it is important. This is one of many messages I tried to impart when I taught in the Department of Women's Studies at San Diego State University in the early 1980s.

Women's studies courses are the seeds from which the forest of feminism has grown. Over thirty thousand courses are offered at American universities, including about seven hundred majors or minors.[2] A study at fifty-five major universities found that every Ivy League school, with the exception of Princeton, "now offers more courses in women's studies than economics, even though economics majors outnumber women's studies majors by roughly 10-to-1."[3]

In contrast, there are virtually no men's studies courses. The few courses labeled "men's studies" are rarely genuine men's studies, but *feminist* men's studies. Feminist men's studies' courses tell men how they can forfeit power, be less abusive toward women, share the housework, and so on. In feminist men's studies, when men have a disadvantage it is seen as men's fault—whether that disadvantage is dying sooner, committing suicide more, doing worse in almost everything in school, being less likely to attend college, paying for children they can see only as "visitors" after divorce, being more likely to be in prison, being subject to male-only draft registration, dying sooner of 9 of the 10 leading causes of death, suffering 94 percent of workplace deaths, or being more of the street homeless than women and children combined. That is, in feminist studies, women's disadvantages are often seen as men's fault; in feminist men's studies, men's disadvantages are seen as men's fault.

Many women's studies departments have become gender studies' departments, but also only in theory. The male perspective is not dealt with—only the feminist perspective on men. Feminists teaching the men's perspective on men and calling it gender studies is like Republicans teaching Democrats' perspective on Democrats and calling it party politics. Just as it is true that no one has less empathy for Democrats than Republican activists do (or vice versa), so it is also true that no one has less empathy for men than feminist activists do. Feminists call it sexism to refer to God as He; they don't call it sexism to refer to the Devil as He.

Women's studies in its current form is not women's studies—it is feminist studies. A genuine women's studies would involve the views of not just liberal women, but also of conservative women (e.g., Independent Women's Forum; Eagle Forum). Every study of gender should include four perspectives: those of both liberal and conservative women and those of both liberal and conservative men. Gender studies now studies only liberal women's view of women's powerlessness and liberal women's perspective on male power. It doesn't look at liberal or conservative men's view of male powerlessness or liberal or conservative men's view of female power.

What, pray tell, is female power and male powerlessness? For starters, from the *male* perspective, many women have male-paralyzing beauty power, sexual power, verbal skills, and victim power, even as men are paralyzed by their biological instinct to protect women.

As a result of the inattention to male powerlessness and female power, men are as ignorant about their own powerlessness and female power as women in the 1950s were about their own powerlessness and male power. And as a result, men today are psychologically about where women were in the 1950s. **The last half century has not been a battle of the sexes, but a war in which only one side has shown up. Men have put their heads in the sand and hoped the bullets would miss.** The less sense this makes now, the more you need genuine men's studies.

The feminist objection to genuine men's studies sounds convincing: "History is men's studies." Wrong. **History is the opposite of men's studies: History books *reinforce* the *traditional* male role of performer.** The function of both women's and men's studies is to *question* traditional roles, not reinforce them. Women had to question the assumption that they must do the child-raising and couldn't do the money-raising. Men need to question the assumption that they must do the money-raising and can't do the child-raising.

Women's studies is necessary to help women see clear alternatives to traditional roles; men's studies is necessary to help men see clear alternatives to traditional roles. Men's studies is *currently* needed more than women's studies exactly because men's role has been less questioned.

History books, by celebrating men only when they perform, trap men into stereotyped roles even more than they trap women, because when we celebrate and appreciate someone for playing a role, we are really bribing them to keep playing that role. Appreciation keeps the slave a slave.

Men's studies is not for men only. It would help both sexes understand dad: why dads are so often afraid to express feelings; why, when dad becomes eighty-five, he is more than thirteen times as likely to commit suicide as mom; why he is more likely to suffer from problems with alcoholism and gambling; why, after divorce, he often feels the children have been turned against him and the courts have turned him into a wallet.

Because half of the children's genes are their dads' genes, as men's studies helps students understand their dads, it also helps them to understand the half of themselves that is their dads. Men's studies, therefore, does not merely change the student's relationship to her or his dad, but the student's relationship to herself or himself. The corollary is that when women's studies portrays men as the dominant oppressors, and the abusers, molesters, and rapists, it leaves women and men feeling shamed about the half of themselves that is their dads—and, for men, the 100 percent that is male.

Men's studies helps every future mom raise her son more effectively and raise her daughter to learn empathy toward men. Her daughter's empathy is eventually extended toward that daughter's sons. In contrast, a women's studies–only approach toward men leaves her daughter with antipathy toward men that can become antipathy toward her sons.

Men's studies helps both sexes understand all the problems men deal with as a result of a heritage that made men able to be loved and respected only if they were able to kill animals, kill in war, or make a killing on Wall Street. It helps both sexes understand all the problems that I discuss throughout this essay. Without men's studies, gender studies misunderstands not just gender but also women, in the same way that if party politics studied only one party, it would misunderstand not just party politics as a whole but also the party it favors.

Men's studies is not the opposite of women's studies. It doesn't say women had rights and men didn't. It explains that none of our grandparents had rights—they had responsibilities. They had obligations. Making money was not about male power and privilege, but about male obligations and responsibilities. Men who fulfilled their responsibilities most effectively received female love. Men who failed received female contempt.

Men's studies does not say women have the power and women oppress men. It helps us understand that neither sex had the right to play the role of the other sex and that therefore, if power is control over our lives, neither sex had power. For example, most dads prior to the early twentieth century had to forfeit any fantasies of becoming writers, artists, or musicians to get paid enough to feed families of ten. Working as a coal miner was not power. Pay was about the power dad forfeited to get the power of pay—the power to have his children live a better life than his. Men's studies helps both sexes understand why, instead of power, both sexes had roles. It also helps both sexes understand that by definition **a role cannot be power**—again, because real power is control over one's own life. Instead, a role implies that outside forces have control of one's life.

Men's studies explains why, in the past, the dominant force was neither men nor women, but the need to survive—and why the "oppressor" was neither men nor women, but the fear of starvation.

If close to a half century of women's studies without men's studies had only given us an understanding of women while neglecting men, the problem would be easily solvable: Create balance with a half century of men's studies without women's studies. But after a half century, feminism is part of our nation's consciousness like syrup in a pancake: Even if it we attempted removal, the pancake is forever reshaped. For example, who doesn't believe that men earn more money for the same work, or that men batter women more than women batter men, or that women do two jobs while men do one? These beliefs have created a deep-seated anger toward men and have resulted in policies like affirmative action extended to women, and women-only scholarships. Of course, if these beliefs were true, anger would be warranted. In this book, I'll explain why none of this is true. But for now let me deal with the anger.

The anger emanating from women's studies has infiltrated all the leading universities. For example, Chris Roney, a dad in Illinois for whom I had done expert witness work so he could become fully involved with his children after a divorce told me that Raquel, one of his six children, was taking a women's studies class at the University of Illinois. I asked Raquel about her experience in the class.

"Warren, the class is very upsetting to me. They keep saying that dads are not good parents, as if there were no exceptions. But my dad is a wonderful parent. His parenting skills and nurturing are much better than my mom's. But in class, by talking all the time about dads as abusers, it makes people afraid of their dads, and by emphasizing divorced dads as molesters and deadbeats, they make it seem as if a divorced dad would only want to raise his daughters if they had bad motives (like to molest them or avoid child support). It's sickening to me."

I asked Raquel what happened when she spoke up. "If I say something positive about men, there is often a pregnant pause—as if I had made a grossly inappropriate comment. And when I write something positive about men in a paper, I get a bad grade. When I write a paper and take the feminist party line, I always get an A; when I don't, I get a bad grade. This isn't right."

Toward a Solution: Gender Transition Studies

The solution? There should be neither a woman's movement nor a men's movement, but a gender transition movement. A gender transition movement would help both sexes make the transition from our genetic heritage of rigid roles to our genetic future of more flexible roles.

The goal of men's studies, then, is not men's studies. Nor should the goal of women's studies be women's studies. Both should ultimately be leading to gender transition studies. And both should be integrating the perspectives of more traditional men and women.

Either women's or men's studies isolated from the other is the use of taxpayer money to *subsidize mistrust between the sexes.* Gender transition studies is the preparation of the sexes to change together and to replace mistrust with empathy.

This doesn't mean we can jump right into gender transition studies. If we do, the agenda will be set by women's studies: Domestic violence will assume men-as-oppressor; contributions to the family will measure women's housework and neglect men's work; discussions of dating will not challenge women to risk sexual rejection, just blame men when they do it wrong; men's health will be neglected; and so on.

Feminists should be the strongest supporters of men's studies. Why? Ultimately the change in women's roles gets stalled when men's don't also change. For example, moms can't break glass ceilings unless dads are caring for the children.

We're all in the male–female boat together; if women are paddling on the left side and men on the right, and a woman says she wants freedom to paddle on the right, the man had better learn the value of paddling on the left or the boat soon will be unable to steer clear of something that will sink it. When either sex "wins," both sexes lose.

2. DO MEN HAVE THE POWER?

"The weakness of men is their façade of strength; the strength of women is their façade of weakness."[4]

There are many ways in which a woman experiences a greater sense of powerlessness than her male counterpart does: the fears of aging, rape, and date rape; less physical strength and therefore the fear of being physically overpowered; less socialization to take a career that pays enough to support a husband and children, and therefore the fear of economic dependency or poverty; less exposure to team sports—especially pick-up team sports—and its blend of competitiveness and cooperation that is so helpful to career preparation; greater parental pressure to marry and interrupt career for children without regard for her own wishes; not being part of an "old boys" network; having less freedom to walk into a bar without being bothered; and many more.

Men have a different experience of powerlessness. Men who have seen marriage become alimony payments, their home become their wife's home, and their children become child support payments for children who have been turned against them psychologically feel like they are spending their life working for people who hate them. They feel desperate for someone to love but fear that another marriage might ultimately leave them with another mortgage payment, another set of children turned against them, and a deeper desperation. When they are called "commitment-phobic" they don't feel understood.

When men try to keep up with payments by working overtime and are told they are insensitive or try to handle the stress by drinking and are told they are drunkards, they don't feel powerful, but powerless. When they fear a cry for help will be met with "stop whining" or that a plea to be heard will be met with "yes, buts," they skip past attempting suicide as a cry for help, and just commit suicide. Thus men have remained the silent sex and increasingly become the suicide sex.

Fortunately, almost all industrialized nations have acknowledged female experiences. Unfortunately, they have acknowledged only female experiences—and have concluded that women have problems, and men are the problem.

Industrialization did a better job of creating better homes and gardens for women than it did of creating safer coal mines and construction sites for men. How?

Industrialization pulled men away from the farm and family and into the factory, alienating millions of men from their source of love. Simultaneously, it allowed women to have more conveniences to handle fewer children, and therefore be increasingly connected to their sources of love. For women, industrialization meant more control over whether or not to have children, less likelihood of dying in childbirth, and less likelihood of dying from almost all diseases. It was this combination that led to women living almost 50 percent longer in 1990 than in 1920.[5] And it was this combination that allowed women to go from living only one year longer than men in 1920 to living more than five years longer than men in 2005.

What we have come to call male power, then—men at the helm of industrialization—actually produced female power. It literally gave women a longer life than men.

I am unaware of a single feminist demonstration protesting this inequality—or any other inequality that benefits women at the expense of men.

Almost as important as life is quality of life. Women who were married to men who were at least moderately successful were the first passengers on the bus from the Industrial Revolution to the Fulfillment Revolution. The passengers created an almost all-female club.

While the male role in industrialization expanded women's options, it retained men's obligations. For example, men voted for women to share the option to vote. But when both sexes could vote, they still obligated only men to register for the draft.

We are at a unique moment in history—when a *woman's* body is affected, we say the choice is hers; but when a *boy's* body is affected, we say the choice is *not* his—the law requires only our eighteen-year-old sons to register for the draft, and therefore potential death-if-needed.

"A Woman's Body, A Woman's Choice" Versus "A Man's Gotta Do What A Man's Gotta Do"

Even as women were touting equality in the 1980s and 1990s, in post offices throughout the United States, Selective Service posters reminded boys of what is still true today—that only boys must register for the draft—that only "A Man's Gotta Do What A Man's Gotta Do." The actual poster is shown here.

If the Post Office had a poster saying, "A Jew's Gotta Do What A Jew's Gotta Do," or if "A Woman's Gotta Do" were written across the body of a pregnant woman. The question is this: How is it that if any other group were singled out to register for the draft based merely on its characteristics at birth—be that group blacks, Jews, women, or gays—we would immediately recognize it as genocide, but when men are singled out based on their sex at birth, men call it power?

The single biggest barrier to getting men to look within is that what any other group would call powerlessness, men have been taught to call power. We don't call "male-killing" sexism; we call it "glory." We don't call the one *million* men who were killed or maimed *in one battle* in World War I (the Battle of the Somme[6]) a holocaust, we call it "serving the country." We don't call those who selected only men to die "murderers." We call them "voters."

Our slogan for women is "A Woman's Body, A Woman's Choice"; our slogan for men is "A Man's Gotta Do What A Man's Gotta Do."

I am unaware of a single feminist demonstration protesting this inequality—or any other inequality that benefits only women at the expense of men.

The Power of Life

We acknowledge that blacks dying six years sooner than whites reflects the powerlessness of blacks in American society.[7] Yet men dying in excess of five years sooner than women is rarely seen as a reflection of the powerlessness of men in American society.

Is the five-year gap biological? If it is, it wouldn't have been just a one-year gap in 1920. (In many preindustrialized countries there is only a small male–female life expectancy gap, and in their more rural areas men sometimes live longer.)

If men lived more than five years *longer* than women, feminists would be helping us understand that life expectancy was the best measure of who has the power. And they would be right. Power is the ability to control one's life. Death tends to reduce control. Life expectancy is the bottom line—the ratio of our life's stresses to our life's rewards.

If power means having control over one's own life, then perhaps there is no better ranking of the impact of sex roles and racism on power over our lives than life expectancy. (See Table 1.1.)

Table 1.1 Life Expectancy as a Way of Seeing Who Has the Power

Females (white)	80.5
Females (black)	76.1
Males (white)	75.3
Males (black)	69.0

SOURCE: U.S. Department of Health and Human Services, Centers for Disease Control and Prevention, National Center for Health Statistics, *Health, United States, 2005, with Chartbook on Trends in the Health of Americans,* Table 27: "Life Expectancy at Birth, at 65 Years of Age, and at 75 Years of Age, According to Race and Sex: United States, Selected Years 1900–2003," p. 167, http://www.cdc.gov/nchs/data/hus/hus05.pdf#027

The white female outlives the black male by more than eleven years. Imagine the support for affirmative action if a forty-nine-year-old woman was closer to death than a sixty-year-old man.

I am unaware of a single feminist demonstration protesting this inequality.

Suicide as Powerlessness

Just as life expectancy is one of the best indicators of power, suicide is one of the best indicators of powerlessness.

ITEM. *From ages nine to fourteen, boys' rate of suicide is three times as high as girls'; from fifteen to nineteen, four times as high; and from twenty to twenty-four, almost six times as high.*[8]

ITEM. *As boys experience the pressures of the male role, their suicide rate increases 25,000 percent.*[9]

ITEM. *The suicide rate for men over eighty-five is 1,350 percent higher than for women of the same age group.*

The breakdown is shown in the accompanying graph.

Public awareness of this suicide gap could help identify the four most vulnerable moments in the lives of our sons and fathers: early

Suicide Rates: Men Versus Women (per 100,000 Population)

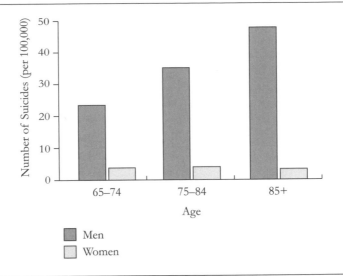

SOURCE: U.S. Department of Health and Human Services, Centers for Disease Control and Prevention, National Center for Health Statistics, *Health, United States, 2005, with Chartbook on Trends in the Health of Americans,* Table 46 (page 1 of 3): "Death Rates for Suicide, According to Sex, Race, Hispanic Origin, and Age: United States, Selected Years 1900–2003," p. 221, http://www.cdc.gov/nchs/data/hus/hus05.pdf#027

twenties; after age seventy-five; after divorce, when men are ten times as likely to commit suicide as their exes[10]; and after the death of a spouse, when widowers are also ten times as likely to commit suicide as widows. I am unaware of a single feminist fundraiser to finance hot lines and public service announcements to encourage these men to express their fears to others rather than turn their guns on themselves.

Her Body, Her Choice Versus His Body, Her Choice

If a woman and man make love and she says she is using birth control but is not, she has the right to raise the child without his knowing he even has a child, and then to sue him for retroactive child support even ten to twenty years later (depending on the state). This forces him to take a job with more pay and more stress and therefore earlier death.

Although it's his body, he has no choice. He has the option of being a slave (working for another without pay or choice) or being a criminal. *Roe v. Wade* gave women the vote over their bodies. Men still don't have the vote over theirs—whether in love or war.

The Clearest Sign of Powerlessness

Subjection of a group of people to violence based on their membership in that group is a clear indicator of that group's powerlessness, be it Christians to lions or the underclass to war. If a society supports violence against that group by its laws, customs, or socialization, it oppresses that group.

In the United States, women are exposed to greater violence in the form of rape. And therefore rape is punished by law and opposed by religion, custom, socialization, and virtually 100 percent of men and women.

In contrast, men's exposure to violence is required by law (the draft); supported by religion and custom (circumcision); and encouraged by socialization, scholarship incentive, and the education system (telling men who are best at bashing their heads against eleven other men that they have "scholarship potential"); via approval and "love" of beautiful women (cheerleaders cheering for men to "do it again"—to again risk concussions, spinal chord injuries, etc.); via parental approval and love (the parents who attend the Thanksgiving games at which their sons are battering each other); via taxpayer money (high school wrestling and football, ROTC, and the military); and via our entertainment dollar (boxing, football, ice hockey, rodeos, car racing, Westerns, war movies, etc.). After we subject only our sons to this violence (before the age of consent), we blame them for growing into the more violent sex.

But here's the rub. When other groups are subjected to violence, we acknowledge their power*less*ness. Men learn to associate violence against them with love, respect, and power. Instead of helping men who are subjected to violence, we bribe men to accept it by giving them money to entertain us by risking death.

This is deeply ingrained. Virtually every society that has survived has done so via its ability to prepare its men to be disposable—to call it "glory" to be disposable in war, and eligible for marriage to be disposable at work.

3. WHAT THE ALL-MALE DRAFT AND THE COMBAT EXCLUSION OF WOMEN TELL US ABOUT MEN, WOMEN, AND FEMINISM

"Every society rests on the death of men."

Oliver Wendell Holmes

ITEM. *Almost 1 out of 4 American men is a veteran.*[11]

ITEM. *In one World War I battle alone (the Battle of the Somme), over one million men were killed or maimed.*[12]

Understanding men requires understanding men's relationship to the Three Ws: Women, Work, and War. As we just saw in Section 2 on Power, only eighteen-year-old boys are legally required to register for future wars. How realistic is it that the boys will, in fact, be drafted? We know only that in twenty-four to seventy-two hours the first induction orders can be in the mail.[13] Should another 9/11 happen tomorrow, that's how fast your life or your brother's or boyfriend's life could change. As I write this, National Guard and Reserve units practice each week setting up the infrastructure to allow 100,000 men to be trained for potential death in boot camps in four weeks.[14] This efficiency is made possible by the preregistration system.

If a boy refuses to register for the draft when he turns eighteen, he can be barred from all federal jobs—from the U.S. Post Office to the FBI.[15] He faces a fine of up to $250,000 and five years in prison.[16] Once in prison, a young man's nubile, young body combined with his reputation for not fighting makes him a perfect candidate for homosexual rape and, therefore, AIDS. In brief, he is subject to being killed. Why? He was too sensitive to kill.

The Multi-Option Woman and the No-Option Man

In many states, an eighteen-year-old boy who has not registered for the draft cannot attend a state school.[17] He cannot receive even a loan for a private school.

Male-only draft registration leaves a woman who doesn't register for the draft able to:

1. Go to a state school.
2. Go to a private school with federal aid.
3. Get married and work; be single and work; have children.

It leaves a man who doesn't register able to:

1. Go to jail.
2. Go to jail.
3. Go to jail.

"Male Obligation" Versus "Female Entitlement"

Before boys and men can vote, they have the obligation to protect that right with the risk of their life; women receive the right to vote without the obligation to protect that right with the risk of anything. **Only women receive the privileges of freedom without a single obligation.** This male–female legal gap creates a male–female psychological gap—a gap between male obligation and female entitlement.

I say "male obligation" Versus "female entitlement" because, even if one believes that women should not be in combat (for whatever reason), there are dozens of other obligations that women could be *required* to register for at age eighteen—administrative roles, technical support, medical support, factory support. But nothing is required of women. And everyone takes that for granted. That's entitlement.

How the Law Affects Men's Versus Women's Moral Maturity

More important, when registering to be a potential killer is a legal requirement for only boys, that **frees a woman from moral dilemmas, allowing her to see herself and other women as more innocent and moral than the young man she sits next to in class.** (Hence we decry "the innocent women and children" killed in war.)

The magnitude of the moral dilemma is greatest at two points in history: when going to war is likely and when our country is engaged in a war the boy considers immoral. Then, every boy must face the moral dilemma of registering to be drafted to potentially lose his life and kill others for something he may consider immoral. For many boys, even if they are in college and think they will never be drafted, the likelihood that their college teachers and peers will consider a war like the War in Iraq immoral and illegal makes registering for it an ethical dilemma. No matter what their level of developmental readiness, only boys are forced to lose their innocence as a rite of passage to adulthood.

My Body, My Business?

For women, it's "our bodies, *our* business"; for men, it's "our bodies, *government* business." For men, G.I. means government issue. A woman's body is a woman's issue; a man's body is the government's issue.

Registering all of our eighteen-year-old males for the draft in the event the country needs more soldiers is as sexist as registering all of our eighteen-year-old females for childbearing by force in the event the country needs more children.

Why Should Women Fight in the Wars Men Cause?

Some feminists say that men cause wars, so it's only right men should fight. This is like saying that women raise children, so it's only right women should go to prison for the crimes committed by children. Parents—not women—are ultimately responsible for raising children, and voters of both sexes are ultimately responsible for their laws and their leaders. And in the United States, seven million more female voters than male voters elect the politicians who create the policies that make or prevent war.

Aren't there more male politicians, though? Yes. Politicians are like chauffeurs—their bodies are in the driver's seat; voters are like the owners in the back seat telling the chauffeur where to go. The politician and chauffeur have some discretion as to how to get there, but the voters—or owners in the back seat—are the ones who must take responsibility for the chauffeurs and politicians they hire, and where they tell them to go.

On the deepest levels, wars are not caused by men, and oppression is not created only by men. Rent *An Officer and a Gentleman*. When I saw *An Officer and a Gentleman* in a theater when it first opened, the women cheered wildly when the female heroine got the officer who had learned how to kill, not the pacifist who refused to kill. As long as women choose the killer genes, they will create children from the genes of killers, not from the genes of pacifists. And if women did not choose those genes, there would be no war from which Europeans would live in America. And if American women only started choosing pacifist men's genes in 1900, they would now be Nazis speaking German. Similarly, if women cared about blacks not being oppressed, no woman would be wearing a diamond mined by companies supporting apartheid. Women who are adult enough to take responsibility for their choices will acknowledge their role in both war and oppression.

Adult Feminists Versus Adolescent Feminists

People who want rights without responsibilities are like adolescents who want the rights to the car without the responsibilities for the payments, the gas, the insurance, or the repairs. **A person who talks more about women's rights than responsibilities is not an** *adult feminist,* **but an** *adolescent feminist.*

How do we get boys to buy into being the disposable sex, even prior to the age of consent?

The Psychological Draft

The psychological draft of boys begins at birth. In the United States it begins with unconsciously teaching infant boys to endure pain when we cut an infant boy's penis without anesthesia even as we leave an infant girl's clitoris uncut; it continues with taking longer to pick up our boy children than our girl children when they cry[18] (thus signaling to only boys that complaining won't solve their problem); it is reinforced with violent sports for boys but not girls.

How are violent sports like football, wrestling, boxing, and ice hockey part of a boy's psychological draft? They teach him to associate being abused with being loved. In most high schools and colleges, the football player is the school's hero—getting the love of the cheerleaders, the admiration of parents, and the respect of other boys. The football player learns to think of it as being a hero when he subjects himself to concussions, broken bones, and spinal chord injuries. Taxpayer money supports this; girls support this; parents support this; other boys support this. That is, he learns that being abused leads to being loved.

The identification of abuse with love, medals that honor men for their deaths, and war films that call it glory—as in the film about the Civil War, *Glory*— are all part of the psychological draft.

You will meet the psychological draft of boys throughout this book. See how often you can identify how we teach boys how they are jerks or oppressors in their overall relationships with women, but how they can become heroes if they risk their life for women, for work, and for war.

The psychological draft of boys prepares girls and boys not only very differently for the armed services, but also very differently for responsibilities *within* the armed services.

Combat for the Disposable Sex Versus Combat for the Protected Sex

"I think women are too valuable to be in combat."
Caspar Weinberger, U.S. Secretary of Defense (under Ronald Reagan)[19]

"It is not appropriate for women to engage in combat to be captured or to be shot, as opposed to pushing a button someplace in a missile silo."
Sandra Day O'Connor, Supreme Court Justice[20]

Combat positions in the armed services are now divided into dangerous versus less dangerous combat positions.[21] In wartime, *only* men can be *forced* into the dangerous combat positions. Restricting women from even volunteering for the most dangerous combat... positions is clearly discrimination against women. But it also discriminates against the men who must fill these dangerous positions. Both discriminations are based on the consensus among male and female lawmakers and the consensus of their bosses (the male and female voters)—boys are the disposable sex; if girls wish to join them, it's their choice—up to a point.

The service is often called "the College for the Poor," yet these dangerous positions are poor preparation for civilian life. Monster.com has few "jobs wanted" ads for cannon artillery positions, armored tank specialists, and infantry positions in civilian life. Poor men hope to be trained in jobs such as computer specialties, office jobs, food preparation, teaching, nursing, social work, flight control, or jet mechanics. When only men are forced to fill the dangerous combat jobs, only men lose the opportunities for these civilian preparation positions.

In addition, cannon artillery and infantry positions are also more likely to reinforce the killer mentality, creating the most psychological disturbances and the most difficulty adjusting psychologically to civilian life. The "restriction on women," then, makes men more disposable in military life and more disposable in civilian life.

His Army Versus Her Army

"Combat training strips you of your self-image so you can be rebuilt to fit the Army mold."

Bruce Gilkin, Vietnam veteran[22]

When every man in the armed services is required to enter combat upon command, and every woman either has the option of combat or is protected from the most dangerous combat, we produce two distinct mentalities. Combat training requires the men to *de*value their lives; women's much greater likelihood to be trained for technical jobs that can be used in civilian life is compatible with *valuing* one's life. The result?

Harassment and hazing are preparation for devaluation—which is why men haze and harass each other: They are amputating each other's individuality because the war machine works best with standardized parts. Harassment and hazing are therefore a prerequisite to combat training in the "men's army"; but in the "women's army," harassment and hazing can be protested—they conflict with valuing one's life.

If the men's and women's armies were physically separate, these differences would be less of a problem. However, when the men are told that the women are equals, but if they harass and haze the women as equals, they have their careers ruined (and often family life destroyed), this only reinforces the men's belief that women want to "have their cake and eat it, too."

Solutions: From Here to Equality

Women constitute 14.5 percent of the total military but 15.4 percent of the officers.[23] **Women receive more-than-equal promotions in** the services despite less-than-equal time in the services (the first women graduated from West Point in 1980).

The dilemma for the military is how to achieve equality without damaging military strength.

How to Achieve Equality Without Damaging Military Strength

The fear of the services is that if women and men are held to equal standards in combat training then either the standards will have to be lowered or, conversely, the standards will be kept the same and about 80 percent of women won't hack it.

The services face another dilemma. If they lower the standards only for women so more women can meet them, will they increase the danger to women? It appears so. The Army has considerably lower standards for women, and 43 of the 1766 Army soldiers who had died in the War in Iraq as of April 23, 2007 are female.[24] The Marines have required women to meet virtually equal standards, and only 6 of the 798 Marines who have died in the War in Iraq are female (as of April 23, 2007). Earning her way to equality seems to protect a woman more than giving her equal status for unequal preparation. In the Army, women constitute 2.4 percent of the deaths; in the Marines, 0.75 percent.

Fortunately, though, there *is* a way of making all combat an equal opportunity option that still preserves combat readiness. Here is my solution.

The Supply and Demand Plan

The plan? The military increases its pay for the jobs it finds the toughest to fill and lowers its pay for the jobs it is easiest to fill. For example, if few recruits want assignments like infantry combat, the pay and benefits are raised until they obtain all the qualified recruits they need; if everyone wants to be a pilot and plenty of recruits are qualified, the pay for pilots is lowered. The result is that women pursuing real equality—sharing the least-desired assignments—would get higher pay. Neither sex is discriminated against; no standards are lowered for any specialty. The psychological result is respect for women because they are earning it, rather than resentment toward women getting equal pay for the safest and most glamorous of the combat jobs (pilot) or resentment for women being more than 14 percent of the military but less than 2 percent of the soldiers making the ultimate sacrifice.

4. WHY DO MEN DIE SOONER, AND WHOSE HEALTH IS BEING NEGLECTED?

MYTH: *Women just naturally live longer than men.*

FACT: *In 1920, American men died only one year sooner than women;*[25] *now the life expectancy gap is 5.3 years (74.8 years for men, 80.1 for women).*[26]

MYTH: *The government neglects women's health research. Evidence: Women's health research receives only 10 percent of all health research funding by the National Institutes of Health.*[27]

FACT: *Men's health research receives only 5 percent of all health research funding by the National Institutes of Health.*[28] *(The other 85 percent is for non gender-specific research, such as cellular, blood, DNA, etc.). For example, a man is slightly more likely to die of prostate cancer as is a woman to die of breast cancer.*[29] *Yet the government spends almost two times as much money on breast cancer as it does on prostate cancer.*[30]

MYTH: *More of the serious, published research is done on men than on women.*

FACT: *In the ten years prior to mid-2006, gender-specific systematic reviews were published on women three and a half times more than on men.*[31] *In the same period, the number of randomized controlled trials (the highest quality research) using only women was nearly twice as large as that for men.*[32] *Since as far back as major computer searches can access complete records (1965) most gender-specific research pertains to women. (For the four 10-year periods beginning in 1965, bibliographic searches find that 16 percent, 13 percent, 18 percent, and 30 percent more gender-specific research was published on women.*[33])

In certain areas women's health research was neglected. We were led to believe that is because we didn't care about women. The opposite was true. Men, and especially male prisoners, military men, and African-American men, were the most likely to be the guinea pigs for the testing of new drugs because we cared less if men and prisoners died. That is, **we used men for experimental research for the same reason we use rats for experimental research.**

While dozens of studies are being done on the possible damage of silicone breast implants, the causes of men dying 5.3 years sooner are virtually ignored. Nor are most of us aware of how quickly men's health is deteriorating. In 1993, the gap between male and female suicide was 3.9 to 1; now it is 4.1 to 1.[34] In Great Britain, there is a recent 339 percent increase in male suicides by hanging alone.[35]

Even as we are increasingly hearing that women die of heart disease as often as men, we are not hearing that when most women die of heart disease, men have been long dead. The *age-adjusted* death rates for the ten leading causes of death are shown in Table 1.2.

Not all of the significant causes of death are neglected. Fortunately, people feared AIDS would affect heterosexuals, and affect women equally to men, and its funding increased. We pay attention to chlamydia, gonorrhea, and syphilis because we believe women are more at risk than men—but in fact, men are more at risk.[36] With suicide, most people know it is predominantly a man's method of disposability, so it is the only leading cause of death that is also neglected.

My list of at least thirty-four *neglected* areas of men's health follows.

Table 1.2   Ten Leading Causes of Death (Age-Adjusted)

	Male-to-Female Ratio
1. Diseases of the heart	1.5 to 1
2. Malignant neoplasms	1.5 to 1
3. Cerebrovascular diseases	1.02 to 1
4. Chronic lower respiratory diseases	1.4 to 1
5. Accidents	2.2 to 1
6. Diabetes mellitus	1.2 to 1
7. Influenza and pneumonia	1.4 to 1
8. Alzheimer's disease	0.8 to 1
9. Nephritis, nephrotic syndrome, and nephrosis	1.5 to 1
10. Septicimia	1.2 to 1

SOURCE: Centers for Disease Control and Prevention, *National Vital Statistics Report* 54, no. 10 (January 2006), Table 17, pp. 69–76, http://www.cdc.gov/nchs/data/nvsr53/nvsr53_05acc.pdf

Neglected Areas of Men's Health

1. A men's birth control pill (There is fourteen times as much published research on female than male contraception in the last ten years despite the need for and scientific viability of a male pill.)[37]
2. Suicide
3. PTSD (post-traumatic stress disorder)
4. Circumcision as a possible trauma-producing experience
5. The male midlife crisis
6. Dyslexia
7. Autism
8. The causes of male violence
9. Criminal recidivism
10. Street homelessness among veterans (85 percent of street homeless are men; about one-third of them veterans)
11. Steroid abuse
12. Colorblindness
13. Testicular cancer
14. Prostate cancer
15. BPH (benign prostatic hyperplasia)
16. Lifespan (why the male–female gap increased from one to seven years; solutions)
17. Hearing loss over age thirty
18. Erectile dysfunction
19. Nonspecific urethritis
20. Epididymitis (a disease of the tubes that transmit sperm)
21. DES sons (diethylstilbestrol, a drug women took in the 1940s and 1950s to prevent miscarriages; the problems it created in daughters were attended to, while the sons' problems were neglected)[38]
22. Hemophilia
23. ADHD (attention-deficit hyperactivity disorder); alternatives to ritalin
24. Workplace deaths (94 percent men) and injuries
25. Institutions turning their backs on HGH (human growth hormone) abuse among male athletes/body builders, the damage of artificial turf

26. Concussions and the cumulative damage from multiple concussions (football)
27. Male testosterone reduction between ages fifty and seventy
28. Infertility (40 percent of infertility is male; NIH has increased female infertility research, but has no research for male infertility)
29. Depression (women cry, men deny; women check it out, men tough it out; women express, men repress); Rand Corporation finds 70 percent of male depression goes undetected
30. Being a victim of domestic violence; unwillingness to report battering
31. Chlamydia as a creator of heart disease in men between the ages of thirty and sixty[39]
32. Estrogen transference to men during intercourse[40]
33. Viagra's effect on heart disease, stress, and marital communication
34. LSD (lower sexual desire) syndrome (seen in more than half of men between the ages of twenty-five and fifty)[41]

What Our Lifespan Tells Us About Who Has the Power

Life expectancy can be thought of as one of the best indicators of real power. When we learn that non-whites have about 80 percent of the chance of whites to reach age eighty-five,[42] we know that it is because of the relative powerlessness of nonwhites. But...

ITEM. *A boy infant is only half as likely as a girl infant to live to age eighty-five.*[43]

ITEM. *When a man is about twenty-five, his anxiety about "making it" is at its height. The odds of a person living out that year are shown in* Table 1.3.

ITEM. *Blacks die earlier than whites from 11 of the 15 leading causes of death. Men die earlier than women from 9 of the 10 leading causes of death, and women and men are tied for 2 of the other 15 leading causes of death.*[44]

A major reason for men's shorter lives has to do with the loneliness and isolation single men feel as a result of not developing the tools to express feelings, especially to other men. And among married men, it is often from the stress of long work weeks or the manual labor that tears away at their bodies when they try to make enough income so

Table 1.3   Odds of Living This Year (Twenty-Five-Year-Olds)

Females (White)	1,754 to 1
Females (Black)	943 to 1
Males (White)	561 to 1
Males (Black)	311 to 1

SOURCE: Tom and Nancy Biracree, *Almanac of the American People* (New York: Facts on File, 1988).

their children can have a better life than they have. This leads less-skilled or educated men to the "death professions."

How do we solve these problems? First, by understanding them. One example: the men's birth control pill.

Toward Solutions: A Men's Birth Control Pill

Nothing freed women more than the women's birth control pill. And, because most women are trustworthy, the female pill also gave considerable freedom to men.

Nothing will free men more than a men's birth control pill. And a men's pill also frees a woman, from her body being the only one subjected to hormone manipulation. It allows a couple to rotate taking the pill, giving each of their bodies a rest. As a man shares this responsibility, the woman experiences him more as a partner from the moment of conception—or a partner in preventing the moment of conception!

I saw the need for a men's pill most poignantly when it was a lead item in my platform for governor of California in 2003. I was flying to Sacramento to introduce it. Next to me were two university students engaged in mile-high flirting. As the pilot's voice overwhelmed theirs, the woman, side-tracked, asked why I was flying to Sacramento.

I explained my proposal for a men's birth control pill. Her response: "I know *three* girls at my university who were afraid their guy was going to break up with them, so they 'mistakenly' went off the pill to get pregnant and get the guy to marry them."

Her flirt-partner, jaw-now-in-lap, stuttered, "*Three* girlfriends?" She verified, then clarified, "*I* would never do this." The guy, though, was still suffering from post-traumatic stress disorder.

It used to be that a woman's body was a woman's destiny. Today a woman's body is a man's destiny: The moment a man puts his penis into a woman's body, he puts his life in her hands. If she becomes pregnant, she can abort or sue for support. He has no say in the abortion and no say in the pay. In many states like Ohio, she can raise the child for as long as eighteen years without ever telling him he has a child, then sue him for eighteen years of unpaid child support.

When I ask men in men's groups if they had originally wanted children—when they first met their future wife—about half say either "no" or "I was lukewarm." Most, though, have children. If I ask how the decision to have children evolved, the answer is often, "My wife became pregnant; she had forgotten to take the pill." That is, few felt they were genuinely full partners in the process.

Perhaps the most important contribution a college student could eventually make is to be a force in the more rapid introduction of a men's birth control pill.[45]

An Equal *Life* Opportunity Commission?

Women have Offices of Women's Health in every state; men have nothing. Women have Equal *Employment* Opportunity Commissions. Men have no Equal *Life* Opportunity Commissions.

I'd like to suggest that an enterprising college student begin an Equal Life Opportunity Commission (ELOC) or an Office of Men's Health to model for the government, giving men an equal chance for an equal life by raising awareness of the dozen "glass cellars" of male disposability and the thirty-four neglected areas of men's health.

More American men die of prostate cancer each year than were killed each year in the Vietnam War or in the War in Iraq. Good research can help us answer dozens of unanswered questions. For example, to what degree are vasectomies—linked to prostate cancer in mice—linked to prostate cancer in men?

Government spending creates only part of the breast cancer–prostate cancer spending gap. If you hear of a "Run for the Cure," is it a cure for breast cancer or prostate cancer? You guessed it. It is impossible to get a figure on the private spending gap, but I estimate it to be approximately 30 to 1.

The difference in support for breast versus prostate cancer can even be seen at the Post Office. The U.S. Post Office prints special 45-cent stamps to raise more than $50 million dollars for breast cancer research.[46] There is a stamp for prostate cancer. The amount contributed to prostate cancer research? Nothing. No stamp raises money for prostate cancer research.

An Office of Men's Health could educate men about why men are seven times as likely as women to be arrested for drunk driving[47] while only three times as likely as women to be hospitalized for alcoholism.[48]

Concrete steps can be taken. Men are less likely than women to have healthcare coverage, a gap that has widened again recently.[49] And 94 percent of those dying from work-related injuries (for example, on construction sites or as truckers, roofers, and cab drivers) are men.[50] Yet, the United States has only *one* job safety inspector for every *six* fish and game inspectors.[51]

With the leadership of today's college students, we can end the era of assessing our sons at birth a 7 percent "male disposability tax"—symbolizing their 7 percent shorter life expectancy.

When either sex wins, both sexes lose.

5. DOMESTIC VIOLENCE: WHO IS DOING THE BATTERING, AND WHAT'S THE SOLUTION?

"Men learn to call pain 'glory'; women learn to call the police."

Don't Men Batter Women More Because Men Have More Power?

This question falsely assumes men batter women more. Here's why that's a false assumption.

If we look at only police reports and all-female self-help groups, it appears that men perpetrate about 90 percent of the domestic violence. But both these figures are dependent on a person's willingness to volunteer a complaint. The women's movement taught us, though, that many women keep feelings to themselves if they feel they will be ridiculed. The only way to know if this might also be true of men is to ask men (rather than wait for the men to call a police station and say, "My wife is beating me—help me" and fear the police will die laughing).

We began including men in questions about domestic violence in 1975, when Suzanne Steinmetz, Murray Straus, and Richard Gelles conducted the first scientific nationwide sample of both sexes.[52] The researchers could hardly believe their results. The sexes appeared to batter each other about equally.

Dozens of objections arose ("Don't women batter only in self-defense?"; "Aren't women hurt more?"). Over a hundred researchers during the next thirty years double-checked via their own studies. About half of these researchers were women, and almost all of the women were feminist academics. Most expected to disprove the Steinmetz, Straus, and Gelles findings.

To their credit, despite their assumptions that men were the abusers, *every* domestic violence survey done of both sexes over the thirty years in the United States, Canada, England, New Zealand, and Australia found one of two things: **Women and men batter each other about *equally*, or women batter men more.**

To the researchers' greater amazement, **women themselves acknowledged they are more likely to be violent and to be the initiators of violence.**[53] **Finally, women were more likely to engage in severe violence that was not reciprocated.**[54]

Studies also make it clear that the women are more likely to inflict the severe violence. How? Women are 70 percent more likely to use weapons against men than men are to use weapons against women.[55] They are more likely to wait until men are asleep, drunk, or otherwise incapacitated. For example, one woman waited until her husband fell asleep, then "sewed him in the sheets, and broke his bones with a baseball bat."[56]

Abuse against men is most common among the elderly, when a frustrated female caretaker starts battering her older, sicker husband. He feels he can't do anything about it because he is dependent on her for his care.

When I first investigated this research, for *Women Can't Hear What Men Don't Say,* my preliminary readers expressed considerable skepticism until I created an Appendix with each of the fifty most significant studies and their findings. The larger and better-designed the study, the more likely the finding that women were significantly more violent.

Since *Women Can't Hear What Men Don't Say* was published in 1999, have new studies have confirmed these findings? Yes. For example, in 2006, Dr. Murray Straus presented data from sixty-eight studies in thirty-two nations, concluding that college women worldwide commit more dating violence than their male counterparts do.[57] More specifically, about a third of dating relationships had some violence, and most dating violence was mutual. The second largest category was that of couples in which the female partner was the only one who was violent. Perhaps the most revealing finding is that when a woman is the dominant partner, she is more likely to be violent than when a man is dominant.

Aren't Women Injured More Than Men?

Despite the fact that women are more likely to use weapons and severe violence against men, 1.9 percent of the men and 2.3 percent of the women surveyed said they had sought medical treatment for an injury due to partner abuse.[58] Here's why I believe that grossly underestimates the injuries to men. When I do a radio show and ask men who have been severely battered to call in anonymously, I ask them if they reported their injury to a hospital or police. The answer almost invariably is "no." Even for a broken arm , if they seek medical attention, they report it as an *athletic* injury. And doctors are not trained to crossexamine the man to see whether the claim of an athletic injury might be a coverup.

But Aren't Men More Likely to Kill Their Partners?

On the surface, the Bureau of Justice reports women are the perpetrators in 41 percent of spousal murders.[59] However, the male method of killing is with a knife or gun, done by himself. Two of the three female methods are "multiple offender killings"—the wife or girlfriend either hires a professional killer or persuades a boyfriend. The problem is, **the FBI does not record these killings as a wife killing a husband; they are listed instead as a "multiple offender killing."**[60] In multiple offender killings there are four times as many husbands as victims than wives, according to the FBI.[61]

The most likely to succeed of these multiple offender killings are contract killings. The FBI reports that some *seventy-eight hundred men were killed without the killer being identified* (versus fifteen hundred women).[62] This number is *almost nine times larger than all of the wives killed by spouses and ex-spouses put together.*[63] However, this "nine times as many" figure is very inadequate since it includes men killed by other men. It only tells us that the number of men killed by women is *potentially* much larger than the other way around.

How likely are we to know about a woman's versus a man's killing? There are three female methods of killing: the two multiple offender types and poisoning. The purpose of all three methods is to not be discovered. Why? So the husband's death appears as an accident so she can collect insurance money. It is rare for a man who has no insurance to be killed by a woman.

In contrast, the next time you read about a husband killing a wife in the newspaper, read further and you'll be surprised to see how often he also kills himself. The suicide indicates that money is not his primary motivation.

As a result of the invisibility of the female methods of killing, women who do kill benefit from the stereotype of women-as-innocent and are treated very differently by the law: 13 percent of spousal murder cases with women defendants result in an acquittal, versus 1 percent of murder cases with men defendants.[64] Similarly, the average prison sentence for spousal murder (excluding life sentences and the death penalty) is almost three times longer for men than for women—17.5 years versus 6.2 years.[65] In the United States, a woman has never been executed for killing only a man.

If Men Are Battered More, Why Do They *Report* It Less?

ITEM. *"Michael, 38, a construction worker and amateur rugby player, barricaded himself in a spare bedroom at nights to avoid beatings from his diminutive wife.*

During a three-year marriage he was stabbed, punched, kicked and pelted with plant pots. Despite his muscular, 15-stone [210 lbs.] build, he was frightened to sleep for fear of attack. 'Nobody would have believed me if I'd told them the constant bruising was from beatings by my wife. I still have the scars from where she tore at my flesh with her fingernails. The screams from my daughter as she witnessed the abuse will haunt me for the rest of my life.'"[66]

If a battered man is believed, he knows that if his wife has been abusing him, she has often been abusing the children; leaving her means leaving his children unprotected from her abuse. And he fears that if he leaves and reports the abuse, she will retaliate that he's also an abuser, and the judge, more likely to believe her, will award her the children.

If Men Are Battered More, Do We *See* It Less?

Most of us are witness to violence against men almost daily, without being aware of what we see. For example, in 100 percent of TV advertisements in which only one sex is hitting or beating the other, it is the woman who is hitting the man.[67] One hundred percent. If you've ever stopped the remote in disbelief and disgust to watch the Jerry Springer show, you'll see women hitting women, and women hitting men, but almost never men hitting women. Many people have seen this, very few have noticed the pattern, and even fewer who notice it question it.

Now check this out in your personal life.

- On your right hand, use one finger to represent each relationship in which you hit your partner (a nonplayful slap or more) the first time—before she or he ever hit you. The number?
- On your left hand, use one finger to represent each relationship in which your partner hit you the first time. The number?

Remember, only one finger per relationship—and only the first time counts. Take out a moment to do this. It's crucial to understanding this topic on the emotional level. Chances are if you ask your class to do this, more women will have hit more men the first time than vice versa. (Just ask each person to write the numbers on a piece of paper and toss the paper anonymously into a pile to someone who tallies the results.)

Why Are We So Blind to Violence Against Men?

We are blind to violence against men because every society that survived had an unconscious investment in training its men to be disposable—whether at work or at war, in coal mines or on construction
sites, as firefighters or as police.

We are more than blind to violence against men: We reward it.
We call it football, rugby, ice hockey, boxing, boot camp, rodeos, car
racing. **Men learn to call pain "glory"; women learn to call the
police.**

The more a man is trained to "be a man," the more he is trained
to protect women and children, not hurt women and children. He is
trained to volunteer to die before even a stranger is hurt—especially a
woman or child. Thus most firefighters are volunteers, and almost all
the volunteers are men. It is not coincidence that all the firefighters
and police officers who died in the 9/11 attacks were men.

Those feminists who say that masculinity is about men believing
they can batter women display the deepest ignorance possible about
men and masculinity. In virtually every culture, manhood rests on men
learning to protect women, not hurt women. **Battering a woman is
the male role broken down.**

Conclusion and Solutions

Men have no shelters to turn to, no hot lines to call, no education to
request a restraining order. They fear that if they call the police, the
police will laugh at them; they don't like "airing their dirty laundry in
public"; they have few men friends, few men's support groups, and a
minimal vocabulary for discussing these issues.

In conclusion, when domestic violence is seen as a two-way street,
it frees us to transfer from a "men must give up their power" model
for treatment to a "walk a mile in each other's moccasins" model for
treatment. It frees us to focus not on a scapegoat oppressor, but on a
mutual responsibility; not on punishment, but on listening skills that
empower our partner—the type I discuss in the first three chapters
of *Women Can't Hear What Men Don't Say*. It frees us not to treat
a slap as terminal cancer, but as a signal that we need to make our
love healthier. We have an opportunity to make a paradigm shift from
the world of victimhood—of learned helplessness defenses, battered

women's shelters and syndromes, mandatory arrest policies, and re-straining orders—to a world of redefining love.

6. THE POLITICS AND PSYCHOLOGY OF RAPE, SEX, AND LOVE

"Men who are unjustly accused of rape can sometimes gain from the experi-ence."[68]

—Vassar College assistant dean of students

Is Rape an Outgrowth of Male Power?

MYTH: *Rape is a manifestation of male political and economic power.*
FACT: *Any given black man is three times as likely to be reported a rapist as a white man.*[69]

Do blacks suddenly have more political and economic power? Maybe rape does not derive from power, but rather from powerlessness.

Is Rape an Outgrowth of Male Violence?

MYTH: *Rape has nothing to do with sexual attraction—it is just an act of violence.*[70] *This is "proven" by the fact that women of every age are raped.*
FACT: *Being at the age of greatest sexual attraction makes the chances of being raped at least 8,400 percent greater than being over fifty.*[71]

When a woman is between the ages of sixteen and nineteen, her chances of being raped are 84 in 20,000; when she is between fifty and sixty-four, her chances are less than 1 in 20,000.[72] Sexual attraction, then, *does* have something to do with who is raped.

What are we really doing when we ignore the role of sexual attrac-tion? We are ignoring our responsibility as a culture for reinforcing men's addiction to female sexual beauty and then depriving men of what we've helped addict them to. We will not be willing to stop re-inforcing men's addiction to beautiful women until we are willing to stop the benefits that beautiful women receive when men's addiction gets boys and men to perform for women, pay for women, pursue women, and give women the option to raise money or raise children even as men have no option but to raise money.

Men's Experience of Pursuing, Paying, and Performing

While the label "date rape" has helped women articulate the most traumatic aspect of dating from women's perspective—and helped attentive men understand that date rape can be as traumatic as stranger rape since it is a violation of trust—men have no labels to help them articulate the most traumatic aspects of dating from their perspective. Now, of course, the most traumatic aspect is the possibility of being accused of date rape by a woman to whom he thought he was making love. If men did label the worst aspects of the traditional male role, though, they might label them "date rejection," "date robbery," and "date fraud."

150 Risks of Rejection: The Anatomy of the Journey from Eye Contact to Intercourse

A study conducted by two feminists found nearly 40 percent of college women acknowledged they had said "no" to sex even "when they meant yes."[73]

Whether it's called dating, "hanging out," or "hooking up," someone has to take the risk of the first kiss, first tongue kiss, and so on. Most women sense that if they don't stop the tongue kiss at some point, the journey from tongue kiss to intercourse is only about a ten-minute ride. So she says "no" by withdrawing her tongue from time to time. And then, instead of the women saying, "When I'm ready to go beyond this, I'll let you know," the man is expected to guess whether the "no" means "no" forever or until the next date, whether she's fulfilling a social expectation to say "no" and really wants him to pursue, or whether the "no" is a "no" until she has more liquor to relax, more coffee to wake up, more talk about her, more feelings from him, more slow dancing, more fast dancing, and so on. The less she has been drinking, the more likely he is to experience about 150 risks of rejection between eye contact and intercourse. And, of course, the 150 risks of rejection are more likely to be experienced if the woman is one of the 40 percent who says "no" when she means "yes."

Robbery-by-Social-Custom: She Exists, He Pays

To shorten the period of potential rejection, men learn to pay for all of the Five Ds—Drinks, Dinner, Driving, Dating, and then, if he is successful at repeatedly paying for the first Four Ds, he gets to pay for the fifth, the Diamond—or, more precisely, a diamond with the right Three Cs (carrots, color, and clarity). Together, the expectation for him to pay for these Five Ds can feel like robbery-by-social-custom: She exists, he pays.

The only other social transaction among humans in which the person paying is not guaranteed to receive anything in return is that between parent and child. Women who do not fully *share* the *expectation* to pay are children-by-choice; they are not women, but girls.

Few men are conscious of how the expectation to pay pressures them to take jobs they like less only because they pay more and how this leads to stress, heart attacks, and suicides that are the male version of "my body, *not* my choice."

"Date Fraud"

If a man ignoring a woman's verbal "no" is committing date rape, then a woman who says "no" with her verbal language but "yes" with her body language is committing *date fraud.*

The purpose of the fraud? To have sexual pleasure without sexual responsibility, and therefore without guilt or shame; to reinforce the belief that he is getting a sexual favor while she is giving a sexual favor, and thus that he "owes" her the Five Ds before sex or some measure of commitment, protection, or respect after sex.

Is Date Rape a Crime, or a Misunderstanding?

PREVAILING PERSPECTIVE. *Date rape is a crime, not a misunderstanding.*

ANOTHER PERSPECTIVE. *Anyone who listens with an equally open mind to both sexes knows it is possible for a man to feel he's just made love and for a woman to feel she's been raped. It's also possible for a woman to feel she's made love in the evening when she's high, and feel raped in the morning when she's sober—without the man being a rapist—or for a woman to feel she's been made love to one evening if the man said, "I love you," but feel raped the next evening if he hasn't called back. But again, that doesn't mean the man raped her.*

The woman who says, "I just want to talk" when she goes to the room but is then responsive to a shoulder rub, a caressed hand, and a first kiss has not *verbally* said, "I've changed my mind," but she has said it nonverbally. Therefore her last *words* were "no" to anything physical, but her last behaviors were "yes" to anything physical. Therein creates the potential for misunderstanding. If only he is asked to take responsibility, we are making him into a criminal for (someone who is a protector, who would say, "are you sure your nonverbal 'yes' means yes") not being her parent.

What's the Difference Between Stranger Rape and Date Rape?

We often hear, "Rape is rape." Right? Wrong. A stranger forcing himself on a woman at knife-point *is* different from date rape. *What* is different? When a woman agrees to a date, she does not make a choice to be sexual, but she does make a choice to explore sexual *possibilities.* Date rape can be differently traumatic because it involves a violation of trust, the disappointment of hope, a mistrust of self, and a type of self doubt that is either nonexistent or different with stranger rape.

Have these legitimate distinctions become bad law? Let's look.

Can a Man be Legally Accused of Rape if He Has Sex with a Woman Who Says "Yes"?

Across the country, campuses now considered "progressive"—from Berkeley to Harvard and Swarthmore—already allow a woman who is drunk to claim the next morning that she was raped even if she said "yes" the evening before![74] Once a woman can claim her "yes" didn't really mean "yes" because she was "under the influence," this opens the floodgates. Ironically, the man's social expectation to pay for the drinks is now seen as evidence he was "plying" the woman with drinks and "luring" the woman to bed. **In an era of equality, we are making her *not* responsible because she is drunk and making him responsible** even though he is also drunk. It is ironic that feminism is pioneering this new *in*equality.

One would think that the universities with the best and brightest women would pioneer the effort to socialize women to ask men out, take initiatives, pay for men's drinks, and so on in preparation for running their own businesses (and their own lives). Instead, they are simultaneously treating these women as children who cannot take responsibility while socializing men to take all the responsibility. These universities then blame businesses for discriminating when these women are less successful in business.

As long as society tells men to be the salespersons of sex, it is sexist for society to put only men in jail if they sell well. We don't put other salespersons in jail for buying clients drinks and successfully transforming a "no" into a "maybe" into a "yes." If the client makes a choice to drink too much and the "yes" turns out to be a bad decision, it is the *client* who gets fired, not the salesperson. We expect *adults* to take responsibility.

Male chauvinism is about protecting women. Male chauvinism and feminism have this in common.

The Politics of Making Date Rape an Epidemic and Making Only Men Responsible

A study sponsored by *Ms.* magazine, the most mainstream publication of the feminist movement, contained a statistic the mass media widely quoted[75] as saying that 25 percent of all women were raped *by the time they were in college.* The study asked this question to get the 25 percent answer[76]: "Have you given in to sexual intercourse when you didn't want to because you were overwhelmed by a man's continual arguments and pressure?"[77]

Notice that these women did not define themselves as raped, just as "overwhelmed." How do I know these women did not necessarily define themselves as raped? **Because 42 percent of these "raped" women said they had sex with these men one or more times after this (the mean was 2.02 times).**[78]

The truth is that *both* sexes participate in unwanted sexual activity. A study by a feminist, reported in the *Journal of Sex Research,* found that **63 percent of the men and 46 percent of the women said they** had **experienced unwanted intercourse.**[79] By feminist definitions of rape as unwanted sex, virtually everyone has been raped. And that's how rape begins to look like an epidemic. It's also how rape gets trivialized.

Why would a college man not want to have sex with a woman? Because, for example, he feels a woman will read into it more of a commitment than he wants. But he has it anyway because he was the one pressing for it before she made that clear, and in the heat of passion he doesn't know how to say "no." In fact, it is exactly that scenario—with the man not calling the next day for fear of further misleading her and the woman feeling rejected because he didn't call after sex—that leads to the woman feeling "raped," and sometimes even reporting it as rape.

Exaggerated claims of rape might be good for politics, but they are bad for women who want to love men. To exploit women for the sake of politics is not my definition of liberation.

Is a Falsely Accused Man a Raped Man?

When a woman says she is raped, it is important to listen, support her, and believe her. Similarly, when a man says he has been falsely accused of rape, *he is also telling us he has been raped.* He is being accused of being one of life's most despicable men. As with Grover Gale, even if he is acquitted, his life can be ruined.

A thirteen-year-old North Carolina girl accused Grover Gale II of raping her four times.[80] By the time Grover spent thirty-six days in jail, he had lost his construction job, fallen into debt, couldn't pay his rent for his family at home, and was on the verge of divorce. Then the girl, whose name still doesn't make the papers, admits she made the whole thing up, saying she was just trying to get her seventeen-year-old boyfriend's attention.[81]

But when Grover returned from jail, his own son was afraid to hug him. Although in debt, the family moved out of state to a small town where no one knew him. He has been raped. Yet he cannot afford counseling and the state won't pay for him to be counseled.

But is Grover Gale an exception? Aren't false accusations of rape rare?

Aren't False Accusations of Rape Rare?

"To my considerable chagrin, we found that at least 60% of all the rape allegations were false."[82]

Dr. Charles P. McDowell, supervisory special agent,
U.S. Air Force, Office of Special Investigations

When the Air Force investigated 556 cases of alleged rape, 27 percent of the women eventually admitted they had lied (either just before they took a lie detector test or after they failed it).[83] Because other cases were less certain, the Air Force asked three independent reviewers to review these cases. They used twenty-five criteria that were common to the women who had acknowledged they lied. If *all three* reviewers agreed that the rape allegation was false, it was ranked as false. Their conclusion? A total of 60 percent of the original rape allegations were false.

Aren't these findings in conflict with the FBI's *Uniform Crime Reports,* which the media has popularized as saying that only 9 percent of rape accusations are false or unfounded?[84] No. The FBI knows the number of women who reported they were raped, but not whether the rapist was found guilty or innocent. In brief, as far as the FBI knows, the percentage of false accusations overall could be anywhere from 0 to 100 percent.

Why Would a Woman Make a False Accusation of Rape?

The Air Force study by Dr. McDowell found that most false accusations are "instrumental"—they serve a purpose. The study's ranking of motivations is shown in Table 1.4.

The Double Standard of "Rape-Shield" Laws

"Rape-shield" laws shield a woman's sexual past from being used against her in court. No law shields a man's sexual past from being used against him in court. These laws evolved when a woman who claimed she was raped was assumed to have already been victimized, and therefore dragging out her sexual past in court appeared to be a double victimization. As courts began to buy this assumption, they

Table 1.4   Motivations Given by the Women Who
Acknowledged They Had Made False Accusations of Rape

Reason	Percent
Spite or revenge	20
To compensate for feelings of guilt or shame	20
Thought she might be pregnant	13
To conceal an affair	12
To test husband's love	9
Mental/emotional disorder	9
To avoid personal responsibility	4
Failure to pay, or extortion	4
Thought she might have caught VD	3
Other	6
Total	100

SOURCE: Charles P. McDowell, Ph.D., M.P.A., M.L.S., "The False Rape Allegation in the Military Community," unpublished paper (Washington, DC: U.S. Air Force Office of Special Investigations, March 1983). A total of seventy-five women who acknowledged they had made false accusations also volunteered their motivations.

began to reason that women needed extra protection in order to have equal protection. By the early 1990s, the Supreme Court upheld this as the law of the land.[85]

We have seen, though, that there are numerous motivations to lie about rape, so we know that it is a violation of due process and equal protection to shield a woman's sexual past during a trial more than a man's. A woman with a history of false accusations—or a man with a history as a rapist—will follow patterns that can help separate the truth-teller from the liar. The purpose of a trial is to determine whether or not there has been a rape, not to assume who needs the shielding during the trial.

Spousal Rape

We have seen that both sexes have sex when they don't want to—even on the first date. But in a marriage this is especially true: *Both sexes engage in "mercy sex."* And that's the difference between having a relationship and not having a relationship—*all good relationships require "giving in,"* especially when our partner feels strongly. The *Ms.* survey can call it a rape; a relationships counselor will call it a relationship.

What About Sexual Harassment?

When a woman touches a man on his rear, he's likely to say "thank you"; when a man touches a woman on her rear, she's more likely to say "sue you."

Why this difference? He's always had to work for sex, pay for sex, risk rejection for sex, perform for sex—so what he gets for no work, pay, rejection, or performing creates gratitude: He says "thank you." She's had men pay for drinks and dinners before they even asked for sex, so when he takes it without asking and without paying, she's more likely to say "sue you."

The federal government has expanded the legal definition of sexual harassment to anything *a woman defined* as a "hostile work environment."[86] Who defines "hostile environment"? Legally, only the woman. *Not even the man's intent makes a legal difference.* Suppose it is her word against his? **Legally, a "bare assertion" of sexual harassment can stand without factual support!**[87] Ironically, Clarence Thomas, when he was chairman of the Equal Employment Opportunity Commission (EEOC), was responsible for creating that decision.

But it's worse than that: A woman doesn't even have to tell the man that he's bothering her. She can now complain *to a girlfriend at work.* The EEOC's decision number 84–1 allows complaining to a girlfriend at work to be "sufficient to support a finding of harassment."[88] That used to be called gossip. Now it's called evidence.

Sexual Innuendo in the Workplace

Guy took a picture of a woman in his office, her face turned the other way, and put it on his file cabinet. His boss ordered him to remove the picture, as "we don't allow pornography." The woman, however, whose picture was the "pornography," was not asked to dress in a less pornographic manner. The workplace sexual reality created by some women is, when photographed, the workplace sexual harassment other women sue men for viewing.

Conclusions and Solutions

The traditional male–female dance that has led to sex has evolved over the millennia. Her role in this tango? Attract/resist. His role? Pursue/persist. Thus far we are subjecting only the excesses in his role to criminal charges. This makes him even more responsible, her even less responsible. Which, ironically, only reinforces the male role of taking responsibility and the female role of being assumed to be the innocent child—again, the common denominator between feminism and male chauvinism.

Does the male–female dance need to be changed? Yes. It has become dysfunctional to both sexes. Men paying, performing, and pursuing may have been functional when women spent their lives raising children and had to select men who could raise money, and therefore select performers who would pursue rather than take "no" for an answer in life (e.g., salespeople who do take the first "no" as the final answer are called "unemployed"). Women keeping sex in short supply before marriage was functional when sex before marriage led to children who couldn't be supported.

Now, though, it is more functional to re-socialize both sexes to responsibly enjoy sex and to share responsibility for paying, performing, and pursuing by expectation—not men-by-expectation, women-by-option. This means changing our socialization for boys to have to take most of the 150 risks of rejection, thus drinking to handle the rejection and buying women drinks in hopes the women will reject them less. It means encouraging our daughters to exercise what I call "original choice power," by taking responsibility to pursue the boys that fit their values, rather than to exercise only "attraction power," which may attract the wrong boys, and "veto power," which can lead to them saying lots of "no's" and still not finding the boys they want.

Finally, it means confronting advertising that reinforces heterosexual men's natural addiction to young and beautiful women and then deprives them of access until they perform, pursue, and pay.

We will never eliminate rape. But we'll have a lot less of it when we make young men conscious of the powerlessness their addiction creates and expect our daughters to share the responsibilities of initiating, paying, and risking rejection, thus leaving men with less need to objectify and to build up the volcano of anger that leaks into sexual harassment and explodes into rape.

7. DOES THE CRIMINAL JUSTICE SYSTEM DISCRIMINATE AGAINST MEN?

Unequal Time for Equal Crime

ITEM. *A man convicted of murder is twenty times more likely than a woman convicted of murder to receive the death penalty.*[89] *Although women are 1 of 8 of those arrested for murder they are only 1 out of 100 of those executed.*[90]

ITEM. *Andrea Yates murdered her five children. She was found not guilty in 2006 by reason of insanity and was given treatment rather than punishment.*[91]

ITEM. *Virginia, one of the leading states in executing males, last executed a female almost a century ago, in 1912.*[92]

ITEM. *In North Carolina, a man who commits second-degree murder receives a sentence an average of 12.6 years longer than a woman who commits second-degree murder.*[93]

ITEM. *The U.S. Department of Justice records the sentence differences listed in Table 1.5 nationwide.*

ITEM. *Being male contributes more to a longer sentence than race or any other factor—legal or extralegal.*[94]

ITEM. *Prosecutors consistently note that women almost always receive lower bail for equal crimes.*[95]

In essence, there are two bails: the male bail and the female bail. Women are also more likely to be released on their own recognizance.

The Execution Club: A Male-Only Club

ITEM. *At least thirty Americans have been executed and later found innocent. All thirty were men.*[96]

ITEM. *One hundred twenty-three men (and zero women) have been consigned to death row and later freed after their convictions were proven unjustified.*[97]

Table 1.5 Number of Months to Which Females Versus Males Were Sentenced for the Same Offense

Offense	Female	Male	% of Added Time Males Serve
Sexual Assault (Including Rape)	41	80	95
Aggravated Assault	25	38	52
Burglary	23	37	61
Larceny	15	21	40

SOURCE: U.S. Department of Justice, Bureau of Justice Statistics, *State Court Sentencing of Convicted Felons, 2002—Statistical Tables,* publication #NCJ-208910, (May 2005), Table 2.6: "Mean Length of Felony State Court Sentences Imposed, by Offense and Gender of Felons, 2002," http://www.ojp.usdoj.gov/bjs/pub/pdf/scscf02.pdf, downloaded August 1, 2006.

Approximately nineteen hundred women commit homicide in the United States *each year.*[98] When women commit homicide, almost 90 percent of their victims are men.[99] Remember, though, that when women kill men it is often via a contract killing, which gets recorded by the FBI not as a woman killing a man, but as a "multiple offender killing."[100]

For nearly four decades now, we have become *in*creasingly protective of women and *de*creasingly protective of men—even if that man is a boy and a legal minor, as was sixteen-year-old Heath Wilkins. Adult Marjorie Filipiak and child Heath both pled guilty to being co-conspirators in a murder. Neither was a hardened criminal. Heath Wilkins got the death sentence; Marjorie Filipiak went free.[101] When Heath Wilkins was found to have been a victim of child sexual abuse, it did not deter the judge from giving him the death sentence.[102] I know of no case in which a *female* minor who was a coconspirator with an adult man in a murder, and was found to have been a victim of child sexual abuse, was given so much as a long prison sentence.

> ITEM. *Any given man in prison is still 1,000 percent as likely as any given woman to die via suicide, homicide, or execution.*[103]

Although women's prisons are safer than men's prisons and designed more for rehabilitation, virtually all the recent press coverage has focused on the plight of the female prisoner—as if that plight were unique to the female prisoner. The result? States such as California are now financing the study of *only* female prisoner health issues.[104] Mothers in Lancaster, Massachusetts, have special facilities in which to see their children; fathers do not.[105] In New York's Bedford Hills Corrections Facility, mothers have a live-in nursery; fathers do not.

Women Who Kill Too Much and the Courts That Free Them: The "Female-Only" Defenses

Neither men nor women are exempt from killing loved ones. The difference is in what happens to them when they do. We have already seen the plea bargain defense and "the contract killing defense." Underlying these defenses is a deep-seated propensity: When women kill, judges and juries search for a reason, and the reason becomes her defense. Thus many of the more than ten defenses I review in *The Myth of Male Power* imply a reason that the woman's crime led to her receiving either no sentence or a reduced sentence: the "battered women's syndrome"; PMS; postpartum depression; being a mother; children need their mothers; the "my child, my right to abuse it" defense; and the "Svengali defense."

No man has successfully used any of these defenses in similar circumstances. Nor do men have any equivalent "male-only" defenses. *Each* of these defenses therefore violates the Fourteenth Amendment's guarantee of equal protection to both sexes under the law. This double standard of self-defense will be wreaking havoc in the legal system for decades.

I'll review just a few of these defenses here. But all of these work only because of our underlying belief in women's greater innocence. So let me start with the "innocent woman defense," the one that underlies all others.

The "Innocent Woman Defense"

At first I had labeled this the "female credibility principle" because of the tendency to see women as more credible because they are thought to be more innocent. However, even when women admitted making false allegations that they were raped or that their husbands abused them, for example, their admission that they lied was often *not* believed. Therefore the belief in the innocent woman ran even deeper than the tendency to believe women.

Take Bessie Reese, for example. Bessie Reese's husband went on a trip and decided not to return to Bessie. Since her husband had gone with James Richardson, Bessie decided to retaliate by poisoning the lunches of the seven Richardson children. All seven children died.[106]

Bessie Reese never became a suspect. She was never given a polygraph test. Was she deserving of such credibility? Not exactly. She had gone to trial for the poisoning of her first husband. (She was set free.)[107] And she was found guilty of shooting her second husband. (She did a short stint in jail.)

James Richardson got the death sentence. Yet James and his wife were eight miles away working in a citrus grove in Arcadia, Florida, when Bessie was serving the children lunch. Richardson was falsely accused of failing a polygraph test—yet the prosecutor who handled the Richardson appeal acknowledges that no one during the original trial ever saw the test.[108]

James Richardson literally watched his own coffin being built. But the death sentence was temporarily commuted in 1972. And then, after James spent two decades in prison, Bessie Reese finally confessed to poisoning the children. But the belief in "the innocent woman" and "the guilty man" was strong enough that even a second signed affidavit by Bessie did not lead to a new trial for James. **Which illustrates the basis of the "innocent woman defense": Women are believed when they say they are innocent of violence and most easily doubted when they say they are guilty of violence.**

It took political protests over the racism of the case (James was black; Bessie was white) to lead to a new trial and Richardson's release (after twenty-one years in prison).

The Visibility of Racism Versus the Invisibility of Sexism

This case became known only as an example of racism. But were it only racism, then Mrs. Richardson, who is black, would also have been investigated. Although Mrs. Richardson was at the same place as her husband when the poisonings occurred, neither she nor Bessie ever became a serious suspect. *Neither* woman became a serious suspect—only the man.

The cost of protecting women who kill is the same as the cost of protecting men who kill: The killer continues to kill—not just disposable men, but precious children.

To this day, Bessie Reese has not been charged with the murders to which she confessed.[109]

The "Arsenic and Old Lace" Case

When Blanche Taylor Moore and her husband went on a honeymoon and he suddenly had to be taken to the hospital, the doctor discovered he had been poisoned by arsenic. The dose wasn't enough to kill him, so Blanche gave him a couple of extra poisoned milkshakes. When the story got out, some people recalled that Blanche's first husband had died from arsenic poisoning. Others remembered a boyfriend had "died of a heart attack." But now the police became suspicious. They dug up her boyfriend's body and discovered his corpse retained a toxic dose of arsenic. Her father's body was then exhumed; it also contained arsenic.[110]

As Blanche's activities became public, people began calling the police saying they had reason to believe that Blanche had killed their relatives as well. Blanche had been assumed innocent for a quarter century. No man in American history has ever been assumed innocent while his mother, first wife, and a woman friend died of poisoning and a second wife almost died of poisoning. Moreover, all this happened in one community, showing that the power of female innocence can make a woman's crimes invisible even when the evidence is right before our eyes.

How the Battered Women's Syndrome Becomes the "Learned Helplessness Defense"

ITEM. *The governor of Ohio releases from prison twenty-five women who had been convicted of killing or assaulting their husbands or companions.[111] Each woman claimed the man had abused her. Within months, other governors had followed suit.[112]*

Until 1982, anyone who called a *premeditated* murder "self-defense" would have been laughed out of court. But in 1982, Lenore Walker won the first legal victory for her women-only theory of "learned helplessness," which suggests that a woman whose husband or boyfriend batters her becomes fearful for her life and helpless to leave him so if she kills him, it is really self-defense—even if she had premeditated his murder.[113]

The woman is said to be a victim of "battered women's syndrome." As we saw in Section 5 on Domestic Violence, when women kill men, the man almost always has an insurance policy. But when asked if a woman could kill for insurance money, Lenore Walker says "no": She claims, "*Women* don't kill men unless they've been pushed to a point of desperation."[114]

Ironically, feminists often say, "There's never an excuse for violence against a woman." When it comes to female violence against men, though, there's *always* an excuse. That sexism is now called the law in fifteen states.

By the 1990s, states such as California and Ohio allowed a woman to kill her sleeping husband because she "*felt* helpless."[115] Allowing a woman to claim self-defense after killing a man who was asleep gave these states a "females-only" definition of self-defense. For the first time in American history, premeditated murder, normally called first-degree murder (the worst kind), was called self-defense—but only if a woman was accused, and only if a man was murdered.

How the "Battered Women's Syndrome" Works in Real Life

Marlene Wagshall waited until her husband Joshua was asleep. She then stood beside their bed, assumed a crouched, combat position that she had trained for, pointed a .357 Magnum at his chest, and squeezed the trigger.[116] Their daughter watched, terror-stricken, as her dad struggled to close the door so she would not see him die. That was the last time their daughter saw her dad.

After eighteen hours on the operating table and the removal of his spleen, parts of his liver, his pancreas, and his upper intestine, Joshua survived, in part. His children, though, were gone—Marlene had kidnapped them.

The grand jury found Marlene guilty not only of attempted murder but also of numerous other counts. However, feminist District Attorney Elizabeth Holtzman reduced the attempted murder charge to second-degree assault and accepted a plea for Marlene to spend *one day in jail.* After one day, Marlene could be free on five years' probation.[117]

Why? Marlene claimed she was a victim of "battered women's syndrome." However, there was no corroborative evidence—no children as witnesses, no hospital records, no accounts of neighbors.

How the "Baby Blues" and "Terrible Twos" Become the "Depressed Mother Defense"

The "Baby Blues" Sheryl Lynn Massip, a mother in her mid-twenties, murdered her six-month-old son by crushing his head under the wheel of the family car. Then she systematically covered up the murder until she was discovered. Then she testified that she suffered from postpartum depression—or "baby blues." Her sentence? Treatment.[118]

The "Terrible Twos" Josephine Mesa beat her two-year-old son to death with the wooden handle of a toilet plunger.[119] She then buried the battered baby in a trash bin. When scavengers found the baby outside her Oceanside, California, apartment, she denied she knew him. When the evidence became overwhelming, she confessed. The excuse? She was depressed. The child was going through the "terrible twos." The punishment? Counseling, probation, and anti-depressants. *She never spent a day behind bars.*[120]

Despite This Evidence . . .

Despite this evidence, state gender bias commissions invariably find the criminal justice system guilty of discrimination against women. However, these "government" commissions are not really government commissions—they are feminist commissions. That is, the government pays the feminist National Organization for Women and the mostly feminist National Association of Women Judges to choose which issues to research and which to ignore.[121] None of the issues discussed here are given serious consideration.

What is considered is that, *for the same crime,* women are more likely to go free on probation; men are more likely to get prison sentences. A common conclusion by gender bias commissions: Women are victims of discrimination because women receive longer periods *probation!*[122] The fallacy is obvious.

Similarly, the commissions are able to see how women's prisons need to pay attention to problems unique to women, but not to problems more common among men, such as guards turning their backs on male-to-male rape. The commissions focus on the overcrowding in women's prisons while barely acknowledging the more intense overcrowding in men's prisons. The commissions do, though, legitimately point out the comparative inadequacy of job-training programs in women's prisons, which does need to be changed.

In Brief . . .

In brief, the underlying problem starts with both sexes' deep-seated belief in the innocence of women, even when the woman confesses. This belief permeates all political parties. Its ubiquity translates into little questioning of the political power of feminism as the one-party system of gender politics. This combination in turn creates legal defenses for women only that are in blatant violation of the Fourteenth Amendment.

Feminism, by taking advantage of our vulnerability to protecting women, has managed to institutionalize the belief that there is never an excuse for violence by men against women, and always an excuse for violence by women against men.

If this double standard of self-defense will be wreaking havoc in the legal system for decades, what can be done? It will change only by the leadership of a bipartisan team of truly courageous attorneys and activists, and only if women play a major leadership role.

8. WHY MEN EARN MORE: DISCRIMINATION? CHOICES?

"Women who have never been married and never had children earn 117 percent of their male counterparts."

There is no single issue that bothers women in the workplace more than the belief they get paid less than men for the same work.[123] And for many women, the psychological damage of being undervalued hurts even more than the economic damage of being underpaid.

For these reasons, when I was on the board of NOW in New York City in the 1970s, I led protests against what I felt was the discrimination the pay gap reflected. And now, since my wife and two daughters (both in college) work, discrimination against women is discrimination against me.

But one question haunted me. "If an employer has to pay a man $1 for the same work a woman would do for 76 cents, why would anyone hire a man?" If women do produce more for less, I thought, women who own their own businesses would earn more than male business owners. So I checked. I found that women who own their own businesses earn only 49 percent of their male counterparts.[124]

Are women less effective? No. When the Rochester Institute of Technology surveyed business owners with MBAs, they discovered money was the primary motivator for only 29 percent of the women, versus 76 percent of the men.[125] Women prioritize flexibility, fulfillment, autonomy, and safety. Women aren't less effective; they have different priorities.

After more than a decade researching this for my book *Why Men Earn More,* I discovered twenty-five of these differences between men's and women's work-life choices. **All twenty-five choices lead to men earning more money and women having better lives** (e.g., more time with family and friends).

I was learning that the road to high pay is a toll road. Real power is about having a better life. The male definition of power—feeling obligated to earn money someone else spends while he dies sooner—is not real power.

Operationalizing real power involves discovering which tolls are worth paying. For example, the average full-time working man works at least three more hours per week than the average full-time working woman. Extra hours pay disproportionately. People who work forty-five hours per week earn more than twice the pay that people who work thirty-five hours per week do (132 percent more pay for 28 percent more time).[126] Is the trade-off worth it? Real power includes properly assessing trade-offs—assessing your family's needs, your talents, your passion, what different careers pay, and your values.

If the first piece of good news for women is that they are doing a better job assessing trade-offs than men, the implication is that men have more to learn from women than women have to learn from men.

There is a second piece of good news for women: **It appears women now earn more than men when they make the same twenty-five**

choices (e.g., a male and female civil engineer both with their company ten years, both traveling and relocating equally, risking equal hazards, working equally egregious weekends). Even part-time working women who work equal hours to men average higher earnings.[127]

If this is true, then when women and men make similar choices, does the pay gap either disappear or get reversed? Yes. For example, **women who have never been married and who have never had children earn 117 percent of their male counterparts.**[128] (This controls for education, hours worked, and age.)

Why? Without husbands, women have to focus on earning more (longer hours, moving, traveling, fields in technology). **Without children, men are *freer* to earn *less*** —that is, they are freer to pursue fulfilling careers (e.g., teaching writing or art) that tend to pay less because the supply exceeds the demand. The supply exceeds the demand exactly because they are more fulfilling.

See if you can find in any text in any other women's studies or gender studies class a list of fields in which women are paid more. In *Why Men Earn More,* you'll see thirty-nine of the major fields in which women are paid at least 5 percent more than men—out of the more than 80 fields that exist like this. And remember, these are not fields in which women necessarily work as many hours, travel as much, relocate as frequently, take as many hazardous assignments, and so on—and those are just five of the twenty-five ways to higher pay women pursue less frequently on average. These, though, are the existing opportunities that become visible only when our binoculars are refocused.

But in the corporate world, aren't male executives paid more than female executives? Yes. Why? According to Irene Lang, president of the feminist research organization Catalyst, men are nine times more likely responsible for bottom-line sales, marketing, and finances, not human resources or public relations. And a study in the *Industrial and Labor Relations Review* finds that male executives are more likely to have had more responsibilities with international rather than local firms or as higher-level executives (e.g., as executive vice presidents versus vice presidents). So an executive is not always equal to an executive.

Comparing men and women with the "same jobs," whether doctor or executive, is still comparing apples and oranges.

But wait. Do companies favor men for these greater responsibilities to begin with? Sometimes. Overall, track records being equal, whoever is more willing to relocate, travel,[129] and work eighty-hour weeks receives greater responsibilities. The male corporate model is built on men's greater willingness to be slaves of sorts. It was created in years when men were the sole breadwinners and executives almost always had children, and therefore had no choice. It was created in years when men bought into the "fathers' catch-22"—loving their family by being away from the love of their families. (Of course, no one pointed this out to men—there has been no men's liberation movement.)

So, are corporations off the hook? No. Changes in the work-life priorities of the next generation of executives imply a need for corporate adaptation. A survey of men and women in their twenties who were asked whether they would accept less pay in exchange for more family time found that 70 percent of the men chose family time, as did 63 percent of the women.[130] Aside from the fact that more men felt this way than women, the deeper message to corporations is that both sexes feel this way.

Is there discrimination against women? Yes. For example: the old boys' network. As well as men's style, men's rooms, men's sports, and so on.

And there is also discrimination against men. Since this is less well known, I'll elaborate. For example, try being a male model and asking for more than one-quarter of what a female model makes. Try getting hired as a male dental hygienist or nursery school teacher, or selling clothing at Wal-Mart (even menswear hires 93 percent women). Send five women and five men without experience to get a job as a cocktail waiter, or even waiting tables at a restaurant. Note that in all the hazardous occupations, such as the armed services, construction, cab driving, and war reporting, women seek protection and men give it, and women end up suffering far fewer injuries and deaths (93 to 94 percent of occupational deaths are suffered by men) even when they are paid the same.[131]

Once a woman knows how to make money, there are dozens of creative ways she can pursue her dream. For example, she can work in computers or engineering for a few years, and make enough to use her savings to take off a year or two to pursue what fulfills more but earns less such as writing a novel. Usually, when you follow your bliss, it's the money you'll miss. Thus, "starving artist" and actors called "waiter." Or she'll find herself marrying a man who is not her soul mate because she's been seduced by his ability to bankroll her bliss.

For men, the mastery of trade-offs is just as important. If his parents have encouraged him to follow his dream, that's fine unless he's heterosexual and wants children. Chances are his dream won't pay much, and women rarely marry men whom they believe will consistently be earning less (they may live with these men, but they rarely marry them).

When women and men know their choices create their pay, they have more flexibility to be nontraditional than if they believe men's greater pay for the same work makes it more cost-beneficial for him to raise money while she raises children. Thus the belief in pay discrimination creates the self-fulfilling prophecy of the gender pay gap. Enjoy the equal opportunity that feminism, capitalism, and male-dominated legislatures have all helped create.

9. ARE WOMEN DOING TWO JOBS WHILE MEN DO ONE?

The Making of the Myth of the Second Shift Woman and the Shiftless Man

When we hear "second shift" we think of a working woman having two jobs compared to her husband's one job. Emotionally, we feel the working woman—and especially the working mom—is often being ripped off, and we may feel anger toward the shiftless dad.

The phrase "second shift" leaped into the public consciousness with the publicity surrounding Arlie Hochschild's book *The Second Shift*[132] in 1989. *Newsweek's* headline publicized it as: "Women's Work Is Never Done,"[133] while *People* announced, "For Working Women, Having It All May Mean Doing It All."[134] *Time* magazine mocked men's "contribution" as "The Myth of Male Housework" versus "For Women, Toil Looms from Sun to Sun."[135] Thus began the Era of the Second Shift Woman and the Shiftless Man.

By the mid-1990s, the anger at men had become so palpable that even sedate publications like *The Economist* were characterizing women's versus men's workload as "A woman's work is never done; a man is *drunk* from sun to sun" (italics mine).[136]

This anger intensified when the United Nations' *Human Development Report 1995* made worldwide headlines with its "findings" that women *everywhere* were overworked and underpaid while their husbands were lazy and unappreciative.

There was a problem with these headlines. Rather, there were many problems. First, they were based on a press release that **excluded every single one of the countries in which the men were found to work more than the women according to the UN's own study.**[137] Second, the media that got the actual 230-page study ignored the contradictions between the study and the press release.[138]

But that's just the beginning. The UN's study was drawn from the studies of experts around the world, but the UN did not report the findings of any study in any country as the authors had reported them. When the UN saw the frequency with which the experts had found that men worked more than women, **the UN asked each author to "amend" his or her study with modifications that would add female labor, not male labor. That is, they asked for an estimate of** *voluntary,* **unpaid community work as well as "basket making, weaving, knitting, sewing, etc. for own** *consumption.*"[139] None of the fifty areas of contribution to the home listed later in this section as predominantly made by men were added.

Statements and a table appearing in the report in fact show that men in the United States worked 59.5 hours to women's 56.4 hours.[140] But the way the UN reported the data allowed it to ignore almost all the male contributions in addition to "amending" to add more women's contributions.

When I questioned the UN staff, they admitted their fabrication, but rationalized it by saying they did this because they felt *they needed to correct people's belief that men worked more.*[141]

Here I will list some of the myths—and therefore, anger at men—
created by *The Second Shift* versus the reality.

MYTH: *Women work an additional month of twenty-four-hour days every year in*
comparison to men. Overall, women work two shifts; men work one.

This myth is generated by ignoring four facts.

FACT: *The average woman does work almost seventeen hours more per week inside the*
home, but the Journal of Economic Literature reported that the average man works
over twenty hours more per week outside the home.[142] *In addition, the average*
man commutes two hours more per week than the average woman.[143] *Counting all*
aspects of work, then, **the average man works five hours per week more than**
the average woman.

FACT: *Hochschild—and virtually all well-publicized housework studies—left out the*
great majority of men's contributions to the home, which are not defined by the
sexist term "housework" but are included in my Male "Housework" List later in
this section.

FACT: *When women earn more income than their husbands, husbands do more house-*
work than their wives.[144] *(To Hochschild's credit, this is documented in The Second*
Shift but obviously is not reflected in the headlines about The Second Shift.)

FACT: *Even when the wife works full-time and year-round, the husband provides*
65 percent of the household income.[145] *As my Section 8 on earnings documents, this*
income gap is not because of discrimination.

What About the Working Mother's Juggling Act?

When we think of the second shift, though, we think especially of the
juggling act experienced by the working mother. The working mother's juggling act *is* fact. But there are also myths.

MYTH: **The working mother has two shifts, but her husband has only one.**

FACT: *The husbands of working mothers are…working fathers.* **Working fa-**
thers' *total* workload exceeds mothers' by four and a half hours per
week *(working fathers': 61.4; working mothers': 56.9).*[146] *Working mothers do*
more work in the second shift; working fathers, though, do more work in the first
shift. Specifically, **fathers work eleven hours more outside the home than**
mothers[147] **do.**

MYTH: *When it comes to free time, married women have less than married men, mothers have* much *less than fathers, and mothers with preschool children?... Forget it!*

FACT: *Married women have almost two more hours of leisure time per week than their husbands.*[148] *Mothers with children age five and older have one hour more of free time per week.*[149] **Mothers *with preschool children averaged three* more *hours more per week of* free time *than dads with preschool children.*[150]**

Dad's free time has *de*creased in recent years by ten hours a week, mom's by four.[151] When the media and academia ignore all this, it sets the stage not only for women shaming men but also for men generating status by shaming themselves and other men. For example, successful woman Jane Pauley publicly shames her husband, Garry Trudeau of *Doonesbury* fame, for not equally sharing housework. Trudeau, in turn, shames other men with cartoons like the one shown here.

However, were we aware of only men's contributions, then my parody of the *Doonesbury* cartoon, also shown here, would make as much sense.

Of course, when we acknowledge both sexes' contributions, then either cartoon without the other makes no sense.

How Did Hochschild Reach Her Conclusion That "Women Work an Extra Month of Twenty-Four-Hour Days a Year"?[152]

Hochschild used mostly 1960s data in a 1989 book to "prove" that men weren't doing any more housework in 1989 then they were in the 1960s! So **headlines were telling the world that men hadn't changed by citing a book that used quarter-century-old data.**

Hochschild's biggest mistake, though, was one made by almost every popularized housework study: She did not adequately measure men's contribution to work around the home. For example, if mom drives the children to daycare, it's called housework; if dad drives the family to grandma's, it's *not* called housework.

The Hochschild List[153]
Chores Traditionally Done by *Women* (à la Hochschild)

Housework

- "Picking up"
- Vacuuming
- Making beds
- Cleaning bathrooms
- Doing laundry
- Routine meal preparation
- Cleanup
- Grocery shopping
- Sewing
- Care for house plants
- Care for pets
- Dealing with the bank

Parenting/Childcare

- Tending a child while sick
- Feeding the child
- Bathing the child
- Driving the child (e.g., to daycare or to doctors)
- Educating the child
- Daily discipline of the child

• Reading to the child

Management of Domestic Life

• Remembering domestic chores and events
• Planning domestic chores and events
• Scheduling domestic chores and events
• Making up the grocery list
• Paying bills
• Sending birthday and holiday cards
• Arranging babysitting
• Preparing birthday parties for the child

Chores Traditionally Done by *Men* (à la Hochschild)

• Putting out the garbage
• Car repairs
• Lawn
• Household repairs

What is left out of the chores traditionally done by men? About 90 percent of the Male "Housework" List.

The Male "Housework" List (or "Honey Do" List), or the Second Shift, Male Style

The biggest fallacy of housework studies is that the word "housework" triggers an image of contributions made mostly by women *in* the home (cooking, cleaning, and so on). **Much of what men do is work *around* the home** (for example, car or roof repairs, outdoor painting and planting, coaching, shoveling snow, driving), not *in* the home. This is true all over the world. What follows, then, is not as much a male "*house*work" list as a list of some of the fifty-four *categories* of *contributions* many men make to the family. (All fifty-four categories, and many more examples in each category, are in *Women Can't Hear What Men Don't Say*. They are rarely mentioned by men, thus the book's title.)

In any given family, some of these activities will be done more by women than by men. If you are in college, put a "D" next to all the contributions made more often by dad and an "M" next to those more likely to be made by your mom. Do a survey of your classmates, email them to me, and I'll report the findings in the next edition of this book.

1. Activities most likely to break an arm, leg, or neck or to crack a skull (e.g., climbing ladders)
2. Activities most likely to trigger heart attacks (e.g., shoveling snow)
3. Activities most likely to cause lower back problems and hernia operations (e.g., moving furniture, hanging heavy pictures)
4. Assembly (e.g., mail order or preassembled furniture or toys)
5. Barbecuing (e.g., cooking, buying supplies, cleaning up)
6. Bodyguard (When women and men walk together in a public place, he unconsciously serves as her bodyguard—if someone tried to harm her, he would try to immediately protect her; if someone tried to harm him, she would primarily protect herself)
7. Camping (e.g., camping equipment buyer, carrier and setter-upper)
8. Car buying and maintenance
9. Carpentry (e.g., putting up shelves)
10. Christmas/Holidays (e.g., Putting up lights on house and tree; tree purchase and set-up)
11. "Male cleaning" (e.g., car washing and waxing; plunging a backed-up toilet; cleaning up dog excrement)
12. Coaching-as-childcare (Sports are one of the greatest teachers. As a coach, dad is making sure he can translate the game into his child's everyday life)
13. Computer buying (Buying implies keeping up with the research to keep up with technology)
14. Confrontations—with neighbors or strangers (e.g., a loud party)
15. Decks (building, sanding, staining, sealing)
16. Disciplining of kids (e.g., "Wait 'til daddy comes home" or tough love–type boundary enforcement)
17. Dragon-killing—modern version (e.g., mouse- and spider-killing, or PC-style: removing spider without hurting it)
18. Driving (e.g., to and from functions, especially when conditions are hazardous, area is unfamiliar, and the couple is both exhausted or high)
19. Emergency *prevention* (e.g., time to change oil, add anti-freeze)

20. When emergencies arise despite prevention (E.g., changing a tire)
21. Post-emergencies: roof repair (shingles, holes, leaks, etc.)
22. Financial research (e.g., life insurance policies, investments, refinancing)
23. Fire-building, wood chopping
24. Garbage
25. Installation/hook-up (e.g., of washer, computer, stereo, cables)
26. Opening jars, doors, big boxes, paint cans
27. Option generating (e.g., dad: "Where'd you like to go to dinner?" Mom: "Makes no difference." Dad: "Chinese?" Mom: "We just had that." Does dad generate the options, mom the vetoes?)
28. Painting
29. Planting (e.g., buying, digging holes for, and moving plants)
30. Plastering, spackling, grouting, caulking, and mortaring
31. Poisons, exposure to
32. Programming (e.g., the VCR, timers, speed dial)
33. Pumping gas, paying for gas, changing oil
34. Remodeling
35. Repairs (e.g., toilets, faucets, sliding and screen doors)
36. Restaurants-for-romance (e.g., checking out restaurants that fit her definition of romance, taking her there, and paying)
37. Shopping for paint, hardware, much of the "bulk" shopping
38. Stereo and video buying, hooking up, trouble-shooting
39. Toy and bike care
40. Weather guard (e.g., giving up his jacket for her; when raining, dropping family near a movie; scraping ice off windshield)
41. Yard work (e.g., lawn mowing, raking, tree trimming, fertilizing)

Myths the Male "Housework" List Destroys

MYTH: *Women's housework is unappreciated.*

FACT: *Both sexes' contributions are unappreciated—the male-style is so unappreciated that there is no equivalent name to "housework," no study, and no headlines.*

MYTH: *Women's housework is unpaid.* .

FACT: *Both sexes do housework for which they are unpaid.*

MYTH: *Countries' GNPs measure men's work, not women's.*

FACT: *Countries' GNPs do not include either sex's unpaid contributions to the family.*

MYTH: *"Women's work" requires women to always be "on call."*

FACT: *Both sexes are "on call," each in their traditional areas of responsibility.*

MYTH: **Women take responsibility, men just help with the housework.**

FACT: *It is rare for either sex to truly share psychological responsibility for the type of contribution traditionally done by the other sex. In homes where only men are breadwinners, women make no financial contribution and men don't complain.*

MYTH: *"A man may work from sun to sun, but a woman's work is never done."*

FACT: *By seeing how men are also "on call" twenty-four hours a day, and also share psychological responsibility that haunts them while they're sleeping, we see how neither sex's work is ever done.*

MYTH: **Men think marriage entitles them to a domestic slave.**

FACT: *Both sexes expect their partner to do chores they used to do themselves before marriage...so the real issue is how marriage tempts both sexes into a division of labor.*

MYTH: **Women nurture men—they even "mother" them; men don't nurture women.**

FACT: *Both sexes nurture each other in different ways. Women's way is called nurturance; the traditional man's "financial womb" is culturally invisible as its own form of nurturance.*

Notice how it isn't necessary to make women wrong in order to acknowledge men. Feminism often acts as if women can receive no credit unless men are made wrong.

The underlying reason books like the *Second Shift* and the UN report could dominate the public consciousness with the myth of the second shift woman and the shiftless man is that feminism has become the one-party system of gender politics, and in all one-party systems there are no checks and balances. Media reporters assigned to cover gender politics are almost all feminists, so press releases that fit the bias get the headlines with little need to double-check sources or seek out experts who would question the research.

10. MARRIAGE, DIVORCE, AND CHILD CUSTODY

Feminism often portrays marriage as a patriarchal institution designed to serve men at the expense of women. Consider another view of marriage—with the controlling force not being men, but survival.

From Role Mate to Soul Mate

For thousands of years, most marriages were in Stage I—survival-focused. After World War II, as death from starvation, disease, and poor sanitation lost its controlling grip, marriages increasingly flirted with Stage II—a self-fulfillment focus. The wealthier the family, the more the focus on self-fulfillment.

In the survival-focused Stage I, most couples were role mates: The woman raised the children and the man raised the money. In Stage II, couples increasingly desired to be soul mates. Why? As couples met their survival needs, they "upped the ante" and redefined love. Sadly, the very qualities that made a "perfect couple" in a Stage I marriage made them "perfect for divorce" in a Stage II marriage (see Table 1.6).

The people with the most freedom to redefine love were the women who had married the most successful men—meaning men chosen for their skill as role mates, not soul mates. Ironically, these women had husbands who made enough money to pay for the psychologists who verified that their husbands were poor soul mates and that the women deserved more. Liberated to seek Stage II goals, these women became dissatisfied. Divorce followed.

Thus the freest, most privileged women became the most dissatisfied—in part because they blamed their husbands for being the men they chose them to be. No one explained that what was needed was a "gender transition movement"—a transition from the old, rigid roles of the past to new, more flexible roles for the future. For both sexes. At the same time.

In the political vacuum, the academic community's political left, impressed with the justice of the civil rights movement and often advocates of Marxism's beliefs that capitalism divided people into oppressors and oppressed, defined women as the oppressed. The women's movement saw men earning more money and called it male power rather than understanding it was the male obligation. They didn't understand that **when over 90 percent of women got married and divorce was rare, discrimination in favor of men at work meant discrimination in favor of their wives at home.** With no one able to see that survival needs also made men's role restrictive and powerlessness, few objected to defining the world-until-then as largely patriarchal and women as an oppressed class.

Table 1.6 Stage I Versus Stage II Marriages

Stage I Roles	Stage II Goals*
Marriage	*Marriage (or Long-Term Relationship)*
Survival	Fulfillment
Role mates: women and men married to create a "whole"	Soul mates: "whole" persons married to create synergy
Division of roles	Commonality of roles
Woman raises children; man raises money	Both sexes raise children; both sexes raise money
Children obligatory	Children a choice
Women expected to risk life in childbirth; men expected to risk life in war	Fewer women killed in childbirth; fewer men killed in war
'Til death do us part	'Til unhappiness do we stay together
Neither party can end contract	Either party can end contract
Women-as-property; men-as-less-than-property (expected to die before property was lost)	Sexes equally responsible for self and other
Both sexes subservient to needs of family	Both sexes balance needs of family with needs of self
Love emanates from mutual dependence	Love emanates from choice
Love less conditional	Love more conditional (no physical and less verbal abuse, listening skills, mutual respect, common values)
Choice of Partners	*Choice of Partners*
Parental influence is primary	Parental influence is secondary
Women expected to marry their source of income ("marry up")	Neither sex expected to provide more than half the income
Premarital Conditions	*Premarital Conditions*
Men addicted to female sex and beauty, then deprived of "fix" until they supply security	Smaller gap between men's addiction to sex and women keeping it in short supply prior to commitment

* Stage II Goals are the ideal; most of these goals are not yet reality for most couples.

Since the late 1980s, the "feminization of poverty" has increasingly been assumed to be a reality. Its credibility heightened when a feminist named Lenore Weitzman reported her findings that women who were divorced suffered a 73 percent decline in their standard of living while their ex-husbands experienced a 42 percent rise in their standard of living.[154] By the time these statistics were found to be erroneous both mathematically and methodologically, based on a small sample, and contradicted by almost all other economists who looked at nationwide samples (such as Duncan and Hoffman[155]), they had become part of the public consciousness. To this day, few people know that by the end of the fifth year after divorce women are on average 10 percent *ahead* of where they were before divorce.

As women complained, men competed to be their saviors. Where one husband had failed, male legislators competed to make government a substitute husband. Soon the government allowed women who divorced to often continue to receive many of the benefits of marriage—the home, money, and children. In contrast, their ex-husbands received none of the benefits of marriage (few ex-wives delivered cooked meals, cleaned, continued sex, or offered emotional support). Instead, divorce to him often meant paying for a home he didn't live in and children he felt were being turned against him.

While divorce led to problems for both women and men, it created deeper problems for children. Divorce's problems for children occurred because, while the women's movement was successfully explaining the value of women at work, no one was explaining the value of men as dads. So divorce left women who wanted to receive child support in exchange for being the primary parent with little political, academic, or philosophical opposition.

The result was a generation in which millions of children were raised by single moms. When I began to research the outcomes for these children for *Father and Child Reunion,* I discovered exactly what was missing when dad was missing.

What Is Missing When Dad Is Missing?

The benefits of dad to the baby begin at birth. The more frequently a father visits the hospital of an infant who is prematurely born, the more rapidly the infant gains weight and the more quickly the infant is able to leave the hospital.[156] More importantly, the more the father visited, the better was the infant's social-personal development and its ability to adapt.[157] In a study of black infants, the more interaction the boy had with the father, the higher his mental competence and psychomotor functioning *by the age of six months*.[158] By the age of three years, psycho-motor functioning is associated with the development of a higher IQ.[159]

Psychologists at the National Institute of Mental Health have found that boys who have contact with fathers display a greater trust level even by the time they are five to six months old.[160] For example, they are friendlier with strangers and more willing to be picked up. They also enjoy playing more and are more verbally open. Students coming from father-present families score higher in math and sci-ence *even when they come from weaker schools*.[161] First grade black and white children of both sexes raised in father-absent families re-corded significantly lower IQ scores than those with fathers pres-ent.[162] Seventy-three percent of adolescent murderers come from mother-only homes.[163]

Suppose, though, there is a divorce? What works best for children of divorce was the primary focus of a decade's worth of research for *Father and Child Reunion*. The following are some key factors.

The Family Arrangements That Work Best for Children

Yes, children do best in an intact family. How do children do in the event of a divorce? After examining more than a hundred of the best studies, I have ranked various family structures from best to worst as follows:

1. Shared parent time (about equal time with mom and dad) with two conditions:
   • Parents live close enough to each other that the child does not need to forfeit friends or activities when visiting the other parent
   • No bad-mouthing
2. Primary father time (primary father custody)
3. Primary mother time

To me the most surprising finding is that children raised by single dads do better in comparison to children raised by single moms. (When socioeconomic variables are controlled for, this is still true, but the gap is less.) These children do better in more than twenty areas of measurement: They do better on the SATs and in almost all academic areas; they get along better with other children; and they are more trusting, have higher self-esteem and better physical health, and do better socially and psychologically.

Children raised by single dads are far less likely to suffer from nightmares, temper tantrums, being bullied, or otherwise feeling like a victim, in comparison to children raised by single moms. In contrast, children raised by single moms are about twice as likely to have ADD or ADHD as are children raised by single dads.

The two characteristics of children raised by single dads that most surprised me are, first, that they are more likely to be assertive, but less likely to be aggressive, and, even more surprising, that they are more likely to be empathetic.

Apparently, even though moms are themselves more empathetic, **giving empathy to a child teaches a child how to *receive* empathy, but not *give* it.** Dads more often require the child to think of others' needs by *enforcing consequences* if the child doesn't, which makes it in the child's self-interest to think of others' needs.

These outcomes occur even though one- and two-year-old children of divorce with developmental disabilities are fifteen times more likely to be given to fathers to raise and even though children who are raised by moms and have problems with drinking, drugs, depression, delinquency, and disobedience are most likely to be given to their dads to "take over" in early teenage years.

The propensity of dads to take on the more challenging children and yet still have positive outcomes speaks highly of dads' contributions. However, children raised by single dads do not do as well as those raised in intact families or those raised equally by mom and dad after divorce.

Caveat: This does not mean that men are better fathers than women are mothers. Single fathers usually have more income and education and tend to be older. And single dads today are similar to female doctors in the 1950s: exceptionally motivated.

One reason that children of divorce on average do so much better with single dads is to the moms' credit—moms are more likely to stay involved. And to dad's credit, dads are more likely to facilitate mom's involvement than mom is to facilitate dad's. In brief, the child living primarily with dad is more likely to live in conditions that come closer to the intact family.

Why this difference? One clue appears to be the bad-mouthing gap. When Glynnis Walker, in her research for *Solomon's Children,* asked children years after divorce which parent bad-mouthed the other, the children were almost five times more likely to say "only mom says bad things about dad" than vice versa. Perhaps as a result, when children live primarily with mom, the children are nine times as likely to feel negatively about dad. Similarly, when mom raises children, the parents are nine times as likely to be in conflict as when children live with their dads.

These findings are significant for two reasons. First, in high-conflict divorces if we conclude that the parental conflict will prevent 50–50 involvement from working, we tend to revert to primary mother time, when in fact it's far more likely that with primary father time the parents will have less conflict and the children will have more of both parents and will do better. Second, once a mother knows the likely alternative to equal involvement is primary father involvement, the incentive is to reduce conflict and have equal involvement—rather than increase conflict to have mother involvement.

Why Are *Both* Parents So Important—Especially After a Divorce?

• **The child is half mom and half dad.** The job of a child growing up is to discover whom it is. Who is it? It is half mom and half dad. It is not the better parent. It is both parents, warts and all. So we are not talking about fathers' rights, mothers' rights, or even the child's right to both parents. We are talking about a new paradigm: **the child's right to both halves of itself.** Psychological stability seems to emanate from the child knowing both parts of itself. Children with minimal exposure to the other parent after divorce seem to feel abandoned and often psychologically rudderless—even when they succeed on the surface (e.g., good grades).

Once this is understood, the damage of bad-mouthing becomes clearer. **Criticizing the other parent is criticizing the half of the child that is the other parent.** As the child looks in the mirror and sees that his or her body language is the body language of the criticized parent, the child fears she or he might also be an "irresponsible jerk," a "compulsive liar," and so on.

• **Checks and balances.** Dads and moms, like Republicans and Democrats, provide checks and balances. Moms tend to overstress protection; dads tend to overstress the "tough" part of tough love. There has to be a balance of power for the child to absorb a balance of both parents' gifts. One parent dominating tends to leave the child with a stereotyped and biased perspective of the values of the minority parent, and ultimately the child is unappreciative of that half of itself. **The minority parent becomes a straw-man or straw-woman, thus that part of the child becomes a straw-self.** The minority parent becomes undervalued, thus that part of the child becomes undervalued to itself.

Checks and balances are best achieved with an approximately equal number of overnights. Why? As children approach adolescence, peer pressure tends to distort values. **The peaceful moments prior to bedtime are often the only time the impact of peer pressure recedes and parents' values can reenter the child's psyche.** The more opposite dad and mom are, the more the child benefits from the contributions of both during these brief windows of fragile moments.

The Future: How Do We Get Men to Raise Children as Much as Women Raise Money?

Imagine "inspiring" women to enter the workplace in the 1960s by telling them, "But if you get a divorce, *your husband will have the option of taking your job.*" Yet this is virtually what we tell men when it comes to raising children.

Here's how dads get the message that their parenting rights are in women's hands.

A Woman's Biology Is a Man's Destiny

In the old days—before abortion rights plus the female-only birth control pill—it was often said, "A woman's biology is a woman's destiny." Today it is more accurate to say, "A woman's biology is a *man's* destiny."

How so? Today, **women have the right to abort or to sue for support.** Only women have what I call ABC rights:

1. Abortion
2. Birth control method (pill, diaphragm, IUD, etc.) and Believability
3. Caring arrangement (adoption, invite dad to parent, parent alone, require dad to pay but prevent him from parenting, parent alone without informing dad but require dad to pay "after the fact")

In contrast, college men have three A rights:

1. Agree
2. Agree
3. Agree

"A Man Can Just Have Sex and Disappear, but a Woman Has to Live with the Consequences, Right?"

Many women have said to me, "Women are more cautious about sex before marriage because a single man can just have sex and disappear; a woman has to live with the consequences." Is that true? No. In fact, a man cannot just walk away: He's legally responsible to support the child. His wages can be garnished—whether or not he would have preferred an abortion. It is the woman who can legally "walk away"— by getting an abortion without even telling him.

Male responsibilities are built into *every* state law. Most states have some version of the Ohio laws that Planned Parenthood does a good job of explaining in a brochure to young men.[164] Here is a summary of an unwed dad's legal responsibilities:

- If the woman decides to keep the child the father must pay for the child for the next eighteen to twenty-one years, even if the mother prevents him from seeing the child.
- A mother can raise the child by herself and sue the man for child support without ever even mentioning to the father that the child is his. She can wait

until the child is twenty-three and then sue him for eighteen years of child support.

• He must pay no matter what he earns, whether the mother is or was a good or bad mother.

A man can "have sex and leave" only if a woman lets him. Two examples:

ITEM. *A Wisconsin court ruled that a man's occupation didn't produce enough income to support two households—his and his ex-wife's. They ordered him to change occupations.*[165]

ITEM. *A father discovers he has been paying child support for a child that he had been fraudulently told was his. The child support was not recoverable.*[166]

In brief, a woman's biology is a man's destiny. Or, to put it more bluntly, **when a man puts his penis in a woman's body, he puts his life in her hands.**

If Men Had "ABC Rights," Here's What They Might Look Like

Men's "A" Right and Responsibility: Abortion (or the Fallacy of "It's a *Woman's* Right to Choose Because It's a Woman's Body")

A woman's body *is* hers to control. When she chooses to share it with a man, she exercises that control. He makes a parallel choice. If together they produce a fetus, equality would dictate joint rights and joint responsibilities. The motto, "It's a woman's right to choose because it's a woman's body at stake" implies that if a man's body is also at stake, he would share that right to choose.

Is a man's body at stake? Any time a man is asked to work to pay child support, he is using his body, his time, his life—not for nine months, but for a minimum of eighteen to twenty-one years. So the motto of the feminist with integrity is, "It's a woman's and man's right to choose because it is a woman's and man's body and life at stake."

A woman has no right to a unilateral choice that affects the rest of a man's life any more than a man would have the right to a unilateral choice that affects the rest of a woman's life. That's why rape is a crime.

ITEM. *When two lesbians fought for primary parent time, the woman whose body was not used was granted it. The feminist National Center for Lesbian Rights and the ACLU both fought for the parent time rights of the woman whose body did not bear the child—calling their advocacy "cutting edge."*[167]

Lesbians' Custody Fights Test Family Law Frontier

By DAVID MARGOLICK
Special to the New York Times

When the body *not* being used is a man's, feminists say that it's exactly because his body is not being used that he doesn't have equal rights; when the body not being used is a woman's, feminists declare she should have equal rights.

Both sides of the contradiction are considered "progressive" and "liberal" for two reasons: A woman's rights are being championed, and feminists are doing the championing.

Men's "B" Rights and Responsibilities: Birth Control *and* Believability

For more than thirty years, the technology to develop a men's birth control pill has been ten to twenty years within reach. But there hasn't been the political will or the belief by the drug companies that men will use it. I explain in *Father and Child Reunion* why men will use it. The men's birth control pill will be as important to men as the women's pill was to women. It is the only guarantee that fewer children will be born without a dad who wants that child.

The existence of a female-only pill is politically possible partly because of the second of those two "Bs" in women's ABC rights—believability. We have socialized men to trust women and have socialized women to expect this trust. If you are a woman, you can get a sense of the power of this trust by imagining there being a birth control pill only for men. The man says, "Don't worry, I'm on the pill." Would you trust him?

Most women of whom I ask this question just laugh.[168] That changes once they get to know a man, but men are socialized to trust women until evidence to the contrary surfaces; women are socialized to be suspicious of men until an individual man earns trust.

Underlying the second "B" is **the unconscious assumption of the moral superiority of women**—that a woman would never consciously or unconsciously become pregnant to get a man to marry her and support her and the child, yet a man would lie to a woman because he "can just walk away." So if she says she's on birth control (and says she doesn't have herpes, and so on) and he still reaches for a condom, he is violating the unwritten code of women being inherently worthy of trust.

Men's "C" Right and Responsibility: Caring Arrangement

How a Woman Can Put a Child Up for Adoption Without Informing the Father...and Why He Can't Stop Her Ed McNamara[169] and his woman friend were having a lovely dinner in a San Diego restaurant after some months of not seeing each other. As she caught him up on the past months, she told him that she and he "just had a baby."

"What?!"

"I've named her Katie."

Ed choked on his fork. "Where, er...is Katie?"

"I've put Katie up for adoption!"

"Adoption? *Our* Katie?!"

"Yes. And guess what? She's been adopted! I thought you'd like to know."

Ed was paralyzed. But not for long....

Ed filed for custody of Katie when Katie was only five *weeks* old. But by the time the case came to trial, Katie had been with her adoptive parents five months. Ed was a contractor's estimator and the judge evaluated Ed as "a good parent who could provide a good, loving home for the child." But the judge ruled the child had already bonded with the adoptive parents. Ed appealed the case all the way to the U.S. Supreme Court.[170]

The woman who does not immediately notify the father of her pregnancy is, in effect, blackmailing the court by preventing it from connecting the child and father without hurting the child. By delaying informing him, she has hurt both the child and father, depriving the child of its natural relationship with its dad—a deprivation that can never be recovered.

Should a Woman Be Required to Notify the Father as Soon as She Discovers She Is Pregnant? If we expect men to be psychologically involved, we need to give men equal psychological time. If we expect men to be *legally* responsible, then close-to-equal time needs to be a legal right. If a man is to be held legally responsible, it is fair for the law to require the woman to make every reasonable attempt to notify the man of her pregnancy within, for example, four to five days.

A "Shared Choice" Movement

A male pro-choice movement does not want the reverse of a "women-only pro-choice" movement; it wants, rather, to *share* the choices—the choice to abortion, birth control method, and childcare arrangements. Equal rights to choose—in abortion, birth control method, or caring arrangement—are men's ABC rights and are as fundamental to men as they are to women. Women-only pro-choice is like men-only business clubs.

The solution to making men equal partners as parents is parallel to the solution to making women equal partners in the workplace: involve men with childcare responsibilities from an early age, make them partners at every stage, create equal rights, expect equal responsibilities, and perhaps create a period of affirmative action to help both sexes make the transition. We owe this to our children.

11. DOES POPULAR CULTURE DISCRIMINATE AGAINST MEN?

"Men have only two faults: Everything they say and everything they do."[171]
Post-Its, by 3M Corporation

Every group should be able to laugh at the foibles that characterize its culture. Red flags go up only when one group is disproportionately singled out.

©1997 Ephemera, Inc.

When we tell a lawyer joke, we visualize men; when we tell a "blonde" joke, we visualize women. Each reflects an attitude toward just that particular subset of men or women. But when we see attacks on all men, or all women, then the best litmus test of whether there is an underlying sexism is to check how we would feel if the genders were reversed.

For example, if we see the commonly found button shown here, we must ask ourselves how would we react if it said, "Not all *women* are annoying; some are dead." Or if we saw the real-life book cover for, *No Good Men,*[172] published by Simon & Schuster, one of the world's most successful publishers, shown here, we must ask ourselves how we would react if we saw *No Good Women* with the picture reversed. (Remember, for each man sleeping with a woman there is a woman sleeping with a man.)

A second litmus test as to whether to raise red flags is to ask, "Is there a market for only one sex being attacked?" For example, when *No Good Men* was successful, the author asked about publishing *No Good Women*. Simon and Schuster did their market research well enough to know women wouldn't buy it, and men wouldn't buy it. The conclusion: No one to pay? No one to publish.

A third litmus test of sexism is to see how we would feel in our gut if that which is being said about "all men" or "all women" were being said about all blacks or all Jews. *Feel* the disgust you experience when you witness these race-equivalents of the *No Good Men* book covers shown here.

Now here's the rub. During periods in our history, the *No Good Blacks* cover would *not* have created that feeling of disgust. Why does it now? African Americans refused to sit in the back of our buses. In Nazi Germany, *No Good Jews* would also not have catalyzed the disgust you doubtless just felt. We might think the difference in our reaction has to do with the perception of men as all-powerful, but it was exactly that perception of Jews that led to the passive acceptance of such slurs in Nazi Germany. **Then we waited for the consequences of that unconsciousness before we created a new consciousness.**

The Only Good Man Is a Dead Man

Cartoons of the type that used to appear mostly in women's magazines are now appearing not only in mainstream magazines but also in perhaps the most mainstream magazine appealing to sophisticated, literary intellectuals in the world, *The New Yorker,* as shown here.

"Well, finally—a man who gets it!"

The New Yorker, July 6, 1992, p. 39.

Perhaps a dozen mainstream films from the late 1980s to the present have one theme in common: Men are insufferable and the only way to change them is to kill them or at least give them a near-death experience. I am unaware of a single film with the same theme about a woman.

In *Ghost,* Patrick Swayze improves with death, as does Albert Brooks in *Defending Your Life.* In *Regarding Henry,* brain damage "kills" the arrogance of an attorney and transforms him into a caring attorney; in *Doctor,* cancer "kills" the arrogant doctor and transforms him into a caring doctor; in *Doc Hollywood,* it takes a car accident and a woman. And then there are the cinematic serial killers of men, Thelma and Louise...

NOW singled out *Thelma & Louise* to celebrate at its twenty-fifth national convention. The keynote speakers, Gloria Steinem and early feminist activist Flo Kennedy, dubbed themselves "the Thelma and Louise of the 1970s." NOW featured T-shirts boasting "Thelma and Louise Finishing School."[173]

When did feminism become a finishing schol for women interested in finishing off men? That wasn't the version of equality I fought for when I was on the board of NOW in New York City.

Not all films portraying men being killed portray the killing as literal. In *The First Wives' Club,* women joyfully kill their exes financially, destroy their reputations, or poison a dad's relationship with his children. Since *The First Wives' Club* was so successful, did formula-addicted Hollywood produce *The First Husbands' Club?* No. "Killing" ex-husbands is a successful formula; "killing" ex-wives is a failing formula. It failed the "is there a market?" litmus test.

Instead, Hollywood understood they could expand the psychological killing of men market to the psychological killing of boys. By 2006, in *John Tucker Must Die,* they were teaching high school girls how to ruin the reputation and break the heart of the school's most popular and respected boy, who had committed the crime of dating more than one of them without informing the others. The lessons learned: Ruining a boy will result in him understanding the girls are right and apologizing. No apologies needed by the girls for ruining him. Boys are learning to be the disposable sex.

In contrast, check out this formula for fiction-based Hollywood films that I document in *The Myth of Male Power:* **Any woman-in-jeopardy who is portrayed as positive and feminine in a fiction**

BENT OFFERINGS By Don Addis

Don Addis, *Bent Offerings,* March 13, 1989, Creators Syndicate, Inc.

film for more than three scenes does not die. Many men may die saving her, but she lives and never loses even a body part.

What motivates this anger? To this day, we hear of *Bride* magazine, but not *Groom* magazine; that is, whether it's the marriage of Princess Di or the latest issue of *People,* for many women the marriage fantasy is about being "swept away." Therefore, **divorce is women's dream of being swept away being swept away.** The anger at the ex-husbands in *The First Wives' Club* is based at least in part on that.

Note, in the examples of greeting cards and cartoons shown in this section, how many are about directing scorn at men by women who feel rejected by men. **Scorn is female porn.** Except that instead of the admiration of women reflected in male porn, note how in the female porn, the women are "killing" men. And calling it a Hallmark moment.

Part of men's porn does come from this fear of rejection too. When a guy fears rejection, he may turn a woman into a sex object ("take a look at that broad"). Why? It hurts less to be rejected by an object than it does to be rejected by a "bright, gorgeous woman who had too much going for her to even look at me." For both sexes, it hurts less to be rejected by an object than by a full human being.

The difference is that the culture supports only women doing this to a much greater degree and has created a culture of contempt for men that is self-fulfilling.

If the cartoon shown here, about divorce, for example, had portrayed two men saying that their divorce was just getting rid of 180 pounds of ugly fat, it would come across as bitter and sour grapes, not as humor, and therefore the cartoonist would never get it published in the *Los Angeles Times,* where it was, in fact, published.

If I'm Single, It's Because There Are No Good Men

A woman who can't find a man can always find a card.

She can send her other single women friends greeting cards that read, "Men: The great ones are all married, the good ones are all engaged...all that are left are some dinkwads, a bunch of geeks, and a couple of slime-buckets."[174] Or "Men are like a box of chocolates.... Most of them are fruits or nuts, and whatever you pick, you'll regret it later."[175]

Bad Mark for Hallmark

When it comes to cards, no one does their market research better than Hallmark, which is why Hallmark knows there is a market for women buying cards like the one shown here, which defines a man in nothing but derisive terms. However, Hallmark has no parallel card defining "woman" as, for example, "Woman. Ingredients: Vanity, entitlement (thinks men should pay for her; thinks the children are hers), confuses love with a diamond, and so on."

Ironically, some of these cards are the creations of a division of Hall-mark called Ambassador. Ambassador gives us the four stages of a relationship: "One: Boy meets girl. Two: Boy romances girl. Three: Boy begins acting like jerk. Four: Girl runs down boy with steam roller."

The picture? A steam roller crushing a man. The punch line? "Don't you love a card with a happy ending?"

What's the deception in cards like this? It's in stage 3: "Boy begins acting like jerk." What that usually means from his perspective is some version of "I'm just not into her." So he begins to not return phone calls and she concludes "jerk." A jerk is rarely someone a woman is crazy about who is crazy about her.

If Hallmark's "Ambassadors" have steam rollers to crush men who reject women, just imagine their military.

Hallmark's military is its Shoebox division. It specializes in the man-bashing cards. Here are three of dozens of similar examples of the way the Shoebox division describes men: "If they can make penicillin out of moldy cheese... maybe we can make men out of the low-lifes in this town";[176] "You're better off when the turkey's gone";[177] and "If men are God's gift to women, then God must really love gag gifts."[178]

The Shoebox division calls itself "A Tiny Little Division of Hallmark." They *were* tiny when they started in 1986. But man bashing was so popular that by 1998 the Shoebox division was Hallmark's largest selling division. Two hundred fifty million dollars a year cashing in mostly on women's anger toward men.[179] The "tiny little" division grew so quickly that Shoebox is now the most recognizable name in the greeting card industry after Hallmark itself.[180]

It is hard to overstate the fame or profit in misandry. (**Misandry is man-hating. You probably haven't heard of it; but now you'll**

MAN • ingredients: vanity, self-centeredness, arrogance, insensitivity, thoughtlessness, insincerity. Plus may contain one or more of the following: communication skills of a chimp, obsessive love for his mother; and/or an ego the size of a landfill.

see it all around you. [Not to worry. It even took Webster's until the turn of the twenty-first century to include it in their Collegiate dictionary. And my spell check still doesn't recognize it!])

Where can you find these man-hating cards? Try the "Love and Friendship" section—a bit like calling the Pentagon the "Love and Friendship" building. The problem runs deeper because it is part of a pattern. Calling itself a "Tiny Little Division" when it is the largest selling division is part of a female pattern of denying one's power. (Which is, like camouflage, a form of power.)

Does Shoebox have greeting cards for men to send? Well, sort of....A man can send a woman a card of a boy (not a man) saying, "Being humble and apologetic does not come easy for me....Unfortunately, being stupid does. Please forgive me."[181] I asked Hallmark if they had an equivalent card for women—with the woman saying it was not easy for her to be humble and apologetic, but easy for her to be stupid. No such card.[182]

Of course, Hallmark's medium conflicts with its message. The message says it is hard for men to be apologetic and humble. Yet Hallmark has found a market only among men who wish to apologize and be humble (say they are stupid).

Does Hallmark know this? Of course. If they didn't, they would be publishing an equivalent card for women. Think about that. Companies are consciously making a profit from women's self-righteousness. When the price is high enough, the prostitute will appear. But their job is to make a profit. The job of the class in which this book is read is to look within.

The title of one of my books—*Women Can't Hear What Men Don't Say*—basically blames men for not speaking their feelings to women. I agree with that, but I also want to acknowledge the rejection men experience when they do. The desire to reject men who express their feelings is so universal that American Greetings reproduced the entire Thelma and Louise "kill-the-whiner card" shown here in fold out form in magazines like *Newsweek* and *Life*. Yes, *Life*.

The Media

Worldwide, when men make an attempt to express adult men's issues in a way that includes criticism of feminism, they feel what might be called "the lace curtain" drawn around them. I will share my story in a minute, but I have been the most fortunate of men. Other men's stories are in *Women Can't Hear What Men Don't Say.* **No other man who has written a book on adult men's issues that has been critical of feminism has done well enough financially to be able to get a second book published with a mainstream publisher.** Here's just a taste of the politics of that process.

How I Met the Lace Curtain

When I was first elected to the board of NOW in New York City, I was twenty-six. I had never written for a national publication. The *New York Times* sought me out, did a major story on me and the men's groups I was running to teach men about feminism, and asked me to write an op-ed piece. I did. They published it, with hardly a word changed. They asked me to do a second. Again they published it with hardly a word changed. And a third....

As long as I was writing from a feminist perspective, the *New York Times* published *everything* I wrote. Once I began question-ing the feminist perspective, the *New York Times* published *noth-ing* I wrote** and did no features on me for almost thirty years. That changed only after I ran for governor of California as a Democrat in 2003 and was covered by the *New York Times,* which led to cover-age on my 2005 book, *Why Men Earn More.* To the *New York Times'* credit, their coverage and editing was fair to my content.

The earlier *New York Times* coverage had led to the *Today* show. During my years speaking from the feminist perspective, I was three times a guest on the *Today* show. Once I began adding men's perspec-tives to the mix, I was never invited back. To this day.

Then, in 1986, I first questioned in public the statement that men earn more than women for the same work. I did that on *Hour Maga-zine,* a show that was nationally televised at the time. Their guests were Gloria Steinem and me, as allies. But I ventured, "Never-married *women* often earn *more* than never-married men, because..." I had no sooner completed the thought than I noticed Gloria, puzzled, look to host Gary Collins as if to signal "cut!" Sure enough, we abruptly cut. The segment was never aired. My status changed from regular guest to never being invited back. I was beginning to notice a pattern!

The Myth of Male Power had just arrived at the studio of *Good Morning, America.* It was creating an in-studio buzz, and my publicists were informed that *GMA* wanted to devote a full half hour to a debate between me and a leading feminist like Gloria Steinem, Betty Friedan, or Susan Faludi. None of the named feminists would do a debate. Why not? For the same reason any one-party system has no interest in debating. When you have the power you have little to gain and a lot to lose.

Apparently, I was politically incorrect. Therefore, it seemed, I would be perfect for *Politically Incorrect,* with comedian Bill Maher, airing around the turn of the twenty-first century. Indeed, they did want people to argue with feminists, and they often called to check me out. But never an invitation. Only after the show had ended a long run did Stuart Pedersen, a paid consultant to the show, explain, "They wanted a male chauvinist who they could make look like a fool."

As it turned out, even on *Politically Incorrect* I had met the lace curtain, and it was drawn around my mouth.

TV's Lace Curtain

CBS's "Throw the Bum Out Week,"[183] aired without any female-bashing equivalent (e.g., a "Throw the Leech Out Week"), reflects a prejudice in the electronic media that is sustained by the more deeply seated prejudice men encounter when divorced. The promotional ad says it all: She's the victim, he's the bum, even though *she's* kicking *him* out—briefcase and all.

The Internet: AOL or AWOL?

Other than talk radio, are there outlets for men's feelings? The Internet originally held out hope. And men began speaking up, especially the nontechie men on America Online, who created forums such as the "Men's Equal Rights" folder. Quite quickly the men's forums on AOL were shut down. Censored.

Is it fair to suggest that if this censorship happened to any other group on AOL it would have made the front pages? Yes. When the *New York Times* discovered AOL had suspended the heated debate between

two opposing discussion groups on Ireland, the suspension made a three-column headline on the front page of the Sunday *New York Times*.[184] And AOL's censorship of men? Ignored by all the major media.

When Dad Tries to Love...

Nothing is more progressive than a dad trying to be equally involved in giving his children the love they need—especially after divorce. Yet the nation's most liberal electronic medium—PBS (Public Broadcasting System)—consistently airs the feminist line on these dads—they're mostly batterers—without question. Here's an example.

The PBS production *Breaking the Silence* (2005) quoted feminist scholars as making claims such as, "In 75% of cases in which fathers contest custody, fathers have a history of being batterers."[185] Fortunately, there is no evidence for that, and when confronted, PBS and the feminist making the 75percent claim could produce none.[186] But it took more than ten thousand protesters to get PBS to agree to do a follow-up story[187] that would presumably be fairer to these dads. When the only electronic medium that is financed significantly by public monies is taken over by employees who portray dads fighting for equality not as responsible dads but as batterers, and then ignore the government data to the contrary, what is the impact?

The impact on college men about to become dads begins with the impact of PBS on our judges and legislators. PBS is doubtless the most-watched serious media by this constituency. Should the college man-becoming-dad also become divorced, the judge may well judge him through an unconscious filter of guilty until proven innocent. If he tries to show the judge government data documenting that, in reality, mothers are more than twice as likely to batter their children as dads,[188] he will be seen as bitter, not as loving. This will be his reality unless he changes it before he or the man sitting next to him in college today fights to love his children tomorrow.

What Can Be Done?

In a capitalist society, one dollar is one vote. Compared to a purchase in a store, a vote in a ballot box is powerless. Hallmark knows how to attract the votes that count.

However, protests affect companies like terrorists affect the United States. Companies are afraid of negative publicity. So when the "Boys Are Stupid, Throw Rocks at Them!" slogan was so popular that the company that produced it was making too much money to stop reproducing it on everything from postcards to T-shirts, Glenn Sacks and others organized to protest the companies distributing the products.[189] The minor result was their removal from many stores.

The major result was the beginning of awareness of the meaning of misandry. Without that awareness, the men around you won't be able to fully love their children, and our sons will experience shame because they are boys.

12. ARE SCHOOLS BIASED AGAINST GIRLS?
OR BOYS?

When boys were outpacing girls in school, we blamed the *schools*. Now that girls are outpacing boys in school, we are blaming the *boys*.

No. We are doing worse than blaming boys. In pop culture we are mocking them (e.g., the "Boys Are Stupid, Throw Rocks at Them!" postcards and T-shirts, versus "Girl Power" and "Girls Rule"). In education we are suing parents for their sons' behavior (e.g., grammar school boys' parents being sued for their sons' "sexual harassment").[190] Boys are being treated like defective girls.[191]

When we weren't blaming boys for doing worse, we were denying they were doing worse. During the Denial Era (the 1970s to about 2006, perhaps ending with *Newsweek's* front cover graphic "The Boy Crisis"[192]), Girl Power programs funded by the government and executed by educators helped teachers overcome their unconscious bias against girls. That's good. But it was for only girls. That's bad.

The part that's good? Educators needed to encourage girls in math, science, self-esteem, assertiveness, and the broadest possible range of career options—all of which is a focus of my own research (e.g., *Why Men Earn More—and What Women Can Do About It*). And when I married my wife, Liz, and one of her daughters had a severe eating disorder, I saw how the awareness of girls' propensity toward eating disorders had led to the funding of programs that may have saved our daughter's life. All of these are among the many blessings of feminism.

Girls, though, don't win from the neglect of boys. Even in 1992, late into the Denial Era, when girls had already been outnumbering boys in college for almost two decades, the American Association of University Women (AAUW) published a study that had enormous impact: "How Schools Shortchange Girls: A Study of Major Findings on Girls and Education."[193]

The report was the catalyst for tens of thousands of schools to pay teachers to be trained to address the way their schools "shortchanged" only girls. In response to this research, all-girl schools were formed throughout the United States even as all-boy schools were protested.[194] Although no group is doing worse than African-American boys in urban areas, after the AAUW study, public schools formed in Harlem for girls (e.g., the Young Women's Leadership School), not boys.

Soon boys' greater need for physical outlets was ignored, leading to cuts in physical education, to cuts in sports programs for boys, and to recess being put on recess.[195]

This boy crisis in education is not unique to the United States. In a worldwide study, the Organization for Economic Co-operation and Development (OECD) found that girls now outperform boys in overall educational markers in all thirty-five of the most-developed countries—the countries in which the influence of feminism is the strongest. These countries include the United States, England, Canada, Australia, Germany, France, and Japan.[196]

Three components of the "lace curtain" (see Section 11 on the media) kept the world ignorant: First, **the AAUW's publicity contradicted much of the actual data from the very studies they commissioned.** For example, the AAUW publicized teachers' need to give girls more attention and respect but ignored the studies it commissioned that found that both boys and girls agree that girls got called on more than boys and that teachers paid more attention to girls than they did to boys;[197] that teachers think girls are smarter; that both sexes feel that teachers like girls more; that both feel that teachers would prefer to be around girls more than boys; and that both boys and girls feel that girls receive more compliments.[198]

The second lace curtain culprit is the major media: No major media pointed out the contradictions. Similarly, it took the *New York Times* almost two decades after women were exceeding men in college to acknowledge it in a significant story.[199] When they did, they devoted more space to how the gap creates problems for the female students ("There aren't many guys to date"[200]) and how it turns men into dominant oppressors ("[The guys] have their pick of so many women that they have a tendency to become players"[201]).In contrast, articles about men being in the majority at the Citadel or in the armed services never mention men as victims because they have few women to date.

Third, the lace curtain is able to keep the world ignorant in part because there is no counterbalance: no organization studying our sons, such as an American Association of University Men (AAUM) pointing to the myriad of data that was signaling the "inconvenient truth" of another crisis in our environment—the "boy crisis." Thus the American media in particular ignored almost all of the worldwide OECD findings that showed boys falling behind girls in all developed countries.

See if you feel these facts should have been ignored (many of which were already apparent in 1992) and whether you feel they currently amount to a "boy crisis."

- Boys make up two-thirds of the learning disabled and 90 percent of the behaviorally disabled. They number nearly 100 percent of the most seriously disabled.[202]
- Three boys for every one girl are diagnosed with ADD/ADHD.[203]
- The number of boys who said they didn't like school increased by 71 percent between 1980 and 2001, according to a University of Michigan study.[204]
- Boys ages five to twelve are 60 percent more likely than girls to have repeated at least one grade.[205]
- In neighborhoods where fathers are most scarce, even among African-American boys *who start* high school, more than *half* don't finish.[206]
- Overall, boys are 33 percent more likely than girls to drop out of high school.[207]
- The percentage of male undergraduates dropped 24 percent from 1970 to 2000.[208]

- Girls receive approximately 60 percent of the As, and boys receive approximately 70 percent of the Ds and Fs.[209]
- Girls are approximately one and a half years ahead of boys in reading and writing competency.[210]
- Boys are 90 percent of the discipline problems in school, as well as 80 percent of the dropouts.[211]
- For every girl who commits suicide, four boys do.[212]
- Boys are the more likely *victims* of violence on school property by about a 3 to 1 margin.[213]
- More girls than boys now take math and science classes.[214]
- More boys than girls (31 versus 19 percent) feel teachers do not listen to what they have to say.[215]

We often pay less attention to boys' problems because, for example, we see that although girls take more classes in math and science, boys are more likely to be engineers, and we conclude discrimination against women still prevails. We don't ask whether boys sometimes choose to major in engineering not because of bias against girls, but because boys know that it will earn them more money than a major in French literature.

As girls are figuring out whether they want children and the option of being financially supported when the children are young, heterosexual boys in college are figuring out how to do the financial supporting if his future wife should want that option. Discrimination against girls at school can never be concluded without considering the social expectations of the family that may in fact lead to boys to earn more money because of discrimination against dads—since dads only have the option of earning money.

The Gap Between the Problem and the Solution

While the AAUW popularized a false version of the low self-esteem of girls, we heard little about the much worse state of the self-esteem of boys in the United States, Canada, Australia, and the United Kingdom uncovered by a study performed by Dr. William Pollack, the Harvard Medical School expert on boys' development.[216] A poignant part of the study was how teenage boys envisioned their future as men. The boys wrote a story based on a drawing of an adult man in a shirt and tie sitting at a desk while looking with a neutral expression at a photo of a woman and children. Only 15 percent of the boys envisioned a contented family man. Instead, "the overwhelming majority constructed narratives about lonely husbands working overtime to support their families, divorced men missing their loved ones, and grief-stricken widowers."[217]

Overall, Pollack, author of *Real Boys,* reports that recent studies find boys' self esteem to be more fragile than girls' and boys' confidence as learners to be impaired.[218]

The Harvard study immediately detected the mismatch between the current problem of a boy crisis and a girl-only solution—specifically that teachers are required to take gender equity courses that have "become especially vigilant, even obsessive, about making sure that the voices of girls" are heard, even as boys are cast as villains.[219]

Solutions That Include Boys

What our sons will be losing are solutions that might already have emerged from an equal amount of attention to boys' problems.

- **Dad involvement. The most reliable predictor of a boy succeeding in school and life is the involvement of his biological dad** (see Section 10 on Marriage). As Michael Gurian has discovered, many solutions for one sex work for both sexes. And as my own research for *Father and Child Reunion* uncovered, both girls and boys raised without an equal amount of dad involvement do worse on almost all academic, social, psychological, and physical health measures. And boys without significant father involvement do even worse than girls. A boy without an involved dad becomes a man with a "father wound"—a man with an Achilles heel and a wounded heart.

  Two solutions to more dad involvement: first, legal changes that *enforce* equal parent involvement after divorce (except when consistent abuse is proven); second, corporations and government developing job-sharing programs at the executive level so that dads who are successful at work are not seduced into "the father's catch-22": loving their family by being away from the love of their family.

- **Mentorship.** When a boy raised in an urban area goes from a mother-dominated home to a female-dominated elementary school, he often has no positive male role models. Is it any wonder he is vulnerable to the negative role model of gangs? For this boy, it is less accurate to say he becomes a man with a "father wound" than to say he never becomes a man.

Two solutions: first, extensive funding and publicity for mentorship and buddy programs for boys; second, parent training to help biological moms who are divorced become true partners with stepdads even as they keep the biological dad equally involved. (Eighty-five percent of stepparents are stepdads.)

• **Active learning.** Girls' brains allow for longer attention spans and therefore benefit more from passive learning such as listening and note-taking. Boy-friendly classrooms imply, for example, role-playing characters in literature, thus giving boys opportunities to be physical, get attention, and perform, or playing music that allows the entire body to move. Whether via the return of physical education and recess or through the integration of role-playing, theater, music, and sport into everything from literature to language, art, and social studies, teacher training can become increasingly creative in integrating the intellectual and the physical.

Rather than choosing between male- and female-inspiring subject matter for reading, integrate both. For example, teach the subtlety of human nature not only by reading character development–type literature like Dickens or Austen, but also have students spontaneously act out the characters *as* they are reading, forming teams that are awarded points by the students for the most successful portrayals of nuanced characters.

• **Male teachers.** An international affirmative action initiative is needed to encourage young men to enter teaching full-time. And corporation-school programs can pair men from business with boys who don't have involved dads. For example, the men can be part-time elementary school teachers in schools with fewer than 50 percent male teachers and part-time mentors for boys from single mom homes. Corporations can constructively channel the male enthusiasm for competition by sponsoring, for example, GM versus GE teams, to see whose mentees can make the most progress in school and life.

• **Dad-in-the-classroom.** In schools with less than 50 percent male teachers and in which many students come from single-mom homes, pay companies to allow men to take a week's leave of absence to teach, thus

exposing students to a variety of male role models and professional opportunities. Give preference for men whose children of divorce are in
that class and who unwillingly have less than 50 percent time with their
children.

Every boy who is a long-term victim of the boy crisis leaves a
woman without a good man to marry, leaves a government without
tax revenue, leaves parents wondering what they did wrong. Just as the
women's movement helped us realize women's full potential, it is now
time for all of us to move toward helping our sons realize theirs.

13. THE FUTURE OF FEMINISM AND MEN

"If someone applauds, men will run in circles and call it a home run."

If the future of feminism and men is to be positive, it will come from
knowing how to navigate the rough waters from a Stage I world
that socialized both sexes only for survival to a Stage II world in
which people who have some handle on survival can focus on creating a balance between survival and fulfillment (see Section 10 on
Marriage).

In a Stage I world, the wound that unified all men was the wound
of their disposability—as soldiers, as workers, as dads. The wound of
believing they are lovable if they kill and die so others might be saved
and survive.

The main social mechanisms that get men to do this are criticism
and appreciation. If someone applauds, men will run in circles and
call it a home run. If someone offers him a Purple Heart he will risk
a buried body.

Blaming the other gender for the world's problems misses the point
as much as blaming our partner for our marital problems misses the
point. The choice of our partner is the single most important statement about the choice of our values. Whenever we blame the other
sex, the mirror will show us the person who chose the genes we are
passing on to the next generation. **Both sexes are the way they are
because that is what made them appealing to the other sex.**

Stage I's rigid roles were not designed to serve men. "No sex before marriage" is not a male fantasy. Dying on front lines serves the country, not the self; half-living in coal mines nourished families, but collapsed men's lungs. Both sexes assumed rigid roles in the hope their children would have a life better than their own.

Throughout the world, wherever there is a division of labor between the sexes, *both* sexes reinforce it in three ways: First, both sexes discriminate against "deviants" (e.g., homosexuals); second, both sexes compete among themselves to be best (for example, cheerleaders and football players competing *among themselves* to become the best cheerleaders and football players); and third, both sexes fall in love with the most successful role players—be they football player with cheerleader or gorgeous young female with a doctor or a rock star.

The division of labor has meant that both sexes had monopolies in their areas of responsibilities: Men's monopoly of the workplace might be called a "manopoly"; mothers' monopoly of the children might be called a "momopoly."

The Stage II Journey

Stage II technology has *reversed* what humans need to do to survive. In Stage I, killing was necessary for the survival of the fittest. In Stage II, with nuclear technology, knowing how to *not* kill is necessary for the survival of everyone.

In Stage I, both sexes fell in love with the members of the other sex who were the least capable of loving. (For example, women married successful men who learned to repress feelings rather than express feelings; men fell for beautiful young women whose love was less mature than older women's.) Now, for the first time in human history, the qualities it takes to survive as a species are compatible with the qualities it takes to love. The challenge for men is to understand why the qualities it takes to succeed at work are inversely related to the qualities it takes to succeed in love.

Thus far, though, we have responded by changing only what women do to survive. While we have used birth control and technology to free women from female-biology-as-female-destiny, we have also used birth control and technology to create *female*-biology-as-*male*-destiny: A pregnant woman can choose to abort or to sue for support.

The freedom of women from biology-as-destiny has not freed men from male-biology-as-male-destiny: We have not demanded that both sexes equally share the hazardous jobs and the risks of dying. We are still socializing men to be our killers, and therefore unlovable...and therefore disposable.

Men have the next layer of work to do because, as we have seen, the process of succeeding enough so women had time to make their Stage II journey only reinforced men's being in Stage I. His income gave her the luxury to contemplate what she didn't like about herself *and him*. But he felt in a catch-22: He feared that if he lost the success that freed her, she'd leave him; yet he also feared that if he stayed focused on being successful, she'd leave him.

The implication? Unless both sexes take the Stage II journey simultaneously, we will tend to produce Stage II *individuals* (usually women), but not Stage II *relationships*. We will suffer another lonely "me" generation. Ironically, the very political genius of feminism that has led to the progress of individual women has impeded the progress of relationships. Here's how.

The Holy Trinity of Feminism's Political Genius
The political genius of feminism is its unspoken "holy trinity":

1. **Always open options for women** (e.g., join armed services).
2. **Never close options for women** (e.g., never *require* women to register for the draft).
3. **When something goes wrong, never hold women responsible** (e.g., "men cause wars" rather than "women are the majority of the voters").

Why is this politically ingenious? If feminism had fought for an adult version of equality—fighting either to require both sexes to register for the draft or for neither to register—that would have alienated all the women who did not want to register. When a political group requires something of its constituency, it reduces its constituency. Similarly, were feminism to fight for both sexes to be equally involved with the children after divorce, that would alienate women who wanted to have the children, the child support payments, and the family home.

The desire for rights without responsibilities is a trait of adolescents ("I want the car, but not the car payments"). Whenever we hear a group talking only about rights, we know we are dealing with adolescents.

The Politics of "Victim Power"

Historically, when a woman complained, she discovered who was interested in rescuing her. It was a way of finding a savior—not just for herself, but also for her children. Men who complained were seen as whiners, not winners, and were distinctly unappealing to women. **Complaining and asking for help, then, is not an evolutionary shift for women; complaining and asking for help is an evolutionary shift for men.**

Men are often confused by feminists complaining because "I am woman; I am strong" does not compute with "I am woman; I am victim."

Changing millions of years of genetic heritage will play many tricks on both sexes. Women will think that being divorced means they are independent even as they seek dependence on the government-as-substitute-husband; men will think that they are helping to make women equal even as they are passing laws to protect women from a dirty joke more than they protect themselves from dying on a construction site.

Part of women's genetic heritage that can contribute to feelings of victimization is that most of women's responsibilities came with little accountability. In the past, lack of permission for divorce kept the woman from being "fired" from her role. If a child stole something, we did not fire the mother for failing in her role. In contrast, if a man coached a team that failed, he would *expect* to get fired. Women had the *option* of setting high standards *for themselves,* and most did; men had the *obligation* of living up to standards *set by others.* **That was what hierarchy was designed to do—to promote men who were accountable and fire those who weren't.**

Feminism reinforced this traditional heritage of women not having anything but their own standards of accountability. A woman was not to be held accountable for how she used child support money. If a woman at work wore a mini-skirt and a low-cut blouse and the wrong man responded, feminists suggested he should be held accountable for sexual harassment, but she should not be held accountable for sexual solicitation. Women were taking on more responsibility, but not more accountability.

Although men's intellect told them that no one who failed to be held accountable could truly be an equal, men's savior instinct could not refuse the sound of a woman crying. So "victim power" was extended to women by mostly men passing laws protecting women against unwanted sexual overtures; preventing pay discrimination against women; *creating* pay discrimination against men (affirmative action); protecting only women against stranger violence (the Federal Violence Against Women Act; rape crisis centers; date rape laws; rape-shield laws) and domestic violence (learned helplessness defenses, battered women's shelters); making certain that mothers were protected to be mothers (Women, Infants, and Children programs; increased enforcement of child support to moms) but not that dads were protected to be dads (no presupposition of shared parenting); and so on. Unlike men, when women feel, women speak. And when women speak for protection, men make laws. And so do women.

The few men who could get in touch with their feelings had no political party for an outlet. Men's concerns do not fall on a continuum between conservatism and liberalism, but in a triangular relationship. Both conservatives and liberals are protective of women, and thus reinforce the traditional male-female sex roles, but they use different rationalizations for that protectiveness.

The conservative expects women to receive special protection via social custom. The liberal expects women to receive special protection via government programs. The conservative assumes most women want the traditional female roles, and the traditional female role requires men to protect women. The liberal assumes men's old roles were power and privilege designed to serve men rather than to be men's way of protecting women, so the liberal feels women need protection to compensate for the male power structure. Both conservative and liberal therefore conclude that men should protect women and no one should protect men.

Are conservatives and liberals in favor of sexual equality? Not really. Special protection with real equality is oxymoronic. In the short run, special protection goes to the privileged. But too often it becomes a double-edged sword. The man who got the Mafia to protect him soon found himself the prisoner of the Mafia's protection. The woman who depends on man-as-protector will find herself male-dependent; when she substitutes the government for a man, she soon becomes government-dependent (even tempted to "marry" government subsidies instead of men). This is why **protecting women creates sexual equality no more than welfare payments creates class equality.**

Is there a legitimate role for protecting women? Yes, there's a need to protect women during transition *just as there's a need to protect men in transition.* But protection-in-transition always requires weaning—or phasing out. **We have been protecting women as a part of women's rights, which has inhibited gender transition.**

The solution? There should be neither a women's movement nor a men's movement, but rather a gender transition movement, a gender transition movement that helps both sexes make the transition from our genetic heritage of rigid roles to our genetic future of more flexible roles.

Toward a Gender Transition Movement

A gender transition movement will be the longest of all movements because it is not proposing merely to integrate blacks or Latinos *into* a system that already exists; rather, it is proposing an evolutionary shift in the system itself—an end to "woman-the-protected" and "man-the-protector." This division is rooted in our biology; it exists among animals.

Gender transition starts by opening the lace curtain and closing down feminism-as-the-one-party-system-of-gender-politics. That combination frees women to hear what men at least could say if the media, academia, and government were not frustrating the already silent sex. It would bring into communication with each other the four major gender perspectives: traditional men, traditional women, transitional men, and feminists.

What does the communication consist of? For starters, how we can allow maximum freedom for both sexes without losing sight of our commitments to our partners and children. Redistributing housework, childcare, and work outside the home within each family; solutions to domestic violence, date rape, and sexual harassment that incorporate men's experiences. Funding the thirty-four neglected areas of men's health; making men's birth control a reality. . . .

An Equal Rights Amendment (ERA) might be relabeled an Equal Rights and Responsibilities amendment (ERA) and made user-friendly to men. Such an amendment's legislative guidelines might suggest that congressional districts be deprived of welfare funding if judges assigned the children to women more than 60 percent of the time in cases of contested custody; it would deprive universities of public monies as long as there were significantly more women's studies courses than men's studies courses; it would deprive TV stations of federal licensing if the FCC found a consistent pattern of male-bashing or consistent attention to women's issues and neglect of men's issues. Being user-friendly to men includes funding research on the denial of dad time, on false accusations, and on violations of due process and the Fourteenth Amendment.

The ERRA would mean a *new* era—an era of shared rights and shared responsibilities.

Life and Death

A gender transition movement would incorporate men's issues. Men's issues are issues of life and death. Why do men whose spouses die or who are divorced commit suicide ten times as often as the women? Why are men in all ten "glass cellars" of disposability (e.g., more of the street homeless than women and children combined, 94 percent of the workplace deaths, dying five years sooner) even as we only discuss "glass ceilings"? Instead of having only an Equal Employment Opportunity Commission (EEOC), men's issues of life and death might best be addressed by an Equal Life Opportunity Commission (ELOC).

Workplace

In the past quarter century, **we warned women against sacrificing their careers but said little about the sacrifices of careers.** Thus we did a poor job preparing women for sacrifices *in* their careers and were blind to men's work sacrifices.

Corporations must ask whether lace curtain biases are making them fearful of hiring women and fearful of mentoring women. When a company can't hire and fire freely, it becomes afraid to hire at all—so it outsources, merges, or "downsizes." Thus forced stability begets instability; the protection of women is undermined by the protection of women. Which is the paradox of protection.

The Family

Nothing needs more alteration than dad's role. Historically, dad's role has been the one that has varied most. Sometimes we want him to hold back Hitler and handle a bullet in his head; other times we want him to hold a baby and put a bottle in its mouth.

The challenge is being willing to give up some of dad's money for more of dad's love—and, in the process, altering the psyche that has made men less lovable. Conversely, **a mother will hold onto her child as if it were her job until we stop using money fathers make to pay for children mothers raise.**

The fact that we *can* direct men by appreciation does not mean we are *willing* to *re*direct men: **Women almost never marry future dads whose future income has little future.** And the process it takes to support a family is often so inversely related to the time and introspection it takes to love a family that dads themselves are often afraid to ask what they're being loved for, and whether they are doing what they love. Fortunately, technology is cooperating. Technology is dad-at-home friendly.

We need to fund research on a men's birth control pill so teenage boys and men have as much right, responsibility, and flexibility as teenage girls and women have. **Equal responsibility for childcare begins with equal choice in child creation.**

One of the most important family issues is that of paternity fraud. DNA tests to ascertain paternity must become the most fundamental of men's reproductive rights. If the sexes' reproductive roles were reversed, and a DNA test were needed to assure a woman she was not spending her life raising money for a child her husband had conceived during an affair, DNA tests at the earliest possible moment would be the most fundamental of women's reproductive rights.

Our policies toward dads won't change without a change in our attitudes toward dads. No research I have done has impacted me more than the research for *Father and Child Reunion* and the findings that showed that **children raised primarily by dads did so much better than those raised primarily by mom.**

We have an image of men as fathers that is more akin to "men just want to impregnate as many women as possible to pass on their genes." That image neglects reality: 85 percent of stepparents are stepdads. These dads are devoting their lives to loving and protecting the genes of other men. We have some rethinking to do about dads.

Our Sons, Our Schools, Our Future

The Stage II elementary school needs to have more male teachers than female teachers in districts in which the preschool children are exposed more to mothers than fathers. In the same way that women in business should not be imitation males, so men who teach should not be imitation females.

Stage I sports was designed to build *defenses against* the outside world, so "our team good, their team bad" was understandable. Stage II sports is designed to prepare us for *trade with* the outside world—for a global economy in which we are all part of the same team.

A Stage II school not only requires team sports for both sexes, but also uses the period after the game to understand the learning experiences of the game ("How does my unwillingness to pass the ball off relate to my larger life?"). Alternative sports like flag football and rotation baseball (each player at a different position each inning) need to be part of the school curriculum. This does not mean that football, even in its one-sex, smash-face form, cannot be financed *privately;* it does imply not financing it publicly. **Male child abuse might be fun to watch, but taxpayers should not be required to pay for it.**

The Stage II school system will help the student understand why individual sports and team sports lead to different life journeys. If Jane focuses exclusively on gymnastics, she learns little about how to negotiate with her peers. And if Dick focuses only on team sports, he has not necessarily prepared himself to be a good self-starter or a good creative thinker—skills needed to start one's own business, or be a writer, artist, or an intellectual who thinks for herself or himself (rather than worrying about being politically correct).

The Stage II male-female journey involves both sexes learning from the male heritage of risk-taking and the female heritage of caution, from the male heritage of learning not to limit oneself for fear of a broken bone and the female heritage of not having to prove oneself by breaking one's bones.

Future Sex

A Stage II middle school and high school balances messages of sexual caution with messages of sexual joy. It doesn't turn sex into fear-based discussions of only safe sex, AIDS, herpes, rubbers, sexual abuse, date rape, stranger rape, harassment, power, and violence, and then tell the boy to take all the initiatives. It understands the sexist bias of saying, "Sex is dirty; boys initiate the dirt." It understands this doesn't leave a boy with a lot of self-esteem; it leaves him with a lot of shame. And it sets up our sons for feeling they have to pay for girls to be equal to them.

Once our sons are paying more for the girls they value more, our daughters begin to think of themselves as valued more the more he pays. And so the dance begins that leads to boys learning to be earning.

Men don't protest the financial inequality in part because of sexual shame and in part because of sexual addiction. But the biggest factor is their role as initiator. **The person who takes the sexual initiatives wants the period of time between the eye contact and intercourse to be as short as possible because the shorter the time between eye contact and intercourse the shorter the period of potential rejection.**

Relationship Language

When I grew up, few people had seen a computer and virtually no one understood computer language. Today, everyone has seen a computer, but few people understand each other. We are living in the Tower of Babel. If in one generation we learned computer language, we can in the next generation learn relationship language and how to understand each other.

Both sexes have in common our desire to be understood. (I've never heard someone say, "I want a divorce; my partner understands me.") To achieve that goal, nothing is more important than the four "relationship language" skills: experiencing empathy ("walking a mile in each other's moccasins"), communicating empathy, giving criticism so it can be easily heard, and hearing criticism so it can be easily given. Of these, our vulnerability to personal criticism is what needs the most work—it is the Achilles' heel by which our love for each other is most frequently wounded.

Relationship language has the potential for stabilizing what technology destabilized. Without it, our yearning for stability will be so great that we will look to others to create it for us: We will beg for stabilizing rules and lists of rights and wrongs from the law, the church, family, and even universities. With relationship language, stability will be a natural byproduct of feeling emotionally safe and supported in a relationship. Once relationship language is mastered, the church and family can be used as *additional support* systems, not as substitute legislative systems.

Our Stage II Challenge

Because every society has such an investment in training part of its population to be disposable in war and in work, the incentives for men to change will only slowly begin to outpace the incentives for men to die as our firefighters, soldiers, lumberjacks, and Alaskan fisherman— so we can feel protected, housed, and fed on the cheap. Therefore, it will take the entire twenty-first century to begin to make the type of progress with men that was made with women between 1970 and 2006. That's the bad news.

The good-or-bad news, depending on your perspective, is that that progress will involve real equality, not pick-and-choose liberation. It will involve moving toward equality of obligation for combat roles, not just the "pick-and-choose liberation" of female opportunity when desired; ceasing to expect men to earn more money than a woman before they are "eligible" and then calling the expectation "power," "patriarchy," "dominance," or "sexism" rather than pressure and obligation; developing affirmative action-type outreach programs for men until men and women have the same life expectancy; giving men special outlets and special incentives to express their feelings and perspectives until men commit suicide no more frequently than women; confronting our monetary incentives to keep men disposable rather than pay, for example, what it would cost to have a house built half by female construction workers; monitoring media sexism that defines relationship issues disproportionately from the female perspective in books, magazines, newspapers, talk shows, and sit-coms; caring as much about battered husbands as battered wives; acknowledging the working dad as much as we acknowledge the working mom; giving fathers as much right to their children as we do mothers; not stopping merely with caring as much about saving males as saving whales, but stopping only when we care as much about saving males as saving females... In the past, we have been challenged by a paradox: **There are few political movements filled with healthy people, yet few healthy changes have occurred without political movements.** Until now, men invested all of their emotional eggs in the basket of the women they loved. So they feared speaking up for fear of losing their only source of emotional support.

In the future, we are challenged with the possibility of a movement producing healthy changes being led by mostly healthy people. This will happen only if men do their homework, study their internal worlds, have the courage to take their perspectives to the external world, and invite women to join them. Men can't say what men don't know, and women can't hear what men don't say.

Notes

1. Augustine J. Kposowa, "Marital Status and Suicide in the National Longitudinal Mortality Study," *Journal of Epidemiology and Community Health* 54 (April 2000), p. 256. The figure is 9.94 times higher in divorced men than in divorced women. The 9.94 figure was obtained from Dr. Kposowa using information from Table 1 on p. 256; personal correspondence, June 29, 2000.

2. The numbers in this paragraph are the best estimates of San Diego State University's Bonnie Zimmerman, president, National Women's Studies Association, interviewed February 11, 1999.

3. Young America Foundation, *Comedy and Tragedy: College Course Descriptions and What They Tell Us About Higher Education Today, 1998–99* (Herndon, VA: YAF, 1998).

4. Lawrence Diggs, "Sexual Abuse of Men by Women," *Transitions* (November/December 1990), p. 10.

5. 1920 statistics from the U.S. Department of Health and Human Services, National Center for Health Statistics (hereafter USDHHS, NCHS), *Monthly Vital Statistics Report* 38, no. 5 (1990), p. 4. The 1990 statistics are from the USDHHS, NCHS, *Monthly Vital Statistics Report,* 39, no. 13 (August 28, 1991), p. 17.

6. See John Laffin, *Brassey's Battles: 3500 Years of Conflict, Campaigns, and Wars from A–Z* (London: A. Wheaton & Co., 1986), p. 399.

7. NCHS, *Monthly Vital Statistics Report* 38, no. 5.

8. USDHHS, Centers for Disease Control and Prevention, National Center for Health Statistics, *Health, United States, 2005, with Chartbook on Trends in the Health of Americans,* Table 46 (page 1 of 3): "Death Rates for Suicide, According to Sex, Race, Hispanic Origin, and Age: United States, Selected Years 1900–2003," p. 221, http://www.cdc.gov/nchs/data/hus/hus05.pdf#027.

9. Ibid.

10. Kposowa, "Marital Status."

11. See U.S. Department of Commerce, Bureau of the Census, *Statistical Abstract of United States: 2007,* 126th ed., (Washington, DC: U.S. Census Bureau, 2006), p. 346, Table 509; p. 344, Table 505; and p. 13, Table 11.

12. See Laffin, *Brassey's Battles,* p. 399.

13. Air Force Lt. Col. Ronald Meilstrup, deputy director of the Selective Service System's Regional Headquarters in Illinois.

14. Bob Secter, "The Draft: If There's a War, There's a Way," *Los Angeles Times,* January 3, 1991, pp. E-1, E-5.

15. Military Selective Service Act. See "Privacy Act Statement," SSS Form 1, Registration Form, September, 1987.

16. Ibid.

17. Jim Schwartz, College Press Service, 1986.

18. Susan Goldberg and Michael Lewis, "Play Behavior in the Year-Old Infant: Early Sex Differences," *Child Development* 40, no. 1 (March, 1969), p. 29.

19. Statement made in 1986 before the Defense Advisory Committee on Women in the Services. Quote confirmed in an interview by Dr. Farrell May 26, 1992, with Kay Leisz, Weinberger's executive assistant.

20. U.S. Congress, Senate, Committee on the Judiciary United States Senate, *Nomination of Sandra Day O'Connor,* Report No. J-97–51, 97th Congress, 1st Session, 1982, pp. 127–128.

21. Interviews by Dr. Farrell on July 14 and 17, 1992, with Maggie Waleland, head of the Presidential Commission on the Assignment of Women in the Armed Forces, and Capt. Jeff Smith, a fellow of the Presidential Commission.

22. Bruce Gilkin, "To Hell and (Almost) Back: A Vietnam Veteran's Struggle with Posttraumatic Stress," *Men's Health* (Summer 1988), p. 44.

23. Research Directorate, Defense Equal Opportunity Management Institute, "Annual Demographic Profile of the Department of Defense and U.S. Coast Guard FY 2005" (2006), pp. 2, 8.

24. Iraq Coalition Casualties website, http://icasualties.org. Each casualty is directly linked to Department of Defense verification of the casualty. Figures are for U.S. forces only.

25. R. N. Anderson, K. D. Kochanek, and S. L. Murphy, "Advance Report of Final Mortality Statistics, 1995," *Monthly Vital Statistics Report* 45, no. 11, Suppl. 2 (Hyattsville, MD: National Center for Health Statistics, 1997), p. 19.

26. For children born in 2003, male and female life expectancies at birth are 74.8 and 80.1 years, respectively. U.S. National Center for Health Statistics, *Statistical Abstract of the United States: 2007* (Washington, DC: U.S. Census Bureau, 2006), Table 96. "Expectation of Life at Birth, 1970 to 2003, and Projections, 2005 and 2010."

27. Interview July 14, 1992, with Vivian W. Pinn, M.D., director of the Office of Research on Women's Health, National Institutes of Health.

28. Ibid.

29. Centers for Disease Control and Prevention, *National Vital Statistics Report* 54, no. 10 (January 2006), Table 17, pp. 69–76, http://www.cdc.gov/nchs/data/nvsr/nvsr53/nvsr53_05acc.pdf.

30. USDHHS, "Estimates of Funding for Various Diseases, Conditions, Research Areas," March 10, 2006, http://www.nih.gov/news/fundingresearchareas.htm.

31. Bibliographic search by Steven L. Collins, Ph.D., of PubMed's controlled vocabulary index (MeSH terms) on June 6 and 7, 2006. Pub Med is a service of the National Library of Medicine. See www.pubmed.gov. A search for "male NOT female" was considered to be gender-specific to men, and likewise for women.

32. Ibid.

33. Ibid.

34. Centers for Disease Control and Prevention, *National Vital Statistics Report* 54, no. 10 (January 2006), Table 12, p. 41, http://www.cdc.gov/nchs/data/nvsr/nvsr53/nvsr53_05acc.pdf.

35. Dr. David Gunnell et al., "Sex Differences in Suicide Trends in England and Wales," *The Lancet* 13 (February 1999), p. 557.

36. USDHHS, "Healthy People 2010 Objectives: Draft for Public Comment," September 15, 1998, pp. 25-16–25-17.

37. Search by Dr. Steven L. Collins, Ph.D., of Pub Med's controlled vocabulary index (MeSH terms) on June 5, 2006. Pub Med is a service of the National Library of Medicine. See www.pubmed.gov.

38. Pamela Newkirk; "A Mother's Nightmare: The Shocking Story of DES Sons," *McCall's* (February 1993), pp. 93–164.

39. Hans-Udo Eickenberg, "Androtropia: Diseases Leading to Early Death in Men," paper presented at the 7th World Meeting on the Aging Male, February 1998.

40. Ibid.

41. Ibid.

42. See the *University of California at Berkeley Wellness Letter* 8, no. 1 (October 1991), p. 1.

43. Ibid.

44. Centers for Disease Control and Prevention, *National Vital Statistics Report* 54, no. 10 (January 2006), Table C, pp. 5 and 10, http://www.cdc.gov/nchs/data/nvsr/nvsr53/nvsr53_05acc.pdf.

45. For a more in-depth exploration, see Warren Farrell, *Father and Child Reunion* (New York: Putnam/Penguin, 2001), pp. 138–148.

46. PR Web, "U.S. Postal Service's Breast Cancer Research Stamp Raises $50 Million for Breast Cancer Research; New Five-Year Goal Set at $100 Million for Breast Cancer Research," http://www.prweb.com/releases/2006/6/prweb394978.htm, June 7, 2006.

47. U.S. Department of Justice, Federal Bureau of Investigation, *Uniform Crime Reports for the United States: 1988.*

48. Unpublished data, USDHHS, NCHS, Centers for Disease Control, National Hospital Discharge Survey, "Number of All Listed Diagnoses from Short-Stay Hospitals, by Age and Sex: 1987." Cited by Jill Braden, Survey Branch of the National Center for Health Statistics, via telephone interview March 15, 1990.

49. U.S Census Bureau, *Health Insurance Coverage: 1997,* Table 2. (Washington, DC: U.S. Census Bureau, 1998).

50. U.S. Department of Labor, Bureau of Labor Statistics, *Census of Fatal Occupational Injuries,* 1997, Table 4. (Washington, DC: U.S. Census Bureau, 1998).

51. U.S. Census Bureau, *Health Insurance Coverage: 1997,* Table 2 (Washington, DC: U.S. Census Bureau, 1998).

52. Murray A. Straus, Richard J. Gelles, and Suzanne K. Steinmetz, *Behind Closed Doors: Violence in the American Family* (New York: Anchor Press/Doubleday, 1980).

53. Ibid. This was the original nationwide random sample that sparked the controversy after finding that 3.8 percent of husbands beat their wives and 4.6 percent of wives beat their husbands.

54. Ibid., pp. 43–44.

55. U.S. Department of Justice, Bureau of Justice Statistics, "Violence by Intimates," NCJ-167237 (March 1998), www.ojp.usodj.gov/bjs/pub/pdf/vi.pdf.

56. "Barbara Spencer-Powell, Overland Park, KS. In Letters," *Time,* January 11, 1988, p. 12.

57. Murray A. Straus, "Men Are More Likely Than Women to Be Victims of Dating Violence," based on data from sixty-eight coordinated studies including 13,601

students at sixty-eight universities in thirty-two nations by the Family Research Lab of the University of New Hampshire, May 21, 2006.

58. Barbara J. Morse, "Beyond the Conflict Tactics Scale: Assessing Gender Differences in Partner Violence," *Violence and Victims* 10, no. 4 (1995), pp. 251–272.

59. U.S. Department of Justice, Bureau of Justice Statistics (hereafter USBJS), *Special Report: Murder in Families* (Washington, DC: USBJS, 1994), p. 3. This survey is much better than the FBI's *Uniform Crime Reports* as an indicator of the percentage of wives and husbands who kill their spouses, since the FBI data has such a high percentage of the killers not identified (31 percent of the female victims' killers, 41 percent of the male victims' killers).

60. U.S. Department of Justice, Federal Bureau of Investigation, *Crime in the United States—2003* (Washington, DC: USGPO, October 2004), Table 2.7: "Murder Victim/Offender Relationship by Race and Sex," http://www.fbi.gov/ucr/cius_03/xl/03tbl2–7.xls downloaded July 31, 2006. The notes adjoining the table state that it only applies to "Single Victim/Single Offender" killings; that is, multiple offender killings are not broken down into gender categories. Only "Single Victim/Single Offender" crimes are broken down into gender categories.

61. The closest the government comes to reporting contract killing is the creation of a "multiple offender" category (e.g., wife plus contract killer), which is what registers more than four times as many husbands as victims than wives as victims. See James A. Mercy and Linda E. Saltzman, "Fatal Violence Among Spouses in the United States, 1976–85," *American Journal of Public Health* 79, no. 5 (May 1989), p. 596, Table 1—see "Multiple Offender" category. Based on 16,595 spouse homicides reported to the FBI from 1976 through 1985. This contract-killing-as-the-female-method perspective is also confirmed by Louis Mizell, the world's foremost expert on contract killings, in an interview on July 18, 1996.

62. USBJS, *Special Report—Violence Against Women.* (Washington, DC: U.S. Department of Justice, 1998).

63. Ibid. shows 900 wives killed by spouses or ex-spouses and 7,824 unidentified male victims, or 8.7 times as many unidentified male victims.

64. USBJS, *Selected Finding: Violence Between Intimates* (Washington, DC: U.S. Department of Justice, Bureau of Justice Statistics, 1994), p. 6.

65. Ibid.

66. Ian Burrell and Lisa Brinkworth, "Police Alarm over Battered Husbands," *Sunday Times* [London], April 24, 1994, pp. 1, 6.

67. Fred Hayward, director of Men's Rights, Inc., *Media Watch Annual Survey, 1991* (Boston: Men's Rights, Inc., 1991).

68. Nancy Gibbs, "When Is It Rape?" *Time,* June 3, 1991, p. 52.

69. USBJS, *Criminal Victimization in the United States: 1987,* publication #NCJ115524 (June 1989), p. 47, Table 41.

70. Susan Brownmiller, *Against Our Will: Men, Women, and Rape* (New York: Bantam, 1976).

71. USBJS, *Criminal Victimization in the United States: 1987,* pp. 18–19, Table 5.

72. Ibid.

73. Charlene L. Muehlenhard and Lisa C. Hollabaugh, "Do Women Sometimes Say No When They Mean Yes? The Prevalence and Correlates of Women's Token Resistance to Sex," *Journal of Personality and Social Psychology* 54, no. 5 (1988), p. 874.

74. See Ira Michael Heyman, Office of the Chancellor, University of California at Berkeley, "Acquaintance Rape," January 20, 1987; John Wiener, "Rape by Innuendo at Swarthmore, Date Rape," *The Nation* 254, no. 2 (January 20, 1992), p. 54; Cathy Young, "What Rape Is and Isn't," *Washington Post* (National Weekly Edition), June 29–July 5, 1992, p. 25.

75. Mary Koss, Christine A. Gidycz, and Nadine Wisniewski, "The Scope of Rape: Incidence and Prevalence of Sexual Aggression and Victimization in a National Sample of Higher Education Students," *Journal of Consulting and Clinical Psychology* 55, no. 2 (1987), p. 162–170.

76. Ibid., p. 167.

77. Ibid., p. 167, Table 3.

78. See Robin Warshaw, *I Never Called It Rape: The Ms. Report on Recognizing, Fighting, and Surviving Date and Acquaintance Rape* (New York: Harper & Row, 1988), p. 63.

79. Charlene L. Muehlenhard and Stephen W. Cook, "Men's Self Reports of Unwanted Sexual Activity," *Journal of Sex Research* 24 (1988), pp. 58–72.

80. Charles Salter, Jr., "A Lasting Shadow," *The News & Observer* [Raleigh, NC], February 17, 1992, p. 1-C.

81. Ibid.

82. Written correspondence to Dr. Farrell from Charles P. McDowell, Ph.D., M.P.A., M.L.S., supervisory special agent of the U.S. Air Force Office of Special Investigations, March 20, 1992.

83. Charles P. McDowell, Ph.D., M.P.A., M.L.S., "False Allegations," *Forensic Science Digest* 11, no. 4 (December 1985), p. 64. The digest is a publication of the United States Air Force Office of Special Investigations, Washington, DC.

84. U.S. Department of Justice, Federal Bureau of Investigation, Uniform Crime Reports Section, *Crime in the United States* (Washington, DC: USGPO, 1990), p. 16. Confirmed in telephone interview on April 29 and May 11, 1992, with Harper Wilson, chief of Uniform Crime Reporting, FBI.

85. See *Michigan v. Lucas,* 111 S. Ct. 1743, May 1991. The Supreme Court ruled that a woman might be shielded from having her sexual past used against her—the "rape-shield" law.

86. Gretchen Morgenson, "Watch That Leer, Stifle That Joke," *Forbes,* May 15, 1989, pp. 69–72.

87. Equal Employment Opportunity Commission, *Policy Guide on Current Issues of Sexual Harassment,* http://www.eeoc.gov/policy/docs/currentissues.html, downloaded July 31, 2006.

88. Richard Pollak, "Persumed Innocent?" *The Nation* 253, no. 16 (November 11, 1991), p. 593.

89. Patrick A. Largan and John M. Dawson, *Profile of Felons Convicted in State Courts,* publication #NCJ-120021 (Washington, DC: USBJS, 1990), p. 9.

90. Victor L. Streib, "America's Aversion to Executing Women," *Ohio Northern University Women's Law Journal* 1, (1997), pp. 1–8; Victor L. Streib, "Death Penalty for Female Offenders, January 1, 1973, through December 31, 2005," Ohio Northern University, http://www.law.onu.edu/faculty/streib/documents/FemDeath Dec2005_000.pdf, accessed July 31, 2006.

91. Angela K. Brown, "Jury Finds Yates Not guilty in Drownings," Yahoo! News, July 26, 2006, http://www.forbes.com/technology/ebusiness/feeds/ap/2006/07/27/ap2908294.html, accessed September 11, 2006.

92. Streib, "Death Penalty for Female Offenders."

93. Matthew Zingraff and Randall Thompson, "Differential Sentencing of Women and Men in the USA," *International Journal of the Sociology of Law* 12 (1984), pp. 401–413.

94. For the smaller impact of racial differences, see Largan and Dawson, *Profile of Felsons,* p. 1, column 2. For the smaller impact of other differences, see Zingraff and Thompson, "Differential Sentencing."

95. See Howie Kurtz, "Courts Easier on Women," *The Sunday Record* [Bergen County, NJ], October 5, 1975.

96. The first twenty-three are documented in Hugo Adam Bedau and Michael L. Radelet, "Miscarriages of Justice in Potentially-Capital Cases," *Stanford Law Review* 40, no. 1 (November 1987), pp. 21–179; the additional seven are in Death Penalty Information Center, "Executed but Possibly Innocent," http://www.deathpenaltyinfo.org/article.php?scid=6&did=111, downloaded August 8, 2006.

97. Innocence Project, "Innocence: List of Those Freed from Death Row," http://www.deathpenaltyinfo.org/article.php?scid=6&did=110, downloaded August 1, 2006.

98. USBJS, *Sourcebook of Criminal Justice Statistics* (Washington, DC: U.S. Department of Justice, 1991), p. 442, Table 4.7.

99. John T. Kirkpatrick and John A. Humphrey, "Stress in the Lives of Female Criminal Homicide Offenders in North Carolina," in James H. Humphrey, ed., *Human Stress: Current Selected Research* 3 (New York: AMS Press, 1989), pp. 109–120.

100. U.S. Department of Justice, Federal Bureau of Investigation, *Crime in the United States—2003,* Table 2.7. The notes adjoining the table state that the table only applies to "Single Victim/Single Offender" killings, that is, multiple offender killings are not broken down into gender categories. Only "Single Victim/Single Offender" crimes are broken down into gender categories.

101. Ron Rosenbaum, "Too Young To Die?" *New York Times Magazine,* March 12, 1989 Section 6, pp. 12–18, 20, 57–58, 61.

102. Ibid.

103. Suicide, execution, and homicide data for 1987 are from USBJS, *Correctional Populations in the United States,* publication #NCJ-118762 (Washington, DC: USBJS, December 1989), p. 105, Table 5.17. Prison statistics for 1987 are from the U.S. Department of Commerce, Bureau of the Census, *Statistical Abstracts of the United States: 1991,* 111th ed. (Washington, DC: U.S. Census Bureau, 1991), p. 195, Table 338.

104. Statutes of 1991, Chapter 692.

105. Fred Strasser and Mary C. Hickey, "Running Out of Room for Women in Prison," Updates section, *Governing* (October 1989), p. 70.

106. Associated Press, "After 21 Years, Man Is Freed in Poison Case," *New York Times,* April 27, 1989.

107. Ibid.

108. Interview on May 15, 1990, with Don Horn.

109. "Victims of the State: Wrongly Convicted Innocents and Other Individuals Abused by the Criminal Justice System," http://www.robertrivera1.com/innocents.htm, downloaded July 31, 2006.

110. Eloise Salholz with Andrew Murr, "Arsenic and Old Lace," *Newsweek,* August 14, 1989.

111. Isabel Wilkerson, "Clemency Granted to 25 Women Convicted for Assault or Murder," *New York Times,* December 22, 1990, p. A-1.

112. For example, Governor Schaeffer of Maryland and Governor Gardner of Washington.

113. Nancy Ray, "Judge Allows 'Battered Woman' Defense," *Los Angeles Times,* September 21, 1982.

114. Wilkerson, "Clemency Granted," p. A-1.

115. California Assembly Bill 785 by Assemblyman Gerald R. Eaves (D-Rialto), took effect on January 1, 1992.

116. Steve Metzger, "The Shooting of Josh Wagshall," *Transitions* 8, no. 2 (March/April 1988), p. 2.

117. Verified in telephone interview with Nancy Young of Elizabeth Holtzman's press office, February 7, 1991.

118. Andrea Ford, "Woman Who Killed Infant Son Allowed to Get Mental Help on Outpatient Basis," *Los Angeles Times*, March 11, 1989.

119. Tom Gorman, "Woman Who Killed Child Remains Free," *Los Angeles Times*, April 26, 1989.

120. Ibid.

121. Norma Juliet Wikler, "Water on Stone: A Perspective of the Movement to Eliminate Gender Bias in the Courts," keynote address, National Conference on Gender Bias in the Courts, Williamsburg, VA, May 18, 1989.

122. Allan R. Gold, "Sex Bias Is Found Pervading Courts," *New York Times*, July 2, 1989.

123. Carol Klieman, reprinted as "Closing Wage Gap for Women May Depend on a Little Research," *San Diego Union-Tribune*, September 29, 1997, section 1, p. 14.

124. U.S. Department of the Treasury, Internal Revenue Service, Statistics of Income Division, unpublished tables E2-1, E2-3, E3-1, and E3-3. Data provided by Dr. Ying Lowry, an economist at the Small Business Administration.

125. Richard DeMartino and Robert Barbato, "Gender Differences Among MBA Entrepreneurs" (Rochester Institute of Technology, United States Association for Small Business and Entrepreneurship, 2001). Table 7; see http://www.usasbe.org/conferences/2001/proceedings/papers/018.pdf

126. U.S. Department of Labor, Bureau of Labor Statistics, unpublished data for 2005 from the *Current Population Survey*, p. 110, Table A-18, "Usual Weekly Earnings of Employed Wage and Salary Workers by Hours Usually Worked on Primary Job and Sex, 2002 Annual Averages." Data provided by Mr. Howard Hayghe, economist, Bureau of Labor Statistics Office of Employment and Unemployment Statistics, telephone: (202) 691-6380. The average worker working thirty-five hours per week earns $384; the average worker working forty-five hours per week earns $894.

Hours Worked	Median Weekly Earnings (2005)
30	$288
31	$304
32	$355
33	$320

(Continued)

Hours Worked	Median Weekly Earnings (2005)
34	$365
35	**$384**
36	$501
37	$475
38	$524
39	$438
40	$605
41	$622
42	$736
43	$721
44	$716
45	**$894**
46	$808
47	$741
48	$808
49–59	$1,047
60+	$1,112

127. U.S. Bureau of the Census, unpublished data from *Employment and Earnings,* Table D-20: "Median Weekly Earnings of Part-Time Wage and Salary Workers by Selected Characteristics."

128. U.S. Census Bureau's Survey of Income and Program Participation, 2001 Panel, Wave 2 (Washington, DC: U.S. Census Bureau, 2005). Available at www.sipp. census.gov/sipp/intro.html (downloaded May 3, 2007).

129. Korn/Ferry International and UCLA Anderson Graduate School of Management, *Decade of the Executive Woman: Survey of Women in Senior Management Positions in the Fortune 1000 Industrial and 500 Service Companies,* (Los Angeles: Korn/Ferry International, 1993), p. 22.

130. Radcliffe Public Policy Center, "Life's Work: Generational Attitudes Toward Work and Life Integration" (Cambridge, MA: Radcliffe Public Policy Center, July 2000). The Harris Interactive Poll was commissioned by the Radcliffe Public Policy Center. See also Joyce Madelon Winslow, "Dads Can Learn from Moms," *USA Today,* July 12, 2000, p.15A.

131. Although 38 percent of the world's journalists are women, only 7 percent of journalists killed are female; see Emily Nelson and Matthew Rose, "Media Reassess Risks to Reporters in Iraq," *Wall Street Journal,* April 9, 2003, p. 10.

Taxicab driving is much less dangerous for women because they work the less dangerous shifts and the safer regions, according to interviews conducted by Alexa Deere or Warren Farrell from April 17–19, 1996, with Yellow Cab Companies in Manhattan, Brooklyn, Los Angeles, and Philadelphia. In 1995, one women and sixty-eight men cabdrivers were murdered on the job according to Guy Toscano, economist, the Office of Safety, Health, and Working Conditions, U.S. Department of Labor.

132. Arlie Hochschild, *The Second Shift* (New York: Avon Books, 1990).

133. Jim Miller, "Women's Work Is Never Done," *Newsweek,* July 31, 1989, p. 65.

134. D. Waggoner, "For Working Women, Having It All May Mean Doing It All," *People,* September 4, 1989, p. 51.

135. John Skow, "The Myth of Male Housework," *Time,* August 7, 1989, p. 62.

136. The Trouble with Men," *The Economist,* September 28, 1996, p. 19.

137. United Nations Development Programme, *Human Development Report 1995* (New York: Oxford University Press, 1995). For the full list of countries (including those in which men were found to work more than the women), see p. 91, Table 4.1: "Burden of Work by Gender, Selected Developing Countries," and p. 94, Table 4.3: "Burden of Work by Gender, Selected Industrial Countries."

138. Telephone interview on February 22, 1996, with Alexandra Bodanza, UN Division of Public Affairs.

139. Luisella Goldschmidt-Clermont and Elizabetta Pagnossin-Aligisakis, "Measure of Unrecorded Economic Activities in Fourteen Countries," UN Human Development Report Office Occasional Papers, a background paper for the *Human Development Report 1995,* p. 1.

140. United Nations Development Programme, Human Development Report Office, "The World's Women 1995—Trends and Statistics," *Social Statistics and Indicators* (NY: United Nations Publications, 1995), Series K, no. 12, pp. 105–6.

141. Telephone interview on February 23, 1996, with Terry McKinley, UN Development Programme, Human Development Report Office.

142. F. Thomas Juster and Frank P. Stafford, "The Allocation of Time: Empirical Findings, Behavioral Models, and Problems of Measurement," *Journal of Economic Literature* 29, no. 2 (June 1991), p. 477, Table 3: "Changes in Time Allocation in Five Societies, 1965–1980s."

143. John Robinson, "Americans on the Road," *American Demographics* (September 1989), p. 10. Men commute four hours per week to women's two hours per week. Of course, working mothers with young children are likely to commute even less, and fathers, because of their income-producing responsibilities, to commute even more.

144. Hochschild, *The Second Shift,* p. 284.

145. U.S Bureau of the Census, Housing and Household Economics Division, Industry, Occupation, and Statistical Information Branch, Table FINC-08: "Earnings of Wife by Earnings of Husband in 1997."

146. F. Thomas Juster, "A Note on Recent Changes in Time Use," in F. Thomas Juster and Frank P. Stafford, eds., *Time, Goods, and Well-Being* (Ann Arbor: Institute for Social Research, University of Michigan, 1985), p. 317, Table 12.1: "Hours per Week in Activities by Age and Sex, 1975–1981 Samples of Rural and Urban Households," 1981 data for ages twenty-five to forty-four.

147. U.S Bureau of Labor Statistics, *Current Population Survey* supplement file, March 1996, Table 2: "Hours Usually or Actually Worked per Week by Working Mothers and Fathers in Husband-Wife Families with Own Children Under 18 in Household, by Age of Children." With children under eighteen, working fathers averaged 45.4 hours per week; working mothers, 34.6. Special unpublished computer run requested by author. Computer run supplied by Bob McIntire.

148. John P. Robinson, "Up Close and Personal," *American Demographics* 11, no. 11 (November 1989), p. 10. Men: 72.9 hours of leisure time; women: 74.7.

149. Ibid.

150. Ibid.

152. Hochschild, *The Second Shift,* p. 3.

153. Ibid., p. 282.

154. Lenore J. Weitzman, *The Divorce Revolution* (New York: The Free Press, 1985).

155. Greg J. Duncan and Saul D. Hoffman, "Economic Consequences of Marital Instability," in Martin David and Timothy Smeeding, eds., *Horizontal Equity, Uncertainty & Economic Well-Being* (Chicago: University of Chicago Press, 1985), Figure 14.3 and Table 14.A.8.

156. Rachel Levy-Shiff et al., "Fathers' Hospital Visits to Their Preterm Infants as a Predictor of Father-Infant Relationship and Infant Development," *Pediatrics* 86 (1990), pp. 291–292.

157. Ibid.

158. Frank A. Pedersen, Judith L. Rubenstein, and Leon J. Yarrow, "Infant Development in Father-Absent Families," *Journal of Genetic Psychology* 135 (1979), pp. 55–57.

159. See L. J. Yarrow, R. P. Klein, S. Lomonaco, and G. A. Morgan, "Cognitive and Motivational Development in Early Childhood," in B. Z. Friedlander et al., eds., *Exceptional Infant 3* (New York: Brunner/Mazel, 1974).

160. Pedersen, Rubenstein, and Yarrow, "Infant Development," pp. 55–57.

161. Bryce J. Christensen, "America's Academic Dilemma: The Family and the Schools," *The Family in America* 2, no. 6 (June 1988). Cited in Nicholas Davidson, "Life Without Father: America's Greatest Social Catastrophe," *Policy Review* (Winter 1990), p. 41.

162. Martin Deutsch and Bert Brown, "Social Influences in Negro-White Intelligence Differences," *Journal of Social Issues* 20, no. 2 (1964), p. 29.

163. Dewey G. Cornell (University of Virginia), in "Juvenile Homicide: Personality and Developmental Factors," final report to the Harry Frank Guggenheim Foundation, New York, 1989.

164. "Males...Babies and Ohio Law," 1987 brochure distributed by Planned Parenthood of Northwest Ohio, 1301 Jefferson Avenue, Toledo, OH 43624.

165. *Marriage of Dennis,* 117 Wisc. 2d 249, 344 N.W. 2d 128.

166. *Matter of Audrey G. [Robert T.],* New York Family Court, Kings County, *New York Law Journal,* August 17, 1989.

167. See Kathleen Hendrix, "A Case of Two 'Moms' Test Definition of Parenthood," *Los Angeles Times,* August 15, 1990.

168. See A. F. Glasier et al., "Would Women Trust Their Partners to Use a Male Pill?" *Human Reproduction* 15, no. 3 (2000), pp. 648–649.

169. Real name. Based on the true story behind the U.S. Supreme Court case of *McNamara v. County of San Diego,* 87–5840.

170. Based on the true story behind the U.S. Supreme Court case of *McNamara v. County of San Diego,* 87–5840.

171. Creative Expression Products/3M (Minnesota Mining and Manufacturing), P.O. Box 33053, St. Paul, MN 55133–3053.

172. Genevieve Richardson, *No Good Men: Things Men Do That Make Women Crazy* (New York: Simon & Schuster, 1983).

173. Diane Mason, "Like Thelma, NOW's Ready to Kick Some," *San Jose Mercury News,* July 10, 1991, p. 9B.

174. "Askew to You" by Recycled Paper Products, Inc., Chicago, IL.

175. "In Your Face Cards" by Recycled Paper Greetings, Inc., Chicago, IL; telephone (801) 272–5357.

176. "Shoebox Greetings"/Hallmark Cards, Inc.

177. Ibid.

178. Ibid.

179. Interview by Warren Farrell, November 11, 1998, with Rachel Bolton, Hallmark Media Relations Manager.

180. Ibid.

181. "Shoebox Greetings"/Hallmark Cards, Inc.

182. Interview by Warren Farrell, November 11, 1998, with Rachel Bolton, Hallmark Media Relations Manager.

183. CBS TV, 1987.

184. Amy Harmon, "Worries About Big Brother at America Online," *New York Times*, January 31, 1999, p. 1.

185. Joan Meier, "Domestic Violence, Child Custody, and Child Protection: Understanding Judicial Resistance and Imagining the Solutions," *American University Journal of Gender, Social Policy, and Law*, 11, no. 2, p. 683, note 80.

186. Professor Joan Meier, personal communciation with J. Steven Svoboda, August 3, 2006.

187. Glenn Sacks, "PBS Agrees to Commission New Documentary." http://www.glennsacks.com/pbs/, downloaded August 2, 2006.

188. U.S. Department of Health and Human Services, Children's Bureau, *Child Maltreatment 2003: Reports from the States to the National Child Abuse and Neglect Data System* (Washington, DC: USGPO, 2004).

189. Glenn Sacks, "Why I Launched the Campaign Against 'Boys are Stupid' Products," *Los Angeles Daily News*, February 4, 2004, www.glennsacks.com.

190. Scripps Howard News Service, "Second-Grader Files Sex Harass Lawsuit," *North County Blade-Citizen* [San Diego], September 30, 1992.

191. Michael Thompson, co-author of *Raising Cain*, in "The Trouble with Boys," *Newsweek*, January 30, 2006, p. 48.

192. "The Trouble with Boys," *Newsweek*, January 30, 2006. Note that even the title of the article that ended the Era of Denial still had an element of blame: "The Trouble with Boys." Imagine an article on anti-Semitism being titled "The Trouble with Jews." To *Newsweek's* credit, the article was excellent and the front cover's graphic "The Boy Crisis" catalyzed the attention to boys.

193. American Association of University Women, *How Schools Shortchange Girls: A Study of Major Findings on Girls and Education* (Washington, DC: AAUW Educational Foundation, The Wellesley College Center for Research on Women, 1992). The updated study is American Association of University Women, *Gender Gaps: Where Schools Still Fail Our Children* (Washington, DC: AAUW Educational Foundation, The Wellesley College Center for Research on Women, 1998).

194. See, for example, Julie N. Lynem, "Bay Area Academies Stress Learning and Self-Esteem," *San Francisco Chronicle*, December 8, 1998, front page.

195. "The Trouble with Boys," p. 48.

196. *The PISA Assessment Framework: Mathematics, Reading, Science and Problem Solving Knowledge and Skills* (Paris, France: Organization for Economic Co-operation and Development, 2003).

197. AAUW/Greenberg-Lake, *Expectations and Aspirations: Gender Roles and Self-Esteem* (Washington, DC: Greenberg-Lake, 1990), *Gender Roles and Self-Esteem* (Washington, DC: Greenberg-Lake, 1990), *Data Report and Banners,* p. 18, as cited in Judith S. Kleinfeld, "The Myth That Schools Shortchange Girls: Social Science in the Service of Deception," a Women's Freedom Network Executive Report, 1998, p. 25, Table 14.

198. Adapted from AAUW/Greenberg-Lake, *Expectations and Aspirations,* p. 18, as cited in Judith S. Kleinfeld, "The Myth That Schools Shortchange Girls: Social Science in the Service of Deception," a Women's Freedom Network executive report, 1998, p. 29, Table 16.

199. Tamar Lewin, "American Colleges Begin to Ask, Where Have All the Men Gone?" *New York Times,* December 6, 1998, pp. 1–28.

200. Ibid.

201. Ibid.

202. Michael Gurian, *Boys and Girls Learn Differently! A Guide for Teachers and Parents* (San Francisco: Jossey-Bass (2001), p. 56.

203. National Alliance on Mental Illness, "Attention-Deficit/Hyperactivity Disorder," http://www.nami.org/Template.cfm?Section=By_Illness&Template=/Tagged Page/TaggedPageDisplay.cfm&TPLID=54&ContentID=23047, Downloaded August 6, 2006.

204. "The Trouble with Boys."

205. Ibid. Data from U.S. Department of Education.

206. Ibid. P. 50.

207. Ibid. Data from U.S. Department of Education.

208. Ibid. Data from U.S. Department of Education.

209. Gurian, *Boys and Girls Learn Differently!,* p. 56.

210. U.S. Dept. of Education data, cited in Ibid. p. 56.

211. Gurian, *Boys and Girls Learn Differently!,* p. 56.

212. Ibid.

213. Ibid., p. 57.

214. Ibid., p. 59.

215. Michael Gurian and Kathy Stevens, *The Minds of Boys: Saving Our Sons from Falling Behind in School and Life* (San Francisco: Jossey-Bass, 2005). Original source: Sommers, *The War Against Boys,* 2000.

216. William Pollack, *Real Boys* (New York: Henry Holt, 1998), pp.165–168.

217. Ibid.

218. Ibid., p. 1.

219. Donna Laframboise, "Why Boys Are in Trouble," *National Post* [Canada], January 5, 1999.

PART 2

Does Feminism Discriminate Against Men?

James P. Sterba

Introduction

The goal of feminism has long been to secure women's equality with men. Historically, this goal has proven to be very difficult to reach. Not until the mid-1800s did feminism become widespread in Europe and the United States. In 1848, French feminists began publishing a daily newspaper entitled *La Voix des Femmes* ("The Voice of Women"). A year later, Luise Dittmar, a German writer, followed with her journal, *Soziale Reform*. Also in 1848, the first women's rights convention was held in Seneca Falls, New York. The convention passed a Declaration of Sentiments modeled after the U.S. Declaration of Independence that advocated reforms in marriage, divorce, property, and child custody law. With black abolitionist Frederick Douglass arguing forcefully on their behalf, all twelve of the Declaration's resolutions drafted by Elizabeth Cady Stanton passed, although the ninth resolution demanding the right to vote for women only passed narrowly upon the insistence of Stanton.[1]

The period from the Seneca Falls Convention until women finally secured the right to vote in 1920 is referred to as the first wave of feminism in the United States. First wave feminists frequently joined forces with and drew inspiration from the abolition and moral reform movements of their times. In what is called the second wave of feminism, beginning in the 1960s, feminists frequently joined forces with and drew inspiration from the black civil rights movement and the anti–Vietnam War movement. As these second wave feminists saw it, suffrage alone had not, and could not, make women equal with men. To be equal, women needed the same educational, occupational, social, and political opportunities that men enjoyed in society.

In 1966, when government agencies refused to take seriously the provision of the Civil Rights Act of 1964 that prohibited discrimination on the basis of sex,[2] a group of feminists led by Betty Friedan founded the National Organization for Women (NOW). NOW then elected Friedan as its first president and launched a broad campaign for legal equality. At the same time, ad hoc groups staged protests, sit-ins, and marches across the country focusing on various issues. One of the most memorable protests was staged at the 1968 Miss America contest, where a "freedom trash can" was set up to dispose of symbols of women's oppression, including bras, girdles, wigs, and false eyelashes, and a sheep was crowned Miss America. Although none of the items thrown into the trash can were burned, from that day on feminists were called "bra burners" thanks to media reports that bra burning was going to be part of the protest.[3]

A third wave of feminism in the United States is usually said to have begun around the mid-1980s. According to the standard account, second wave feminism was advanced by white middle-class heterosexual women who presumed that all women were just like them, with the same interests and needs, thus enabling these white middle-class heterosexual women to speak for all women everywhere. But then, in the 1980s, poor and working-class women, women of color, lesbians, and Third World women entered the picture and challenged the theories held by the second wave feminists. The challengers contended that these theories were biased and had left them out. As a result, third wave feminism was born, and feminists became attentive to differences of race, class, sexual orientation, and national origin.[4]

There are at least two problems with this standard account of third wave feminism. First, many second wave feminists were clearly already paying attention to differences among women. In 1970, a press conference was held headed by women's movement leaders Gloria Steinem, Ti-Grace Atkinson, Flo Kennedy, Sally Kempton, Susan Brownmiller, Ivy Bottini, and Dolores Alexander to express solidarity with the struggles of gays and lesbians against discrimination. In 1971,

NOW issued a policy statement recognizing gay and lesbian rights as a feminist issue.[5] Moreover, second wave feminists were already hearing from women with different voices. As Marilyn Frye notes, Tony Cade's anthology *The Black Women* was published in 1970; the Furies Collective and Diana Press were publishing feminist work on class, race, and sexuality in the early 1970s; Jill Johnson's *Lesbian Nation* was published in 1973; and Maxine Hong Kingston's *The Woman Warrior* was published in 1975. According to Frye, "the period of obliviousness to race and class and culture and nationality was *before feminism*, it was not some stage of feminism *before the 'others' turned up to complain.*"[6]

A second problem with the standard account of third wave feminism is that it fails to emphasize how difficult it is to transcend barriers of race, class, sexual orientation, and national origin or, to put the problem in moral terms, how difficult it is to really put oneself in the position and mind-set of others, and then take appropriate action. Sometimes taking these differences into account is presented as something that now enlightened third wave feminists easily do rather than as something that remains quite difficult to achieve. The task requires challenging one's own perspective with the variety of relevant alternative perspectives presented to us by others, putting the best construction on those alternative perspectives, and facing their challenge head-on with a willingness to give up one's own perspective, either in whole or in part, if the evidence overall favors doing so. Accordingly, taking race, class, sexual orientation, national origin, and other relevant differences into account is never an easy task, even though it is required by the feminist goal of equality. Feminists can no more reach their goal of equality by ignoring relevant alternative perspectives provided by women than they can by ignoring relevant alternative perspectives provided by men. Difficult though it is to carry out, feminists must take all relevant perspectives into account as they advance toward their goal of equality between women and men.

Of course, this means that feminists must also take seriously criticisms that maintain that feminism has gone beyond its goal of equality and is now seeking to unfairly discriminate against men in favor of women. Feminists can no more ignore this challenge than defenders of affirmative action can ignore a similar challenge that affirmative action, a practice that is also said to be grounded in an ideal of equality, in fact, discriminates against white males.⁷ Such challenges must be faced head-on if a commitment to the goal of equality is to be legitimately maintained.

This is why I have taken up this debate with Warren Farrell. Farrell started out his career as a defender of feminism. At that time, he published *The Liberated Man* and had been elected three times to the local board of directors of NOW in New York City. Then in the mid-1980s, Farrell had a change of heart and began speaking and publishing books that were critical of feminism, starting with two award-winning international best-sellers, *Why Men Are The Way They Are* (1987) and *The Myth of Male Power* (1993), followed by a Book-of-the-Month Club selection, *Women Can't Hear What Men Don't Say* (2000), *Father and Child Reunion* (2001), and *Why Men Earn More* (2005), which was recently featured in the *New York Times* and on *20/20*.

Farrell's work constitutes a formidable challenge to feminism that needs to be addressed. His critique is broad and wide-ranging. He argues that feminism has supported discrimination against men with regard to military service, healthcare, domestic violence, rape, the criminal justice system, the workplace, divorce, child custody, popular culture and the media, and public education. As the subtitles of this essay clearly indicate, I shall also discuss each of these issues, sketching out a feminist perspective and taking up critiques that Farrell and others have raised against that perspective. In each case, I shall show that feminism has not discriminated against men or, more precisely, that, in each case, feminism has not been appropriately used by its defenders to discriminate against men.⁸ While there are many forms of feminism, they do share some common ground, and part of that common ground, I will try to show, is that feminism does not discriminate against men.

1. DO WE NEED MEN'S STUDIES—OR IS HISTORY MEN'S STUDIES?

The first women's studies program in the United States was founded in 1969–70 at San Diego State University. As of 1998, there were over six hundred such programs nationwide.[9] From the mid-1970s, men's studies courses also began to be taught at colleges and universities around the country. The First National Conference on Men and Masculinity was held in the United States in 1975. An association of men and women was formed at the time, which has since changed its name twice and is currently called the National Organization for Men Against Sexism (NOMAS).[10] NOMAS today describes itself as an activist organization of men and women advocating a perspective for enhancing men's lives that is pro-feminist, gay-affirmative, anti-racist, and committed to justice on a broad range of social issues, including class, age, religion, and physical abilities.[11] Although today there are some men's studies programs across the country, most of those who teach men's studies courses and belong to organizations like NOMAS are, in fact, associated with women's studies or gender studies programs rather than with men's studies programs.

Early on, second wave feminists did defend the need for women's studies on the grounds that "history is men's studies."[12] However, what was meant by this claim is that the history that was taught at the time was simply the history of men, not the history of *both* women and men. Women were clearly left out of that history. Women's studies was thus proposed as the needed corrective; it would provide the missing history of women.

However, women's studies soon began to do more than provide just the missing history of women. It began challenging the roles to which women have been confined in society. As Warren Farrell rightly points out, women's studies began to question women's roles in society.[13] As Farrell puts it, feminism began to tell women that "they have rights to what was the traditional male role."[14] But what about telling men that they had rights to what was the traditional female role? Feminism never opposed that. Feminists want men and women both to share the responsibilities for whatever roles there should be in society. So while feminists were opposed to men's studies as history that left women out, they were not opposed to men's studies as a field that questions men's roles in society. In fact, it is really impossible to question women's roles without questioning men's roles. The lives of women and men are intimately related in society. If you really want to change the roles of women in society, you must want to change the roles of men as well. Feminists never objected to a men's studies that advocates changing

the traditional roles of men so as to better realize feminism's own ideal
of equality between women and men.

2. DO MEN HAVE THE POWER—AND IF SO, WOULD THEY WANT TO CHANGE?

Feminists have long held that men have the power, that is, the dominant power in society. Feminists have never held that women are without power, just that the power *distribution* in society unfairly favors
men over women. Actually, one way to understand the feminist ideal
of equality is as an ideal of equal power or as an ideal of equal opportunity to acquire power in society.[15] Given that Warren Farrell proposes
that we should think about power as having control over one's own
life, we could restate the feminist ideal as one of having equal control
over one's own life or equal opportunity to acquire control over one's
own life.[16]

Farrell goes on to distinguish two stages of human history: Stage I,
in which women's and men's roles are simply functional for survival,
and Stage II, in which women and men can go beyond survival to
seek self-fulfillment. Farrell thinks Stage II is now a possible stage for
human history because of effective birth control, increased wealth,
and the possibility of divorce. In Stage II relationships, Farrell claims
that successful women who are married to successful men face three
options when considering whether to have children—option one:
work full-time; option two: mother full-time; and option three: some
combination of working and mothering. By contrast, the successful
men who are married to these successful women have just one option:
work full-time, which really means that they have no options at all.[17]

According to Farrell, for thousands of years, in Stage I marriages,
neither men nor women had power in the sense of control over their
own lives; they simply had roles and responsibilities. Only in Stage II
marriages, in which people have options, does Farrell allow that we
can properly speak about them as having power in the sense of control over their own lives.[18] So in Farrell's example of the "multi-option
woman and the no option man," only the woman would have power

in the sense of having control over one's own life. That makes her, Farrell tells us, "more than equal" to her husband.[19]

Yet surely this is an odd way to characterize human history or the options faced by two-career couples today when deciding whether to have children. Why should we think that having roles and responsibilities precludes having power, even power understood as control over one's own life? Even if we think of people's roles and responsibilities as primarily directed at benefiting others, fulfilling those roles and responsibilities usually brings status and privilege to those who fulfill them, as Farrell himself acknowledges.[20] This, in turn, enables them to have control over their own lives.

Consider Bill Clinton. Even with all the adversities of his two terms in office, fulfilling the role and responsibilities of president of the United States surely brought him considerable status and privilege, which, in turn, enabled him to exercise considerable control over his own life, maybe even more so after his terms in office were over. So there is no incompatibility between having roles and responsibilities and having control over one's own life. In fact, the former is frequently a useful way of acquiring the latter.[21]

In addition, while having options usually does increase the power one has over one's own life, Farrell has not fairly characterized the options facing the successful woman and the successful man when they are deciding whether to have children. Consider Jill and Tom, both with equally promising jobs at top law firms.[22] Suppose they both enjoy their work and regard it as important. What options do they have with respect to having children? Jill could choose to continue working full-time. Yet given the long hours her job now requires, this would only permit her to be minimally involved with rearing her child, and she should regard that as undesirable, other things being equal.[23] Of course, that option would look better if Jill knew that Tom was willing to give up his job to care for their child full-time. Yet even if Tom were so willing, Jill should still judge that option not to be in the best interest of Tom or their child. Other things being equal, a better option is for both Jill and Tom to continue with their law careers toward partnerships under reduced workloads so that they can equally share their childcare and housekeeping responsibilities. The option of Jill working part-time and mothering part-time while Tom continues working full-time toward partnership usually requires that Jill move to a lower-paying, nonpartnership track at her firm. Jill should regard that option as undesirable both because of its effects on her career and because it means that Tom would not be as involved in childcare and housekeeping as she would be. Tom should also reject the option of his working part-time and fathering part-time, which usually requires him to move to a lower-paying nonpartnership track at his firm, for the same reasons that Jill should reject that option for herself. Accordingly, other things being equal, Tom should also prefer the option in which both of them continue with their law careers toward partnerships under reduced workloads so that they can equally share their childcare and housekeeping responsibilities. Thus, if Jill and Tom are equally respectful of each other's interests as well as the best interest of their child, contrary to what Farrell claims, they would each entertain exactly the same options when deciding whether to have a child, even though the circumstances in which they find themselves may preclude them from being able to act upon what they regard as their best option.

It is also a mistake to think that most of human history has been stuck in Stage I, in which people are just struggling to survive. In fact, much of human history, and most of recorded history, is the story of what people and societies have done when motivated by goals that have included but have also gone beyond that of survival. This means that we can criticize such people and societies for not having more equality between women and men. Even among societies that Farrell would surely regard as survival focused, such as American Indian nations, some organized themselves in ways that tended toward equality for women. For example, among the Seneca, women did the farming and controlled what they produced while sharing the childrearing with their men. As a result, Seneca men could not hunt or wage war unless the women agreed to allocate the food they controlled for those purposes. In 1791, Seneca women explained to American Army officers who were attempting to negotiate a peace treaty that "you ought to hear and listen to what we, women shall speak, as well as to the sachems [male chiefs] for we are the owners of this land—and it is ours."[24]

Suppose, then, that we convince men that there was an unfair distribution of power favoring men over women in the past that still persists today—would they be willing to correct for the imbalance? How could men resist this demand for fairness? Of course, many men who seem to gain from discriminating against women suffer themselves from other forms of discrimination directed against them, which may leave them feeling relatively powerless.[25] Feminists have recognized this and have appropriately responded to it by opposing all forms of discrimination, not simply discrimination against women. As I noted earlier, feminists have taken into account differences of race, class, sexual orientation, national origin, and other relevant differences in formulating their theories. Similarly, at the practical level, feminists have to unite with others in opposing all forms of discrimination. Needless to say, it would help if feminists could show that correcting the imbalance of power between men and women really did serve the interests of men as well. Yet even when this is not obtained, an appeal to fairness should suffice for those who wish to be moral, especially given the willingness of feminists to join forces against all forms of discrimination.

Today, however, there are some special difficulties with shifting power to women in society stemming from the fact that women are not normally associated with a number of the significant forms of power in society. Exemplars of religious power, physical power, economic power, and political power are all normally men. Women who enter these domains of power are perceived as oddities. A number of years ago, there was quite a stir when Barbara Harris was the first woman to be consecrated a bishop in the Episcopalian church. When Margaret Thatcher was prime minister of Great Britain, journalists referred to her as "the iron maiden" and "Atilla the Hen," thus expressing the incongruity of a woman holding such a high political office. Of course, women do have power or influence on the basis of sexual or personal attractiveness, and mothers are frequently said to have dominant power in the home, although the extent to which mothers have power in the home may be overrated. One study showed that only 16 percent of females and 2 percent of males named their mothers as the most powerful individual they personally knew.[26] The general problem with women acquiring power is that masculinity is traditionally associated with power and femininity is traditionally taken to be its opposite. Hence, the more women are seen as powerful, the more they are seen as unfeminine or unwomanly. Obviously, something has to change here if women are to have equal power or the equal opportunity to acquire power in society.

3. WHAT THE ALL-MALE DRAFT AND THE COMBAT EXCLUSION OF WOMEN TELL US ABOUT MEN, WOMEN, AND FEMINISM

In countries around the world today, the male-only draft and the combat exclusion of women are common practices. A few countries, like Israel and Eritrea, draft both men and women, but most countries today, irrespective of whether they have a draft or not, still maintain the combat exclusion of women in some form or other.[27] While widely adopted, David Benatar regards these practices as the main example of a "second sexism" that inflicts men today.[28] Taking it a step further and speaking specifically of the United States, Warren Farrell believes that "there is no form of sexism that is more damaging, more unconstitutional" than the male-only draft and the combat exclusion of women.[29] Significantly, most contemporary feminists, except for those who are opposed to war under all circumstances, also oppose a male-only draft and the combat exclusion of women.[30] However, they disagree with Benatar and Farrell with respect to the grounds for their opposition. Benatar and Farrell see the male-only draft and the combat exclusion of women primarily as forms of discrimination against men, whereas most feminists see these practices simply as forms of discrimination against women. This makes a difference because it suggests different strategies for ridding ourselves of these unwanted practices.

In the United States, the combat exclusion of women was imposed by legislative action in 1948.[31] Women, of course, had been excluded from combat before that time, but the 1948 legislation was a significant step taken to exclude women permanently from combat. Interestingly, a combat exclusion provision was not part of the original bill that was introduced in 1947 to establish a regular corps of women in each of the services. The bill initially passed the Senate without any provision for the combat exclusion of women. It was only during discussion of the bill in the House that an amendment explicitly excluding women from serving on combat ships and aircraft was introduced. The amended bill then passed in the House and later again in the Senate with little discussion of its combat exclusion provision.

As it turns out, this little considered amendment to the 1948 act authorizing regular corps of women in each of the services, unchallenged by subsequent Congresses, became the constitutional basis for the defense of the male-only draft. In *Rostker v. Goldberg* (1981), William Rehnquist, arguing for the majority of the Supreme Court, held that since the purpose of the draft was to provide conscripts for combat, a male-only draft did not violate the equal protection component of the Fifth Amendment because women were restricted by legislation from serving in combat roles. No one even considered challenging the constitutionality of the combat exclusion itself, or whether a draft might not be an important backup mechanism for filling the 150,000–250,000 noncombatant positions in the military for which women were still needed at the time.

Today, the most frequent argument that is given for excluding women from combat is that they have less strength, stamina, and muscle than men. Of course, it can be pointed out that much combat activity today does not require a great deal of strength. Even if it did, however, that would not be a reason for excluding all women. Surely some women are stronger than some men are. So if strength were really what counted, then strength, and not sex, would be the appropriate criterion.

There are also numerous examples of male-dominated activities in which women have met or exceeded all the physically desirable requirements for those activities but were still excluded from participating. For example, in 1961 NASA invited women pilots to join the race for space against the Russians. Jerrie Cobb, a professional pilot who had logged seven thousand hours in the air, accepted the invitation. She floated for 9 hours and 40 minutes in a pitch dark isolation tank before hallucinating; male subjects who tested before her had lasted only 4 hours and 30 minutes. Mary Wallace Funk, the holder of several world records in flying, beat John Glenn on the stress tests, bicycle analysis tests, and lung power tests. She also beat Wally Shirra on the vertigo test while setting a record in the bicycle endurance test and the isolation test, where she lasted 10 hours and 30 minutes before hallucinating. But then without explanation, NASA canceled the women's tests, with the consequence that male astronauts rocketed into our history books while more qualified women were denied their due.[32]

Moreover, there is now available a solid body of evidence that women's physiology makes them more tolerant of G-forces than men and so more suitable to be fighter pilots than men. According to a U.S. Air Force study, because women are smaller on average than men, the shorter distance between their hearts and their brains makes easier for their hearts to counteract the G-forces trying to draw blood out of the brain and keep the brain supplied with blood. So, in this regard, women are, on average, clearly more physically qualified than men to be fighter pilots, which is one of the most prestigious combat positions in the U.S. military.[33]

Yet obviously not all women meet or exceed the general physical qualifications expected of men in all branches of the military. In the U.S. Army, for example, only 32 percent of women can met or exceed the minimum male test scores on the Army Physical Fitness Test.[34] Nevertheless, an Army study of forty-one women showed that 78 percent of the women in the study qualified for "very heavy" military jobs after six months of weight lifting, jogging with seventy-five-pound backpacks, and performing squats with hundred-pound barrels on their shoulders.[35] Given that girls raised in the United States are usually two years behind boys in learning the skills needed for physical competence, it is surprising what such catchup programs are able to accomplish.[36]

In this context, it is also important to recognize that from the very beginning it was the superior qualifications of women that led the U.S. military to turn to women in order to save the all-volunteer force.[37] The women drawn to military service were smarter and better educated than the men were. For example, according to one study, over 90 percent of women recruited had high school diplomas, compared to 63 percent of the men, and women also scored 10 points higher on service exams.[38] In addition, proportionately more female than male cadets have been selected as Rhodes and Marshall scholars, and proportionately more women entering West Point have been National Honor Society members and high school valedictorians and salutatorians in all but two years since integration in 1976.[39] As one U.S. Defense Department report put it, "The trade-off in today's recruiting market is between a high quality female and a low quality male."[40]

Yet while defenders of men's rights, like Farrell and Benatar, and most feminists today are united in their opposition to the practices of the male-only draft and the combat exclusion of women, they disagree over the most fundamental reasons for opposing those practices. Farrell and Benatar maintain that the male-only draft and the combat exclusion of women is primarily a form of sexism that benefits women. But how could this be, when denying women access to combat roles denies women access to the most prestigious positions in the military and hinders their advancement both within and without the military?[41]

To see what allowing women to take on the risks of combat can do, consider the example of Eritrea. In Eritrea's long-drawn-out war with Ethiopia, Eritrean girls learned to use weapons and studied military tactics and survival techniques. When they were old enough, they fought along side men at the front. As a consequence, young Eritrean women today have powerful role models in their mothers, who fought in this thirty-year-long war of independence from Ethiopia that was won in 1991. After the war, women were able to enter the National Assembly and serve in other political positions for the first time. Today, Eritria's ambassador to the European Union and ministers of justice and labor have been women. It is harder to prevent women from occupying positions of social and political power once they have served their country in combat.[42]

To see the effects of excluding women from combat, consider the case of Israel.[43] In Israel today, both women and men are required to serve in the Israel Defense Force (IDF), but women are generally excluded from combat roles. Thus, 70 percent of women in the military are assigned to secretarial jobs. Men's willingness to sacrifice their lives for their country confirms their status as good citizens and provides them with "symbolic capital" that they then carry with them into civilian life. The good citizen is the retired soldier or officer who can prove his service to his country by having served in combat. Having served in combat is an important part of one's resume when applying for almost any job. For example, being a colonel with combat experience is more important than being an educator when applying for a lucrative school principal position. Combat experience, so useful in the general market, is even more useful in the political arena.

Accordingly, a retired general (or any high-ranking officer) has almost instant access to high-level political positions. These are the benefits that men reap because of their combat experience in the Israeli military, but that women are denied because they are kept from combat experience in that same military.

Of course, Farrell and Benatar allow that excluding women from combat does disadvantage those women who want to serve in combat roles; they just think that to focus on these disadvantages is to ignore the much greater disadvantage suffered by vast numbers of men who are forced into combat.

Needless to say, feminists do not deny that there are costs to men from the system that discriminates against women in the military. It is also clear that these costs are not borne equally by all men. Some men suffer very little from combat duty, and then go on to become high-ranking officers and later important government officials, while other men become cannon fodder.

Let us focus on the cannon fodder—those men who sacrifice their lives in the wars that are fought under patriarchal systems. Surely, such men do not appear to have benefited from the patriarchy of their societies.[44] Why then cannot we say that such men have suffered from sexual discrimination?

Just because some men are disadvantaged by patriarchy in the military, it doesn't follow that they have suffered from sexual discrimination. One reason why it doesn't follow is because it is men, not women, actually a particular group of men, a subset of those currently in the military—who are keeping the male-only draft and the combat exclusion of women in place.[45]

Sometimes the leadership of the U.S. military maintains that it is not them, but rather public opinion, that is keeping these practices in place: "What we have learned is that the American public...is very, very reluctant about the idea of women engaging in hand-to-hand combat."[46] But here the leadership of the U.S. military is clearly reading its own views into public opinion; as early as 1990, after the U.S. incursion into Panama, a CBS/*New York Times* poll asked, "Do you think women members of the armed forces should be allowed to serve in combat if they want to?" Of those polled, 72 percent answered "yes," and only 26 percent answered "no."[47] In another poll, a majority of Americans agreed that women should be drafted in a national emergency.[48]

Where the opposition in the United States to removing the male-only draft and the combat exclusion of women is concentrated, therefore, is among those men who now are in the U.S. military. For example, 45 percent of first-year midshipmen at the U.S. Naval Academy expressed the view that women did not even belong in the military, and 38 percent of fourth-year midshipmen felt the same.[49]

This same view is also found among the highest commanders in the U.S. military. For example, Air Force Chief General Merrill McPeak testified before the Senate Arms Services Committee in 1992 that if he had to choose between a qualified woman and a less qualified man to fill a combat role, he would go with the man. "I admit it does not make much sense but that is the way I feel about it," McPeak responded.[50] Another U.S. general expressed a similar view:

> War is a man's work. Biological convergence on the battlefield [women serving in combat] would not only be dissatisfying in terms of what women could do, but it would be an enormous psychological distraction for the male, who wants to think that he's fighting for that woman somewhere behind, not up there in the same foxhole with him. It tramples the male ego. When you get right down to it, you have to protect the manhood of war.[51]

As retired Army Chief of Staff General William Westmoreland once put it, "No man with gumption wants a woman to fight his nation's battles."[52] Or, in the words of former Marine Commandant General Robert Barrow when testifying before the Senate Arms Services Committee in 1993, "I may be old-fashioned, but I think the very nature of women disqualifies them [from combat]. Women give life. Sustain life. Nurture life. They don't TAKE it."[53]

As these quotes indicate, support of the male-only draft and the combat exclusion of women in the United States is concentrated in the military elite. It is the military elite that is keeping the male-only draft and the combat exclusion of women in place.[54] So it cannot be that the members of the military elite are engaging in sexual discrimination against themselves by supporting the male-only draft and the combat exclusion of women. Discrimination, the only kind we can meaningfully complain about, must be imposed upon us by others, not by ourselves. People cannot do something to themselves and then cry discrimination because of the consequences of what they have just done to themselves.

Another reason why the harmful consequences that the male-only draft and the combat exclusion of women imposes on other men are not a form of discrimination is that these harms are simply the side effect of a practice that is well designed for the overall benefit of men. In addition, bear in mind that even in a nondiscriminatory military, some men would still be "cannon fodder." What a military that discriminates against women offers men is greater status and benefits, especially in nonmilitary life, albeit with a somewhat greater chance of becoming "cannon fodder." On its surface, however, it does not appear to be a bad deal.[55]

Consider also that even in a society without any sexual discrimination, some women and some men will still be worse off than they are in our own society, namely, those men and women who are served very well by the discriminatory gender practices in our own society. Nevertheless, those men and women would not have been sexually discriminated against because, by hypothesis, they are in a society in which there is no sexual discrimination. Similarly, although some men may be disadvantaged in a military because of the male-only draft and the combat exclusion of women, they would not thereby have suffered from sexual discrimination because the purpose of the male-only draft and the combat exclusion of women is not to discriminate against any men, but rather to serve the overall benefit of men, and it is appropriately designed for that purpose.[56] Of course, some men in the military may suffer from racial or class discrimination, even when they do not suffer from sexual discrimination.

So although Benatar and Farrell and other defenders of men's rights are surely right to oppose the male-only draft and the combat exclusion of women, the grounds they give for their opposition are grossly mistaken. These practices do not constitute sexual discrimination against men of the most damaging sort, as Farrell claims. Given that these practices are primarily maintained in place by men in the military, they cannot constitute discrimination against themselves. Nor do they intend to discriminate against other men. Accordingly, the male-only draft and the combat exclusion of women need to be opposed, as feminists have claimed, because they constitute discrimination against women and because of the harmful consequences that discrimination has on the military itself. Accordingly, the best strategy for eliminating these practices is to get men in the military to stop discriminating against women. There is little need to concern ourselves with sexual discrimination against men, at least regarding the male-only draft and the combat exclusion of women.[57]

4. WHY DO MEN DIE SOONER, AND WHOSE HEALTH IS BEING NEGLECTED?

In 1986, the U.S. National Institutes of Health (NIH) introduced a requirement that grant applications include women in medical testing and research. The next year, NIH reaffirmed the requirement, as well as emphasizing the need to include minorities. Unfortunately, these new requirements were generally ignored.[58] Then in 1990, the U.S. House Caucus on Women's Issues joined by Henry Waxman, chair of the House Energy and Commerce Subcommittee on Health and Environment, was able to get the General Accounting Office (GAO) to investigate whether NIH had implemented its own 1986 testing requirement concerning women. The GAO's negative report led the NIH, which was at the time up for reauthorization, to establish the Office of Research on Women's Health (ORWH).[59] In 1993 the U.S. Congress went further, passing the NIH Revitalization Act, which made the ORWH a permanent part of NIH and required the inclusion of women and minorities in medical research.[60]

In *The Myth of Male Power*, Warren Farrell argues against the need for the ORWH on the grounds that medical research in the United States has not neglected women. If anything, Farrell claims, it is men who have been neglected.[61] But Congress did not just act on a whim in creating the ORWH. There was plenty of evidence that women had been neglected in medical research. For example, the National Institute of Aging's Baltimore Longitudinal Study of Aging that started in 1958 included virtually no data on women, even though two-thirds of the population over age sixty-five are women.[62] Other studies have also neglected women: the Multiple Risk Factor Intervention Trial (MR. FIT), a study to evaluate the impact of various activities on the risk of heart attack, which was done with 12,866 men and 0 women; the Health Professionals Follow-Up Study examining the relation of coffee consumption and heart disease, which was done with 45,589 men and 0 women, and the Physicians' Health Study on the effects of aspirin on the risk of heart attack, which was done with 22,071 male but 0 female physicians.[63]

With respect to the Physicians' Health Study, Farrell claims that it was matched by the Nurses' Health Study, which similarly sought to determine the effects of aspirin on the risk of heart attack, in which eighty-seven thousand female registered nurses participated, but what Farrell doesn't mention is that the Nurses' Health Study, unlike the Physicians' Health Study, was only an observational investigation, not a more costly randomized clinical trial.[64] In fact, the report of the Nurses' Health Study itself pointed to the need for just such a randomized clinical trial study of women.[65]

In addition, women have not been included in drug trials in the United States, even though they consume roughly 80 percent of pharmaceuticals. Drugs such as Valium were never tested on women, even though two million women now take the drug each year.[66] The GAO report found that fewer than half the publicly available prescription drugs in the United States had been analyzed for gender-related differences in response.[67] As a result, frequently prescribed drugs and dosages were based on men's conditions and average weights and metabolisms. This led to twice as many adverse reactions to drugs in women as in men.[68] For example, some clot-dissolving drugs that are useful for treating heart attacks in men were found to cause bleeding problems in women, and some drugs that are commonly used to treat high blood pressure tended to lower men's mortality from heart attack while raising women's. Other drugs (e.g., antidepressants) varied in their effects over the course of a women's menstrual cycle such that a constant dosage of an antidepressant may be too high at some points in a woman's cycle and too low at others. Still other drugs (e.g., acetaminophen, an ingredient in many pain relievers) are eliminated in women at slower rates than they are eliminated in men. Not only did drugs that were developed for men turn out to be potentially dangerous for women, but drugs that were potentially beneficial for women may have been eliminated in early testing because the test group did not include women.[69]

Similar problems plagued AIDS research. As late as 1991, neither of the two U.S. institutions that distributed funds for AIDS research had funded a major project to address whether women with AIDS experienced different symptoms from men.[70] As a result, the official definition of AIDS did not originally include many of the HIV-related conditions in women because what was known about HIV disease was derived principally from research on men. In fact, most early studies on women were largely restricted to preventing the transmission of HIV from mother to child.[71] This resulted in little information on the progress of the disease in women themselves. As a consequence, most healthcare workers were unable to diagnose AIDS in women until the disease had advanced significantly, such that, on average, men died thirty months after diagnosis, while women died only fifteen weeks after diagnosis.[72]

The GAO found that 13.5 percent of the NIH budget supported research on women's health.[73] Farrell claims that this does not imply that women's health was neglected in research because, he says, an even smaller percentage of the NIH budget was spent on men's health while the rest was spent on gender-neutral health issues.[74] But the very research that we have been discussing—the National Institute of Aging's Baltimore Longitudinal Study of Aging, MR. FIT, the Health Professionals Follow-Up Study, the Physicians' Health Study, and the research on AIDS—all purported to be gender neutral, when, in fact, as we have just seen, they all favored men over women by failing to determine when a medication would have a different effect on women or when the etiology of a disease would be significantly different in women. Moreover, "women's health," often means just "women's reproductive health," so that even research so focused can neglect other aspects of women's health.

The investigators of these studies have defended the limiting of research subjects to men on the grounds that men are less costly and easier to study. They have pointed out that women's hormonal cycles also present methodological problems that complicate analysis. They have also been concerned that including women of childbearing age might endanger fetuses if the women subjects were to get pregnant during the clinical trials or soon after.[75] But if particular drugs are going to be marketed to women and used by them even, in many cases, during their pregnancies, then these drugs need to be adequately tested on women first.

Women's health has been neglected in still other ways. For example, standard instruments for heart surgery have been designed to go into bigger male arteries, thus making surgery on women riskier and more difficult to perform. Sometimes surgeons have to use surgical instruments on women that were designed for use on children.[76] It is also the case that men are more likely than women with the same medical needs to receive a transplant at every age category. The discrepancy between the sexes is most pronounced in the group from forty-six to sixty years old, with women having only half the chance of receiving a transplant as men of that same age.[77]

But what about NIH's greater funding of research on breast cancer compared to prostate cancer? Although about as many women die of breast cancer each year as men die of prostate cancer, NIH spends about four times as much on breast cancer research as on prostate cancer research. Farrell takes this disparity to be a clear example of the government unfairly favoring women's health over men's health.[78] However, it is important to point out here that the women who are dying from breast cancer are much younger, on average, than the men who are dying from prostate cancer. So the discrimination here, if it is that, would more likely be age discrimination than sex discrimination. It is also significant that more money is spent on AIDS research, which, as we noted, has been primarily focused on men, than is spent on breast cancer and prostate cancer research combined. So rather than seeing discrimination, what we are more likely seeing is the relative success of different groups lobbying for limited research funds. The AIDS lobby, with its growing number of AIDS victims, has been most successful. The breast cancer lobby, helped by the support of well-known people who have been afflicted with breast cancer, from Betty Ford to Gloria Steinem, has been next most successful. The prostate lobby, to date, has been least successful, and it clearly needs to do a better job in presenting its case in the competition for funding. The same holds for proponents for research in the seventeen other areas from a male birth control pill to sexual impotence where, Farrell claims, men's health has been neglected.[79] They just need to compete harder for funding.[80]

Farrell takes his clearest example of discrimination against men in health care to be the seven-year advantage in life expectancy that women have over men today.[81] Throughout human history from antiquity until the beginning of this century, men, on average, have lived slightly longer than women. By 1920, women's life expectancy in the United States was one year longer than men's (54.6 years vs. 53.6 years). Since about 1960 women have had a life expectancy that is about seven years longer than men's. Today the life expectancy for a woman is 78.8 years, versus 71.8 years for a man.[82] Similar male/female life expectancies can be found in other developed countries.

How can we account for this difference? Is it the result of discrimination against men, as Farrell claims? Well, we know that the differences are most pronounced in two age groups: ages fifteen to twenty-four (in which the male death rate is close to three times that of females) and fifty-five to sixty-four (in which the death rate for men is twice that for women).[83] We also know that much of the mortality differential in the fifteen to twenty-four age group is excessive male mortality from motor vehicle accidents.[84] That men smoke and drink more than women are additional factors. One study indicated that 75 percent of the change in the sex mortality differential between 1910 and 1962 can be attributed to cigarette smoking.[85] But even if smoking, drinking, and motor vehicle accidents are key factors, we can still ask, Why do men smoke, drink, and have more motor vehicle accidents than women do?

Farrell thinks that the answer can be found in the greater stress found in men's lives.[86] But studies of stress appear to show that women have more stress in their lives than men do. In one global study of people ages fifteen to sixty-five, 21 percent of women claimed to experience an immense amount of stress, compared with 15 percent of men. More single women than single men (17 percent vs. 12 percent) feel intense stress daily; the same was found for more married women than married men (21 percent vs. 17 percent), more widows than widowers (21 percent vs. 10 percent), and more separated or divorced women than separated and divorced men (28 percent vs. 20 percent). In another study, working women over age forty are more likely to report high levels of stress when compared to their younger female counterparts and to working men in general.[87] So, it does not appear that a difference in stress explains the difference in longevity between women and men.

Yet whatever the cause of the difference in projected longevity, as long as it is not purely physiological, feminism should make it disappear. Feminism proposes to create true equality between women and men, starting with true equal opportunity, and it is very likely that this equality of women's and men's life experiences will eliminate the current difference in longevity between them. If women's and men's lives become quite similar in terms of their benefits and burdens, this should lead toward equal longevity. In this equalization, women and men, however, will not have all of the opportunities that they now have. Rather, while some currently exclusive opportunities (like the chance of becoming a construction worker) will become common ones, other exclusive opportunities (like the opportunity to have a rewarding career/job together with a caregiving and housekeeping spouse at home) will be eliminated, in favor of new common ones (like the opportunity to have a rewarding career or job while equally sharing the childcare and housekeeping responsibilities at home). In this way, feminism, although not responsible for the longevity gap between women and men, does have a promising strategy for getting rid of it. Moreover, the reduction of the gap appears to be already underway. The U.S. National Center for Health reported in 2006 that the longevity gap between women and men had shrunk to five years, and if current trends continue, with women's and men's lives becoming more and more similar, in fifty years the gap could disappear.[88]

5. DOMESTIC VIOLENCE: WHO IS DOING THE BATTERING, AND WHAT'S THE SOLUTION?

Domestic violence has a long and sordid history. In Ancient Rome, wife beating was sanctioned under the Laws of Chastisement.[89] In Europe, squires and noblemen regularly beat their wives, and peasants followed their lords' example. The church also approved these methods of subjugating women. Priests counseled wives who were beaten by their husbands to win back their goodwill through increased devotion and obedience.[90] In a medieval theological manual, a man was permitted to "castigate his wife and beat her for corrections."[91] In his "Rules of Marriage," Friar Cherubino of Sienna recommended

> When you see your wife commit an offense.... Scold her sharply, bully and terrify her. And if this still doesn't work... take a stick and beat her soundly....[92]

In Russia, during the reign of Ivan the Terrible, the state church issued a Household Ordinance that spelled out how a husband might properly beat his wife. Nor was a man prosecuted for killing his wife if it "happened upon correction."[93] In France, under the Napoleonic Code, wife beating was not a legal grounds for divorce unless it could be proven to be attempted murder or unless the husband also wanted a divorce.[94]

Although history is replete with individual and local opposition to domestic violence and also periods where it was made illegal, as under the Puritans in the Massachusetts Bay Colony from 1640 to 1680, it wasn't until the 1960s and the 1970s, with the second wave of feminism, that widespread opposition to domestic violence got underway.[95] In the early 1970s, several countries—among them Scotland and Iran—made wife beating illegal.[96] In 1975, a new penal code was adopted in Brazil that prohibited husbands from selling, renting, or gambling their wives away.[97] Also in 1975, the queen of the Zulus was given interim custody of her two children after claiming in affidavits to the Durban Supreme Court that her husband had whipped her while she was pregnant.[98] However, the year before, the former prime minister of Japan, Eisaku Sato, was awarded the Nobel Peace Prize, even though his wife was quoted as saying in an interview, "Yes, he's a good husband, he only beats me once a week." In 1974, the Nobel Peace Prize committee did not consider wife beating sufficient grounds for withholding their award. In Japan itself, Sato became even more popular following the revelation of his wife beating.[99]

The times, however, were changing. From the early 1970s, NOW decided to make battered women a priority issue in the United States.[100] By 1981, there were five hundred battered women's shelters in the United States.[101] By 1983, over seven hundred shelters were operating nationwide, and by 1989, there were twelve hundred.[102] Today, there are five thousand.[103]

Still, according to recent statistics, nearly one-third of U.S. women report being physically or sexually abused by a husband or boyfriend at some point of their lives. Forty percent of all women who are murdered in the United States are killed by their male partners. Thirty-five percent of all visits by females to emergency rooms for injuries sustained in intentional or possible intentional violence are for injuries from domestic assaults, which is seven times the number for males.[104]

According to a common feminist interpretation of domestic violence, men batter because they expect to be in control of their families.[105] These expectations come from the way they were raised, which prepared them for male privilege and power, and they have learned to exercise that privilege and power through violence. Men who batter their wives believe that marriage gives them control over their wives and that hitting is an acceptable means of maintaining that control. As researchers Emerson Dobash and Russell Dobash put it, "Men who assault their wives are actually living up to cultural prescriptions that are cherished in Western society, aggressiveness, male dominance, and female subordination—and they are using physical force as a means to enforce that dominance."[106] According to this feminist perspective, the domination of women is a cultural prescription and violence against women is a means to that end, one that has usually been sanctioned by the law. Of course, not all men batter their wives; many of those who do not, according to this feminist perspective, find other ways to assert their male dominance. Clearly, this is a perspective, supported by data, which must be taken into account in any moral assessment of the problem of domestic violence. There is, however, a conflicting perspective supported by other data that also must be taken into account.

That perspective put forth by men's rights advocates maintains that women batter men, too. According to Warren Farrell,

> If we look only at police reports and all-female self-help groups [in the United States], it appears that men perpetrate about 90% of the domestic violence. But when we study male-only self-help groups we get a different picture. Only 6% of the men involved say they were the perpetrators; 81% said their wives were the perpetrators, 13% said it was mutual.... [According to nationwide studies of domestic violence

of both sexes, however,] women and men are said to batter each other about equally, or women batter more [and] women were more likely to initiate violence and much more likely to inflict severe violence.[107]

One such nationwide study in the United States, cited by Farrell,[108] the 1992 National Alcohol and Family Violence Survey, which was based on a nationwide probability sample of 1,970 cases and conducted by Dr. Glenda Kantor of the Family Research Lab at the University of New Hampshire, gave the frequencies shown in Table 2.1 for minor and severe violent acts between husbands and wives.

Table 2.1 Frequency of Violent Acts Between Husbands and Wives

	Husband to Wife	Wife to Husband
Minor Violent Acts		
Threw something	4.1%	7.4
Pushed/grabbed/shoved	10.4	10.9
Slapped	2.6	3.8
Severe Violent Acts		
Kicked/bit/hit with fist	1.3	3.4
Hit/tried to hit with something	1.6	3.8
Beat up	0.8	0.6
Choked	0.8	0.6
Threatened with knife or gun	0.4	0.7
Used knife or gun	0.2	0.1

According to this study, the overall frequency of minor violent acts is 5.7 percent for violence of husbands to wives and 7.3 percent for violence of wives to husbands. For severe violent acts, the overall frequency is 0.85 percent for violence of husbands to wives and 1.4 percent for violence of wives to husbands. Many other national studies provide comparable results.[109] How then should we take this data into account in a moral assessment of the problem of domestic violence?

The first thing to note about this data is how jarring the idea that women batter at least as much and at least as severely as men is in the light of what we know about the long history of domestic violence. As I indicated earlier, domestic violence of men against women just began to lose its legal justification in the 1960s and 1970s. Of course, it could be that we are in a completely new world created by the feminist movement of the 1960s and 1970s, and now that the legal supports for men battering women have been removed, we are seeing a new equality between men and women, manifested in equal battering.[110] Advocates of men's rights, like Farrell, claim that feminists don't want to recognize the current reality of equal battering as they press on for more and more advantages for women.[111]

Not surprisingly, similar arguments can be found in racial politics. Some opponents of affirmative action, for example, maintain that racial discrimination has basically come to an end and that current defenders of affirmative action are now trying to go beyond equality to secure unfair advantages for certain minority groups.[112] In both cases, the argument is that equality has been achieved or already exists and, hence, that there is no need for a corrective that favors one group over the other.

Curiously, the study most cited by proponents of this equal battering view of domestic violence conducted by Suzanne Steinmetz, Murray Straus, and Richard Gelles was actually published in 1975.[113] This means that the transition from a practice of permitting and protecting men's battering of women to one of equal battering would have had to occur virtually overnight. That is surely unlikely to have been the case.[114]

To see why it wasn't the case, we need to look more carefully at the studies that have been done on domestic violence. First of all, as Farrell himself notes, not all of the studies show equal battering. The National Crime Survey indicates that when victimization occurs 85 percent of the victims will be women and 15 percent will be men.[115] Such surveys of criminal behavior tend to show less frequent and more severe violence in general and higher rates of violence by men. By contrast, surveys of family conflict, especially those that use the Conflict Tactics Scales (CTS) developed by Straus, do show approximately equal rates for men and for women. But, as Straus himself admits, surveys that use his CTS focus on "the number of assaults... [ignoring] the contexts, meanings and consequences of [those] assaults."[116]

Straus goes on to defend the significance of these abstracted results with the following analogy:

> The criticism that the CTS does not take into account the context and meaning of the acts is analogous to criticizing a reading ability test

for not identifying the reasons a child reads poorly (such as limited exposure to books at home or test anxiety) and for not measuring the harmful effects of reading difficulty (such as low self-esteem or dropping out of school).[117]

But does this analogy hold? Can acts be usefully specified as violent apart from the contexts, meaning, and consequences of those acts? For example, what would be the significance of saying that police officers and those they arrested for serious offenses were "equally violent" if all we meant by that was that each had struck the other an equal number of times, ignoring the fact that most of those arrested probably lacked any justification for using force? Wouldn't such abstracted results be regarded as fundamentally distorting apart from the contexts, meaning, and consequences of the acts they claim to characterize? While the results on a well-designed reading ability test do have an independent significance apart from their causes and consequences, accounts of the uses of force apart from their causes and consequences do not appear to have a similar significance.[118]

There are other reasons why the CTS, particularly as used by Straus and his associates, is a poor measure of domestic violence. The introduction to the standard CTS reads as follows:

> No matter how well a couple gets along, there are times when they disagree, get annoyed with the other person or just have spats or fights because they're in a bad mood or tired or for some other reason. They also use many different ways of trying to settle their differences. I'm going to read some things that you or your (spouse/partner) might do when you have an argument. I want you to tell me how many times... in the past 12 months you...[119]

The scales are thus applied only to couples that are living together, or at least have an on going intimate relationship. Accordingly, they fail to measure the violence that occurs among separated and divorced couples. It turns out that a higher percentage of women are stalked, physically abused, and harassed after relationships end. In a random U.S. survey, eight times as many women as men reported being stalked by a current or past partner, and an estimated 90 percent of women killed by their intimate partners have been stalked first.[120] In a random

Canadian survey, 39 percent said that violence occurred for the first time after separation, 24 percent said that violence became worse, and 37 percent said it stayed the same.[121] In this study, 60 percent of the women compared to 25 percent of the men required medical attention. According to a U.S. National Crime Victimization Survey, violence against separated women is more than eight times higher than violence against married women.[122] Straus himself concludes that studies of family conflict that usually use his CTS include very few severe cases and thus "may provide an erroneous basis for policies and interventions."[123]

According to Daniel Saunders, another problem with these studies is that they neglect to include sexual abuse.[124] Rates of sexual abuse of women by an intimate partner were more than five times higher than those of men, two to sixty times higher in high school surveys, and twenty times higher in a random U.S. survey.[125] Thus, the inclusion of sexual abuse demonstrates clear gender differences. In response to the criticism that the CTS did not include sexual abuse items, some such items were added to the latest version of the scale (CTS-2).[126] However, Jack Straton estimates that since more women are raped by their husbands than are only battered by them, adjusting Straus's own results to include sexual violence would make the ratio of male-to-female intimate violence more than 16 to 1.[127]

In addition, domestic violence studies that use the CTS to measure violence between men and women frequently fail to take into account the difference in motives between men and women. Studies of domestic homicide, for example, show clearly that women are much more likely to use violence in self-defense than are men.[128] Saunders points out that one study found that 60 percent of husbands killed by their wives had "precipitated" their own deaths; that is, they were the first to use physical force, strike blows, or threaten with a weapon. Only 9 percent of wives killed by their husbands had struck first or issued threats. These figures were based on "provocation recognized by the courts." Homicides by women are generally part of an attempt to stop their partners from either further harming the women themselves or their children or to prevent an attack they see as imminent and life threatening.[129] In one study, women who killed their male partners reported experiencing a much higher level of fear than did men who killed their female partners.[130]

In contrast with women, men are motivated to kill their female partners by jealousy and a need to control, particularly when a relationship appears to be, or is being, terminated.[131] Husbands are motivated by self-defense seven to ten times less frequently than wives are.[132] Some scholars attempt to counter this evidence that women are acting in self-defense by pointing to a study that shows that 53 percent of women hit first.[133] But a woman might hit first in an attempt to ward off the greater violence that she expects from her husband because of prior abuse; a woman might also hit first with no expectation or intention of inflicting serious injury on her husband.

In addition, the physical consequences of domestic violence are generally far greater for women than for men, given that men, on average, are forty-five pounds heavier and four to five inches taller than women.[134] The 1985 National Family Violence Survey asked respondents if they had been "hurt badly enough as a result of a conflict between you to need to see a doctor." Over seven times as many female victims as male victims reported that they had such an injury.[135] In another study, men's reactions to women's violence against them usually did not reflect the negative consequences reported by women. Of the men who described their response to the violence of their female partners, the largest proportion said they were "not bothered" (26 percent) followed by those who felt that the woman was "justified" (20 percent) and those who "ridiculed her" (17 percent) or were "impressed" (3 percent). Others felt "angry" (14 percent) or "surprised" (6 percent) and there were a variety of other reactions (8 percent). Only 6 percent felt victimized.[136] Similarly, in a study of college couples, women who used physical force did not believe that they would or could seriously injure their partners.[137] Straus himself recognized the need to adjust violence rates for injury when he stated in his 1997 study, "The injury adjusted rate for assaults by men is 6 times greater than the rate of domestic assault by women."[138]

While feminists have appealed to patriarchy to explain men's greater violence against women, Farrell has attempted to undercut this appeal by pointing to studies that show the level of violence in lesbian relationships in the United States to be similar to that in heterosexual relationships.[139] But this is to ignore the unfavorable legal and social constraints on lesbian relationships or, more generally, on homosexual relationships. Despite the progress of the gay and lesbian civil rights movement, many in the United States still view homosexuals as perverse, a threat to children, and psychologically disturbed. Homosexuals in the United States are subject to high rates of anti-gay violence and harassment and discrimination in housing and employment and are prohibited from serving openly in the military or getting legally married.[140] Why should we not expect the impact of this hatred and violence directed at homosexuals to affect their intimate lives just as it affects other aspects of their lives? Of course, patriarchy and heterosexism are not unrelated. In the current cultural environment in the United States and elsewhere, attempts to increase the equality between men and women are often opposed because it is thought that they would make men more like women (more nurturing, more caring) and that this in turn would make them more like homosexuals.[141] Similarly, homosexuality is feared, particularly by men, because they think that it will make them more like women (more feminine or more effeminate). Yet even though patriarchy and heterosexism are connected in these ways, they still tend to lead to violence in somewhat different ways. Accordingly, we shouldn't expect that all the intimate violence suffered by women can be traceable directly to patriarchy.

Nor need feminists deny that sometimes men are unjustly battered by women. Patriarchal structures do not always put husbands into a position of dominance over their wives. Sometimes circumstances are reversed, as when wives are physically stronger than their husbands and are also the breadwinners in their families. In such circumstances, women may use their greater strength to batter their husbands and use their greater economic resources to make it difficult for their husbands to leave. In such cases, domestic violence law should protect these battered men just the way that sexual harassment law currently protects those relatively few men who are sexual harassed in the workplace.[142]

What needs to be opposed, however, is the use of CTS-based domestic violence studies to undercut the funding for battered women's shelters. Drawing on these studies, some men's rights advocates have argued either for significantly reducing the funding of battered women's shelters or for equal funding of shelters for both men and women. In Minnesota, a suit was filed by the National Coalition of Free Men requesting that funding of domestic violence programs be terminated on the grounds that they discriminate against men.[143] In Chicago, these studies were used to block funding for a shelter for battered women and their children.[144] In New Hampshire, the state where Straus has been at the University of New Hampshire for virtually his entire academic career, state funding was diverted to open up a men's shelter, but almost immediately it had to close down for lack of clients.[145] More broadly, advocates of men's rights use CTS-based studies to argue that things are really equal between men and women and so there is no justification for any socially funded policy that provides a benefit for women unless that policy also provides an equal or comparable benefit for men.

Interestingly, a comparable argument is made in racial politics. Arguing that racial discrimination against minorities no longer exists, opponents of affirmative action have opposed even outreach programs that attempt to make minorities aware of employment and educational opportunities about which they, and not members of the white majority, tend to be unaware. Of course, if we were all equal, then only equal treatment would be justified from that point. But when things are not equal between men and women, as in the context of domestic violence, where women are battered far more than men are, a differential corrective is required. Of course, those relatively few men who are battered by women should not be neglected. What is important, however, is that we should not be deceived by false claims of equality, and so fail to recognize, as feminists have argued, that the major problem of domestic violence is men's battering of women.[146]

6. RAPE, DATE RAPE: HOW SHOULD WE RESPOND?

Four thousand years ago, the Code of Hammurabi punished a man who raped a woman betrothed to another with death. If a married woman was raped, the code specified that both the woman and her attacker were to be killed, unless it turned out that her husband wished that his wife be spared.[147] Under ancient Hebrew law, however, a wife who was raped could not be so spared because she was thought to have committed adultery. Nevertheless, that same Hebrew law allowed that if a man raped a woman who was neither married nor betrothed, he could escape punishment altogether by simply marrying the woman and paying fifty silver shekels to her father.[148] In these ancient codes and in subsequent law, rape was considered to be primarily a crime against a woman's father, her husband, or the man to whom she was betrothed rather than a crime against the woman herself.

In England, before the Norman Conquest of 1066, the penalty for rape was death and dismemberment, but this punishment was only inflicted when a man raped a highborn and propertied virgin whose father was a powerful lord.[149] In the thirteenth century, under Edward I, the Statutes of Westminster expanded the crime of rape to include married women as well as virgins, with no difference in punishment.[150] In the eighteenth century, Chief Justice Matthew Hale of the King's Bench defined "rape" as "the carnal knowledge of any woman above the age of ten against her will," and he recommended that juries be instructed that rape "is an accusation easily to be made and hard to be proved, and harder to be defended by the party accused, though never so innocent." His recommendation was followed into the twentieth century.[151] Hale is also known for introducing a marital rape exemption into the law.[152] Subsequently, the English law of rape was adopted wholesale by the American colonies, and it later became the law in the United States with very little change until the twentieth century.

In the United States, under the impetus of the feminist movement of the late 1960s and 1970s, rape law began to change. First, an "utmost resistance" requirement for nonconsent was reduced to one of "reasonable resistance." Second, a collaboration requirement that was much stricter than anything demanded for other offenses was removed. Third, rape-shield laws were introduced both by the federal government and by states to protect the victim of rape from an irrelevant examination of her past history. Fourth, beginning in the 1980s and continuing in the 1990s, a number of states in the United States have removed the marital rape exceptions from their laws.[153]

Part of what drove the impetus to change rape law in the United States was a new recognition of the frequency of rape. In 1982, *Ms.* magazine published an article entitled "Date Rape: A Campus

Epidemic?" Preliminary research suggested that this kind of rape was even more common than rape by strangers. To investigate that possibility, *Ms.* approached the National Institute of Mental Health (NIMH) for funding to do a major national study. NIMH put the magazine in contact with Mary Koss, then a psychology professor at Kent State University who had already done research in this area. A survey was administered to more than sixty-two hundred undergraduate women and men on thirty-two college campuses. It was the largest scientific investigation ever undertaken on the subject, and it revealed that 1 in 4 female respondents had an experience that was said to meet the legal definition of rape or attempted rape.[154]

Warren Farrell and others, however, have challenged the results of Koss's study. Farrell claims that in order to arrive at the figure that 25 percent of all women were raped by the time they were in college, Koss used affirmative responses to the following question: "Have you given in to sexual intercourse when you didn't want to because you were overwhelmed by a man's continual arguments and pressure?"[155] But this is to misinterpret Koss's study. First, Koss's 1 in 4 figure is not a measure of rapes alone, but rather a measure of rapes or attempted rapes. Second, although this question was in Koss's study, a positive answer to it was not used to support Koss's 1 in 4 conclusion about rape or attempted rape, but rather to support a finding of sexual aggression. Only positive responses to the following four questions were taken as evidence of rape or attempted rape:

1. Have you had a man attempt sexual intercourse (get on top of you, attempt to insert his penis) when you didn't want to by threatening or using some degree of force (twisting your arm, holding you down, etc.) but intercourse did not occur?
2. Have you had sexual intercourse when you didn't want to because a man gave you alcohol or drugs?
3. Have you had sexual intercourse when you didn't want to because a man threatened or used some degree of physical force (twisting your arm, holding you down, etc.) to make you?
4. Have you had sex acts (anal or oral intercourse or penetration by objects other than the penis) when you didn't want to because a man threatened or used some degree of physical force (twisting your arm, holding you down, etc.) to make you?[156]

Of course, it is true, as Farrell points out, that if you ask college students whether they have experienced "unwanted sex," high percentages of both men and women will respond that they have.[157] But Koss's study is not about unwanted sex generally, but about a specific kind of unwanted sex that purports to satisfy the legal definition of rape or attempted rape. That is what her 1 in 4 figure claims to measure.

In a subsequent interview with the *The Blade*, Koss allowed that her question about alcohol and drugs was "ambiguous."[158] But even if we drop the positive responses to that question from Koss's study, we still get a 1 in 5 figure for rapes or attempted rapes.

Nor is it clear that we should want to exclude a question about alcohol or drugs from an assessment of rape. Harvard University maintains that rape "includes intercourse with a person incapable of expressing unwillingness or who is prevented from resisting, as a result of the intake of alcohol and other drugs."[159] Is such an understanding of rape objectionable?

Farrell thinks that it is, and he criticizes Harvard and other universities for incorporating such provisions into their prohibition of rape. But if a man signed away his car or house while he was dead drunk, would we think he had appropriately consented? I don't think any court in the land would hold a man to such an agreement. So why should we assume that a woman consented to sexual intercourse under similar circumstances? In addition, most states include just such a provision in their rape law.[160] In these jurisdictions, an intoxicated person cannot legally consent to sexual intercourse.

In 1974, the state of Michigan, responding to the lobbying efforts of feminist groups as well as low conviction rates for rape, passed the first rape-shield law in the United States. Other states quickly followed, and in 1978, the U.S. Congress enacted a federal rape-shield law. These laws varied widely in their requirements. Their single common feature is that they all attempt to keep evidence of the victim's past sexual conduct out of the courtroom except under certain conditions.[161] General rules of evidence exclude the introduction of evidence that is irrelevant and prejudicial. In the past, however, the sexual history of the victim of rape had almost always been taken to be relevant to determining whether she consented to sexual intercourse in the case at hand. This is now recognized to have been a serious mistake, and rape-shield laws have been introduced to limit this access to the sexual history of the victim.

Farrell objects to all such rape-shield laws on the grounds that they a flagrant violation of the right to due process (because they shield one party more than the other) and on the grounds that they violate the equal protection clause of the Fourteenth Amendment.[162] But this is to misunderstand what these laws, however ineffectively, are attempting to do.

As Farrell himself admits, rape is an underreported crime. According to the National Crime Victimization Survey, there were over 150,000 rapes or attempted rapes reported in the United States in 2002.[163] It is further estimated that more than three times that number of rapes actually occur. Of those rapes that are reported, only a very small percentage ever make their way to trial.[164] Only between 2 and 5 percent of reported rapes lead to convictions.[165] One reason these percentages are so low is that irrelevant and prejudicial information about the rape victims' past history is still introduced as evidence in trials, and this has led to biased verdicts, which, in turn, has made rape victims more reluctant to have their cases tried or even to report their rapes to the authorities. The purpose of rape-shield laws is to prevent just this sort of irrelevant and prejudicial evidence from being introduced in trials and, thereby, to lead to more convictions in rape cases, which, in turn, would lead to more rape cases being brought to trial, and more cases being reported to the authorities.

Consider how irrelevant and prejudicial the blanket use of the past sexual history of the victim of rape has been. This history was used because it was assumed that if a woman had said "yes" to sex with other men in the past that strongly suggested that she also said "yes" to her accused rapist. Employing this assumption in rape trials, however, unfairly restricts the sexual freedom of women. To eliminate this unfairness, we must rely primarily on evidence from the present sexual encounter to determine whether or not a woman has consented to sexual intercourse, and do the same for men as well. If both women and men are thus treated fairly in this regard, as rape-shield laws purport to do, Farrell has no grounds for thinking that there will be any violation of their due process or equal protection rights in this regard.[166]

False Allegations of Rape

Another reason Farrell is concerned about the protection that rape-shield laws provide is that he believes that a significant number of rape allegations are false.[167] But even if a significant number of rape allegations were false, it still wouldn't justify abandoning the protections of rape-shield laws and unfairly using women's sexual histories against them.

Yet what reason do we have to think that a significant number of rape allegations are false? Here Farrell cites a study done at the U.S. Air Force Academy in 1985 by Charles McDowell. He regards this study as the "most shocking finding" of his book, *The Myth of Male Power*.[168] Unfortunately, the study is not in the public domain, and until I used the Freedom of Information Act, I had basically only Farrell's summary of its results to go on. According to Farrell, when McDowell investigated 556 cases of alleged rape, 27 percent of the women admitted they had lied (either just before or after they took lie-detector tests). On the basis of twenty-five criteria that were taken to be common to the women who had lied, McDowell is then said to have determined that a total of 60 percent of the original rape allegations were likely to be false.[169]

Other studies, however, have produced somewhat different results. The FBI reports that 8 percent of rape allegations in the United States are unfounded.[170] In 1992, the *Washington Post* reported that in the Maryland counties of Anne Arundel, Montgomery, and Prince George, the percentage of unfounded rape claims were comparable to unfounded claims about other crimes. However, the *Post* also found that in two relatively small jurisdictions, Howard County and the city of Alexandria, the percentage of unfounded rape claims was significantly higher than for other types of unfounded claims.[171]

It is important to recognize here that "unfounded" does not mean "false." Rape allegations are considered by police to be unfounded for a variety of reasons other than being false. Such reasons include not reporting the assault promptly, being provocatively dressed, hitchhiking, going alone to bars or cocktail lounges, and walking alone at night.[172] Police have judged cases to be unfounded even when victims sustained bruises, black eyes, cigarette burns, and bitten nipples, as long as there was a previous sexual relationship between the parties. Police are more likely to believe a rape allegation if there is more than one offender, if weapons were used, or if the victim had a reputation for chastity.[173] In Oakland, California, in 1990, following disclosure that 25 percent of reported rapes and attempted rapes were deemed unfounded by the police, 228 cases were reopened for investigation. The police admitted that in some cases victims were not even interviewed or contacted after the initial reports were made. It turns out that many of these victims were women of color, prostitutes, drug users, or women who were acquainted with the assailants.[174] So it is highly likely that many of the rape allegations that are deemed by the police to be unfounded are not false allegations at all.

With regard to the 1985 study by McDowell at the U.S. Air Force Academy, it is important to note that McDowell does not maintain in his study all that Farrell claims he does.[175] McDowell is also mistaken about the main claim that he does make in his study. He claims that of the 556 rape allegations that were investigated, 220 were determined to be actual rapes, 80 were determined to be false allegations, and 256 could not be "conclusively verified as rapes."[176] From this data, McDowell concludes that 27 percent of the rape allegations were false. But 80 is not 27 percent of 556. It is only 14 percent of 556. That is still a high percentage, but it is not 27 percent.

Nor does McDowell make all the claims in the study that Farrell says he makes. Farrell tells us that the women in McDowell's study admitted that they had lied either just before or after they took lie-detector tests, but McDowell does not say this in his study.[177] As we will see when we look at more recent public investigations at the U.S. Air Force Academy, the circumstances under which these women withdrew their allegations are quite relevant to whether they did so freely. Farrell also tells us that McDowell was able to isolate twenty-five characteristics common to those women cadets who are said to have lied and then use those characteristics to determined that 60 percent of the original rape allegations were likely to be false. But while Mc-Dowell does claim to have found twenty-five characteristics that were common to those women cadets who are said to have lied, he did not apply them to the cases that were "not conclusively verified as rapes" to arrive at a 60 percent figure for rape allegations that were likely to be false. Moreover, when you see what characteristics McDowell claims are common to women cadets who are said to have admitted making a false allegation of rape, you can see why he might have been a bit hesitant to apply them to the undetermined cases. Here are some of those characteristics:

1. Complaint is made to a hospital or medical authorities in order to justify tests for pregnancy or venereal disease.
2. Victim relates the incident either in a monotone or with excessive zeal and relish.
3. Victim alleges she was assaulted by more than one person.
4. Victim claims she offered vigorous resistance but was forcefully overcome.
5. Victim claims rapist did not perform oral or anal sex.
6. Victim presents letters allegedly from rapist in which death or rape threats are made.
7. Victim has previous record of having been assaulted or raped under similar circumstances.

I find it very hard to believe that these are characteristics that distinguish those who make false allegations of rape from those who do not and that such characteristics can be usefully employed to resolve the status of cases about which we are in doubt. In any case, McDowell made no attempt in his study to apply his twenty-five characteristics of women who are said to have admitted making a false allegation of rape to determine the truthfulness of other allegations of rape about which there was doubt, unlike what Farrell claims.

As it turns out, we also have more recent public investigations of rape and sexual assault at the Air Force Academy that paint a quite different picture from the one provided by McDowell and Farrell.[178] According to a report issued in 2003, "the highest levels of the Air Force leadership" knew, or should have known, about allegations of rape and sexual assault from at least 1993 and possibly from 1976 when the academy first began admitting women. However, the brass did not take any effective action, the report said.[179] Women at the academy were counseled that if they were raped they had two choices: "Pretend it didn't happen and deal with it or report it." But if you report it and ask for an investigation "your entire life at the academy is over, and you'll probably get kicked out."[180] Women who did ask for an investigation were frequently immediately penalized either for drinking or socializing at inappropriate times, and these rule violations were then used against them to undermine their credibility.[181] Even before this recent report was completed, four top officers in charge of the academy were replaced, and Air Force officials told U.S. Senators investigating the academy that they were now offering amnesty for lesser offenses, like drinking or socializing at inappropriate times, to encourage women who have been victims of sexual assault to come forward without fear of punishment, something they falsely claimed they had been doing all along.[182]

What is particularly interesting for our purposes here is that the total number of rape and sexual assault cases that the Air Force investigated over the ten-year period from 1993 to 2003 is between 57 and 61.[183] By contrast, in the nine years from 1976 to 1985 covered by the McDowell study that Farrell cites, when even fewer women were admitted each year to the academy, the study claims to have investigated 556 cases of alleged rape! This would mean that there were more than ten times more alleged rapes and other sexual assaults investigated in the nine years covered by the McDowell study than in the ten years covered by the more recent investigations. How could this be?[184] Why weren't officials at the Air Force Academy boasting about how much better things are at the academy in the last ten years or so (bad as they are) compared to how they were in the not too distant past? At the very least, these recent public investigations of the academy have cast serious doubt about the accuracy of the McDowell study on which Farrell relies. Accordingly, if we want a sense of the number of false accusations of rape across the country, we do better to rely on the FBI's 8 percent figure for unfounded accusations, bearing in mind that this figure itself needs to be significantly discounted because of the difference between unfounded and false accusations, as discussed earlier.

Farrell thinks "the most important single change we can make" to solve the problem of rape is "to resocialize women to take the initiative sexually."[185] There is good reason, however, for thinking that this is not at all the best place to start. As rape cases show, forwardness by a woman in the current cultural environment can be understood by a man to be sufficient grounds to press her to go all the way, even if that was not her intention, and unfortunately, some judges and juries see it that way as well. Consider the recent Kobe Bryant rape case, in which the woman was forward enough to agree to go to his room and enter into consensual kissing with him; then, she claims, after things turned violent, she clearly indicated that she didn't want to go on to intercourse. If this is what actually happened, we can see that her forwardness dramatically increased, rather than decreased, the likelihood that she would be raped.[186]

A better first step for avoiding rape is to use the law, education, and other social institutions to instill in men that they are expected to secure explicit consent from their partners before engaging in the act of sexual intercourse. In other words, getting men to stop at "no" is not enough; we must further demand that they secure a clear "yes" before engaging in sexual intercourse. While there is much that can be done to accomplish that goal, at a minimum, changes in the law would help to realize this positive standard of consent. Let me suggest just two improvements that might help beyond a requirement of an explicit "yes" before engaging in sexual intercourse.

We know that the vast majority of nonstranger rapes are unprotected, first-time sexual encounters.[187] Similarly, a study of college rape victims by Mary Koss found that more than 60 percent of acquaintance rapes occurred in the context of "nonromantic" or "casual dating" as opposed to "steady" dating.[188] What this suggests is that a great deal of misunderstanding lies behind these rapes. Suppose then we had a crime of reckless sexual activity that prohibits a person from intentionally engaging in unprotected sex (i.e., intercourse without wearing a condom) with any person other than his or her spouse when the two people had not on a previous occasion engaged in sexual intercourse.[189] The crime would be punishable by imprisonment for up to three months or with a fine. The only defense against this crime would be that the person with whom the defendant had unprotected sex expressly asked to engage in unprotected sexual activity or otherwise gave unequivocal indications of affirmatively consenting to engage in sexual activity that is specifically unprotected.[190]

Applying a condom usually requires some break in the action. That is likely to give both parties the opportunity, especially when the parties do not know each other that well, to correct any misunderstandings, reassess the situation, and make sure both want to continue.[191] Surely such a law would reduce the incidence of date or acquaintance rape, which correspondingly would significantly reduce the incidence of rape overall. Kobe Bryant would have been clearly guilty of this crime, and many men would have learned an important lesson if Bryant had been convicted of it.

It is also worth pointing out here that Bryant was married and that studies of rapists have found that many of them are married as well, or have steady regular sexual partners.[192] For such men, it is not the case that they rape because they have no nonviolent way of having sexual intercourse. When it is not simply a misunderstanding, the exercise of power is fundamental to what they are doing to the women they rape. That is why both requiring an explicit "yes" for sexual intercourse and requiring a condom for first-time sexual intercourse could serve to provide needed barriers to protect women from this illegitimate exercise of power against them.

Another change in the legal system that could help to lower the incidence of rape would be to have special courts with judges who specialize in hearing such cases, just as in many urban areas in the United States, there are now special units within the District Attorney's office that specialize in domestic or child abuse.[193] If the judges who hear rape cases were more knowledgeable about rape and its history, they would, for example, be better able to apply rape-shield laws and thereby be better able to secure more just verdicts.

7. IS THE CRIMINAL JUSTICE SYSTEM SEXIST?

From the very beginning, women in U.S. prisons have been treated differently from men. At the Auburn State Penitentiary in New York, women were kept in a cramped and windowless attic room and were not even allowed out of the room for exercise. Food and water were brought in daily and refuse was carried out. According to a prison chaplain writing in 1830, "To be a male convict in this prison would be quite tolerable, but to be a female convict, for any protracted period, would be worse than death."[194] In the Indiana State Prison at Jeffersonville, a male prisoner revealed that young female prisoners "were subjected to the worst of debasement at the hands of prison officials and guards" at the same time that older female prisoners were "obliged to do the work of all." In this prison, the warden established a concubinage, and sadistic beatings, rape, and illegitimate births were part of the ordinary prison routine. [195] By the late nineteenth century, a reform movement led to separate prisons for women that remedied at least some of the inequalities to which women were subjected.[196]

In the late 1960s, with the second wave of feminism, U.S. courts began to address still other inequalities that disadvantaged women in prison. In *Liberti v. York* (1968), the court held that a female plaintiff's indeterminate sentence of up to three years for breach of the peace violated the Equal Protection Clause of the Fourteenth Amendment because the maximum prison term for men convicted of the same offense was only one year. In *Commonwealth v. Stauffer* (1969), the court found that Pennsylvania was not justified in sentencing women to a state penitentiary while sentencing men to county jails for the same crimes. In *Mary Beth G. v. City of Chicago* (1983), the court rejected the city of Chicago's practice of routinely strip-searching women, but not men, as a violation of the Equal Protection Clause. In *Bukhari v. Hutto* (1980), the court held that no justification existed for disparate treatment based on the fact that it would cost more to provide the same programs at women's prisons as there were at men's prisons because of the smaller number of female prisoners. Probably the most influential and wide-ranging of these court decisions was *Glover v. Johnson* (1979), which held that women's constitutional rights had been violated because they were provided with fewer and poorer educational and vocational programs and less adequate facilities and equipment and because they were denied access to supplemental programs, like work passes and incentive good time.

Despite the long history of how women have been disadvantaged by the U.S. criminal justice system, Warren Farrell thinks that women are now unfairly favored over men in the system.[197] He cites the number of months to which women and men are sentenced for burglary, larceny, and aggravated assault, but fails to sufficiently take into account whether there are other relevant facts about these men and women that explain the differences in sentences.[198] He also fails to note that the average prison term for wives who kill their husbands is twice as long as it is for husbands who kill their wives.[199] He does note that 30 percent of women in prison for killing their husbands had histories of violent offenses, but he seems to fail to realize that this implies that an astonishing 70 percent of the women in prison for killing their husbands have no history of violent offenses at all.[200] In fact, 50 percent of them have no previous record at all.[201]

To support his case that the criminal law favors women over men, Farrell offers us two high-profile cases.[202] The first is the McMartin preschool case. The second is the mail-fraud case against Jim Bakker, the televangelist.

In the first case, Farrell claims that a grandson and his grandmother, Peggy McMartin, were "both indicted on fifty-two counts of child molestation. His grandmother's bail was one third of his and he spent nearly five years in jail before the jury finally ruled that the two were not guilty. She—the director—spent less than two years in jail."[203] In the second case, Farrell claims that although "community property laws were supposed to make equal rights and responsibilities for the couple's profits or debts" when Jim Bakker and Tammy Faye Bakker's "business got into trouble, Jim got forty years in prison and Tammy Faye got none."[204] In both of these cases, Farrell claims, the women were unfairly favored over the men by the criminal justice system. But this conclusion is not borne out by a careful examination of the cases.

In the McMartin case, there was no one named "Peggy McMartin." There was a Virginia McMartin, whose grandson Ray Buckey did spent five years in prison before he was found innocent, but his grandmother never spent any time in prison, although she was initially charged with conspiracy in the case. But that charge was dropped before the first trial took place. The director of the preschool was Peggy Buckey, and she and her son Ray, who is Virginia McMartin's grandson, did spend time in prison—she spent about two years before she was acquitted in the first trial, and he spent about five years before he was acquitted in both the first trial and then in a second trial in which he was the lone defendant. However, there is explanation for their difference in treatment that has nothing to do with a difference in sex.

To begin with, both Ray and his mother, together with three other teachers at the school, were held without bail through the longest preliminary hearing in history—eighteen months. Although before the preliminary hearing both Ray and his mother were charged with fifty-nine counts, after the hearing, Ray was only charged with fifty of those counts to which thirty-one new ones were added, for a total of eight-one, later reduced to eighty. His mother, after the hearing, was only charged with eight of her original fifty-nine counts to which fifteen new ones were added for a total of twenty-three, later reduced to twenty-two. At that point, Ray's mother, after spending about two years in prison, was granted a bail of $500,000, which, with the help of friends, she was able to make, while Ray was denied bail and remained in prison until the end of the two trials. He was denied bail because of the greater number of felony counts against him and because of past testimony by alleged victims who accused him of threatening to kill them or their parents if they spoke of the alleged molestations.[205] So, as the court saw it, there were reasonable grounds for treating Ray Buckey differently from his mother and grandmother in the McMartin preschool case that had nothing to do with a difference in sex.

In the case of Jim and Tammy Faye Bakker, after Jim Bakker gave up control of his televangelist ministry Praise the Lord (PTL), and especially after he was convicted of fraud while running PTL, Jim and Tammy's family property was so reduced that when she later divorced him while he was in prison, there was virtually nothing at all for them to divide. So Tammy did suffer physically, emotionally, socially, and economically from her husband's downfall. Nevertheless, she was not implicated in his crime and so was not sent to prison along with him.[206]

Jim Bakker kept two sets of books on his mail-fraud scheme at PTL, and so only two of his closest associates at PTL knew about the scheme, and they turned state's evidence against Bakker to get shorter sentences. Jerry Falwell, who took over PTL after Bakker, made the group's financial records available to the federal government, which then used them to make its case against Jim Bakker and his two closest associates at PTL. The government's case was airtight. Bakker had virtually no defense. If the government could have implicated Tammy on the basis of PTL records, it would have done so. If Bakker's two closest associates at PTL who turned state's evidence could have implicated her that could have further reduced their sentences. However, not a shred of evidence emerged against her. She was not spared a jail term because she was a woman, as Farrell suggests, but rather because she was in no way implicated in Jim Bakker's crime.

Self-defense is another area of the criminal law in which women have not fared well. In particular, women who kill their batterers have generally not been acquitted of homicide charges on grounds of self-defense.[207] In this area, experts on battered women's syndrome are now being used in support of self-defense claims that would otherwise be difficult for jurors to understand.[208] Battered women's syndrome is used to explain why women don't leave the men who batter them and why they reasonably believe that killing their abusers is their only possible means of escape from a life-threatening situation.[209] With or without such testimony, however, it has been difficult to get acquittals for battered women when they kill their batterers in nonconfrontational contexts, despite the similarities of these women to hostages or prisoners of war who kill their guards to escape or to nations that attack their enemies, reasonably anticipating that their enemies were about to attack them.[210]

Farrell does not reject the use of the battered women's syndrome in cases of self-defense. He just argues that fairness requires that there should be a battered men's syndrome available to men in certain cases of self-defense. Theoretically, Farrell is right; there should be such a defense available to men in certain cases of self-defense. Yet practically, given what we know about domestic violence (see Section 5), we also know that there will be very few men who would ever be in a position to avail themselves legitimately of such a defense.

Farrell does offer us one case in which he thinks that the battered men's syndrome is applicable. According to Farrell's account, Tom Hayhurst's mother had abused him, his siblings, and his father, who had eventually committed suicide. Each of the children had moved away, except for Tom's sister who was developmentally disabled. But when Tom's mother was seriously injured in a car accident, according to Farrell,

[s]he asked Tom to return home to help her and his disabled sister. Tom left his job in Arizona and took care of his mom without pay. This left him with too little money to afford an apartment. Because he knew he couldn't handle living with his mother, he lived in a van in the driveway. However, as the court report reads, "She began verbal and physical abuse of him brandishing a knife, and throwing objects at him." "Finally," Tom explains, "I just blew it. I grabbed a crowbar and hit her." The blow of the crowbar killed her.[211]

Yet Farrell's accounting does not reveal all the relevant facts in this case.[212] Nor does it accurately present the final encounter between Tom and his mother that led to her death. At the time of her death, Tom's mother was seventy-four years old and used a walking stick, not the type of person one would think of as a threat to one's life. Tom was forty-one and able-bodied. Upon returning home, however, he had begun drinking "all day, every day...consuming a fifth or more of gin or vodka daily." On the day he killed his mother, Tom awoke in his van, "polished off a glass of vodka, [and then] went into the home to make some coffee." In their final confrontation, Tom's mother accused him of hiding her walking stick. According to court records, here is what Tom said happened:

> I told her she was crazy. She said something like, "I don't want you around here anymore." I told her, "Just leave me alone." She wouldn't stop. She got in my face. She had a glass jar and threatened to hit me with it. I just blew it. I grabbed the crowbar. I hit her. Everything was like in a fog, like a dream. It was like I wasn't there.[213]

In light of this fuller, corrected account, it is clear that battered men's syndrome would not be a useful defense for Tom's killing of his mother for a number of reasons. First, Tom's mother was an old handicapped woman, not easily seen as an inescapable threat to Tom's life. Second, Tom himself was drinking heavily, thus diminishing his ability to respond reasonably. Third, his mother was asking him to leave her house, and she was only threatening him with a glass jar, not with a knife, as in Farrell's account. She hardly represented a lethal threat, nor even a threat that he could not have easily avoided by just leaving her house.

The judge in this case gave Tom a standard sentence for second-degree unpremeditated murder and wished him "good luck," telling his brothers that "he'll end up in some forestry gang and that is all right." There is no basis for thinking that Tom was acting out of justified self-defense in killing his mother, as battered men's syndrome would attempt to show in the cases in which it is appropriately applied.[214] Although I am sure there are some cases in which battered men's syndrome could be appropriately used, the fact that Farrell has not produced even one such case should say something about their frequency.

No one would deny that one of the purposes of a criminal justice system is to support the existing distribution of wealth and income in a society. If that distribution is unjust, however, as it is in the United States, where especially minorities and the poor are denied the opportunities they need for a decent life, then this means that the criminal justice system is flawed as well.[215] Leaving this problem aside, we have noted how, historically, women have fared badly compared to men in the criminal justice system and that efforts to improve women's situation under the criminal law are still ongoing. Given then what I have argued in this section and in the previous sections on domestic violence and rape, there is no reason to think that at the present time, due to the influence of feminism, the criminal law has reversed itself and now favors women over men.

8. WHY MEN EARN MORE: DISCRIMINATION? CHOICES?

Virtually every feminist critique of the workplace begins by noting the pay gap between men and women. Today, on average, women working full-time in the United States earn only 72 cents for every dollar men earn. Put another way, a college-educated woman working full-time earns $44,200 a year compared to $61,800 for her male counterpart—a difference of $17,600. For a woman working thirty years, the difference exceeds half a million dollars.[216] Moreover, if part-time workers are included in this comparison, the gap in the United States rises, with women earning only about half of what men earn.[217] As feminists see it, a significant part of this gap is because of discrimination.

What feminists see as discrimination, however, others, like Warren Farrell, see as women's choices. If women were only to choose differently, Farrell claims, they would earn as much as men.[218] As Farrell sees it, women and men in the United States with equal experience and qualifications, doing the same job for the same hours under the same conditions, get paid the same. As evidence for his view, Farrell points to the fact that never married women (who not have children) earn approximately the same as never married men (who do not have children).[219] Farrell recognizes that there is a significant pay gap between married women (especially when they are mothers) and married men (especially when they are fathers). He just takes this gap to be the result of women's choices and claims that it would disappear if women were only to choose differently.

Farrell goes on to suggest twenty-five ways how, by choosing differently, women can level the salary playing field with men.[220] Among his recommendations are that women choose careers in technology or science, work longer hours, accept more responsibilities, be more willing to relocate and travel, and take jobs that are dangerous and in unpleasant environments. Farrell thinks that if we were to conduct a study that controlled for all twenty-five of these ways of earning more, we would not find any pay gap between men and women.[221] Of course, researchers have controlled for some of these factors and still found that a significant pay gap of about 20 percent, but no study has controlled for all twenty-five of Farrell's factors, something it would be very difficult to do in any case.[222] So Farrell's hypothetical claim about what would make the pay gap disappear remains untested and may even be untestable. He does, however, offer as further evidence for his view the existence of 39 fields in the United States (exemplifying some of his twenty-five pay-increasing features) in which women earn at least 5 percent more than men.[223] What Farrell does not mention, however, is that the study of the U.S. Bureau of Labor Statistics from which he extracted these 39 fields contains over 320 other fields in which men do earn more![224]

Moreover, if women were to follow Farrell's twenty-five ways to earn more and they wanted to have children, they would need to find a mate who is willing to stay home and be the primary caretaker. Are there men like that around? Farrell insists that there are. In *Why Men Earn More,* his most recent book, he tells us that 70 to 80 percent of men he has surveyed in audiences from 1980 to 2004 have said they would be full-time dads "if their wives wanted to advance their careers and they made it clear that they would value them even more if they were full-time dads."[225] However, in an earlier book, *The Myth of Male Power,* published in 1993, Farrell tells us something a bit different. There he claims,

The first time I asked a group of men whether they would choose to parent full-time for six months to a year...and more than 80% said that being a full-time with their newborn child would be their preference if they were not hurting the family economically and their wife approved, I assumed I was either dealing with a group of liars or a self-selected sample. When I received only a slightly smaller percentage from an association of construction subcontractors [in 1992], I began to understand the degree to which men had not even thought about their options.[226]

Not only does this earlier quote appear to contradict Farrell's later assertion that he has been asking groups of men about their willingness to be full-time dads since 1980, it also suggests that the choice Farrell is offering men is a much better option than the one that most women have in the United States. Farrell's hypothetical choice to men involves no economic loss at all from choosing to parent full-time for six months to a year. In contrast, in the United States, as Farrell himself is at pains to point out when he is promoting his twenty-five ways to earn more, if a woman were to take that much time off to parent, it would almost be sure to have a negative impact on her career and earning power, and so constitute just the kind of economic loss that Farrell is assuming that men hypothetically choosing to parent would not have to make.[227] So Farrell's alternative for women of finding a full-time dad may not be much of a real-world alternative after all.[228]

Nor are Farrell's twenty-five ways to earn more of much help to the single mother who can't afford to relocate or work long hours because she must take care of her children, or to the woman who would risk losing custody of her children if she were to pursue any of Farrell's suggestions, or to the mother who is now reentering the job market after a number of years' absence because she chose to raise her children.

Nor, for that matter, is a full-time dad that great an option, even for those women who happen to find one. In effect, this option tends to simply reverse the situation in traditional households in which the mother is the full-time homemaker and the father is the full-time breadwinner. Studies have shown, however, that this traditional arrangement is not preferable to one in which the tasks of parenting and breadwinning are more equally shared. Although it is theoretically possible for couples to be equitable when the roles of homemaker and breadwinner are kept separate, when couples organize their marriage into separate spheres, it is very difficult psychologically to separate the rhetoric about equality (in which we say that we are equal in our separate roles) from reality (in which we still regard the breadwinner role as having the greater importance). Almost all the research in the United States on couples with separate spheres of influence finds that each partner does not share equal power.[229] One study found that the partner who provides more income has more decision-making power, and the greater the difference in incomes, the more decision-making power the higher earning partner tends to have.[230] Very frequently, this greater decision-making power translates into greater power over one's life in Farrell's sense. Accordingly, once we recognize that both traditional marriages and Farrell's flip-flop alternative to traditional marriage are both problematic, we can come to appreciate the need for a different solution to the pay gap between men and women in the United States than the one Farrell advocates.

A more promising alternative, favored by feminists, is to provide institutional supports for parents that would make full-time or equal-time employment possible and attractive to both women and men. There is also considerable evidence that doing this would effectively reduce the pay gap in the United States. Most significantly, this way of decreasing the pay gap between men and women has the big advantage of providing women with the same real-world opportunities as men to have a career while at the same time allowing them to be significantly involved with the care of their children, thereby helping to create a truly equal opportunity world, one that does not exist at the present time, at least not in the United States.

There are four elements to this feminist plan:

1. A maternity leave policy that provides employed mothers job security and publicly financed wage replacements at the time of childbirth or adoption.
2. An additional parental leave policy that provides both parents periods of paid leave during their children's youngest years.
3. Parents should also be entitled to time off in order to attend to short-term needs that occur throughout their children's lives, such as routine illness or a school-related emergency, without lost pay.

4. There should also be a policy that subsidizes the costs of child-care available to all families on a variable scale depending on family income, the number of children, and their ages.[231]

Such a plan would go far beyond the U.S. Family and Medical Leave Act of 1993, which only provides for an *unpaid* leave at the time of childbirth, adoption, or serious family medical conditions, but not beyond programs currently in place in Western Europe.[232]

It might be objected that this feminist plan for reducing the pay gap between men and women would raise the cost of doing business, cause inefficiencies, and result in the misallocation of resources.[233] But there is evidence that either this does not happen, or need not happen. One study shows that the cost of replacing skilled workers in the United States is typically 0.75 to 1.5 times the worker's annual salary.[234] So there are significant costs to the employer when women leave the workplace to care for their children. Flexible work schedules have also been shown to increase productivity.[235] One U.S. study found that most supervisors think their part-time workers are more productive and are less likely to quit or miss work than full-time workers are.[236] Anyway, how could we ever expect that policies that produce overworked men and underemployed women would be the most efficient that could be devised?

Furthermore, the problem employers in the United States face when competing with other U.S. employers who do not want to incur the costs of family-friendly programs can be remedied by state and federal governments requiring all U.S. employers to support such programs and by adequately funding these programs at the state and federal level; the problem with international employers who do not want to incur the costs of family-friendly programs can be dealt with by international agreements, including provisions in trade agreements and guaranteeing basic rights to all workers, or, in the short run, it can be dealt with in the ways that Western European employers are doing while still remaining profitable.[237] The use of state and federal government intervention and funding in the United States to support such family-friendly programs can also be justified, as it is throughout Western Europe, on the grounds that well-raised children are a public good that should be supported with public interventions and funding. [238]

It would also be helpful if men, as well as women, participated in these family-friendly programs, thus bringing about an equal sharing of the homemaking and breadwinning roles. Accordingly, such programs should include generous incentives for fathers to participate in them. Such an equal-sharing transformation of men's roles would only require half as much as the flip-flop transformation (in which men become full-time homemakers and women become full-time breadwinners) that is required for Farrell's solution to the pay gap.

Beyond failing to provide the family-friendly supports that would enable women to compete with men on equal terms in the workplace, another factor contributing to the pay gap is the direct discrimination against women in the workplace that imposes burdens and restrictions on them far greater than anything comparable to what men suffer in the workplace.[239] In 1996, Chevron Corporation settled for $8.7 million for discrimination against women in promotions and jobs. In 1997, faced with overwhelming evidence that men made more than women and that women almost never had a chance to move up the corporate ladder, Home Depot settled for $87.5 million. In 2002, American Express Financial Advisers settled and entered a consent degree for $31 million and court oversight for denying promotions and account assignments, as well as equal mentoring, training, and pay for women. In 2003, a female employee received $3.8 million in a federal jury award against Goodyear Tire and Rubber for failure to provide equal pay. In 2004, Morgan Stanley settled for $54 million for failure to promote and provide equal pay for women.[240]

Farrell's response to the charge that women are discriminated against in the workplace is to concede that they are, but then to argue that men are discriminated against, too.[241] Nursing and K–12 education are cited as fields in which men are discriminated against in favor of women. But while there is evidence that men sometimes do suffer from discrimination in these fields, there is also evidence that overall they are doing better in such fields than women are.[242] According to one study, instead of facing a glass ceiling to advancement comparable to the glass ceiling women face in male-dominated fields, men in female-dominated fields are enjoying a "glass escalator" that advances them more rapidly than women in those fields. Of course, we shouldn't downplay any discrimination that men suffer in the workplace. At the same time, we must recognize that the overwhelming preponderance of sexual discrimination in the workplace is suffered by women, not by men, and even when it is men who are discriminated against, overwhelmingly it is men, not women, who are doing the discriminating.[243] Nothing can make this clearer than by turning to the problem of sexual harassment in the workplace.

Sexual Harassment

As is well known, there is a high incidence of sexual harassment in the workplace in the United States. In research conducted by psychologists, 50 percent of women questioned in the workplace said they had been sexually harassed. According to the U.S. Merit Systems Protection Board, within the federal government, 56 percent of eighty-five hundred female civilian workers surveyed claimed to have experienced sexual harassment. According to the *National Law Journal,* 64 percent of women in "pink-collar" jobs reported being sexually harassed and 60 percent of three thousand women lawyers at 250 top law firms said that they had been harassed at some point in their careers. In a survey by *Working Women* magazine, 60 percent of high-ranking corporate women said they have been harassed; 33 percent more knew of others who had been.[244] Similarly, in a survey of ninety thousand female soldiers, sailors, and pilots, 60 percent of the women said they had been sexually harassed. Only 47 percent of the Army women surveyed said that they believed their leaders were serious about putting a stop to sexual harassment.[245] According to another study, 66 percent of women in the military experienced at least one form of sexual harassment in the past year.[246] Another study found that 50 percent of women at the U.S. Naval Academy, 59 percent of women at the U.S. Air Force Academy, and 76 percent of women at the U.S. Military Academy experienced some form of sexual harassment at least twice a month.[247] According to a 2002 study by the U.S. Department of Defense, over 60 percent of women in the military experienced some type of sexual harassment, down form 78 percent in 1995.[248] Interestingly, sexual harassment claims filed by men with the Equal Employment Opportunity Commission (EEOC) have grown from 9 percent of all cases filed in 1992 to 15 percent in 2003. However, most of these claims involve male-on-male harassment; harassment of men by women is far rarer.[249]

Unable to deny the frequency of the sexual harassment of women as evidenced by these studies, Farrell seeks to undercut the significance of its frequency by providing a bowdlerized definition of its nature. According to Farrell, sexual harassment most frequently consists of sexual initiatives by men toward women below them at work that fail by not leading to courtship.[250] Alternatively, Farrell characterizes sexual harassment as a distasteful joke.[251]

Unfortunately, Farrell's definitions of sexual harassment bear virtually no resemblance to the legal definition put forward by the EEOC in 1980 and exemplified in court cases since that time. The EEOC distinguished between two different types of sexual harassment:

1. Quid pro quo ("this for that") sexual harassment, in which sexual favors are made the condition of employment benefits (such as a boss telling his secretary to sleep with him or he will fire her).
2. Hostile environment harassment, which creates an intimidating, hostile, or offensive work environment.

To help us understand how the courts have interpreted the hostile environment type of sexual harassment, consider the following cases. In *Christoforou v. Ryder Truck Rental* (1987), a supervisor at the truck rental company at a Christmas party fondles a worker's rear end and breasts, propositions her, and tries to force a kiss. All of this is unwelcome. Here the court ruled the encounter to be "too sporadic and innocuous" to support a finding of sexual harassment. Or consider the case of *Rabidue v. Osceola Refinery Co.* (1986). Joan Rabidue worked at an oil refinery where pictures of nude and scantily clad women abounded, including one, which hung on a wall for eight years, of a woman with a golf ball on her breasts and a man with his golf club, standing over her and yelling "fore." At her workplace, a coworker, never disciplined despite repeated complaints, routinely referred to women as "whores," "cunts," "pussy" and "tits." Here again, the court found this not to be sufficiently hostile an environment to constitute sexual harassment. Finally, consider the case of *Harris v. Forklift Systems, Inc.* (1993). Teresa Harris was a rental manager at Construction Systems. Her boss, Ben, told Teresa on several occasions, in the presence of other employees, "You're a woman, what do you know" and "We need a man as the rental manager." Again in front of others, he suggested that the two of them "go to the Holiday Inn to negotiate [Teresa's] raise." Ben occasionally asked Teresa and other female employees to get coins from his pants pockets. On other occasions, he threw objects on the ground in front of Teresa and other women and asked them to pick the objects up. He made sexual innuendos about Teresa's and other women's clothing. On one occasion, while Teresa was arranging a deal with one of Construction's customers, Ben asked Teresa in front of other employees, "What did you do, promise... some [sex] Saturday night?" Soon after, Teresa quit her job at Construction. In this case, even the U.S. Supreme Court did not find this to be sexual harassment. The court merely struck down the district court's ruling that in order for there to be sexual harassment, Harris needed to show that her boss's conduct had "seriously affected her psychological well-being."

It is obvious from these cases that the courts are interpreting the legal definition of sexual harassment in a very demanding way. Even so, many legal cases have still been found to meet these stringent requirements for sexual harassment, and large settlements have been paid out. For example, Dupont Corporation in 1998 paid out $3.53 million in a jury award to a peroxide departmental operator who was driven out of her job because of her sex. In 2002, the New York City Police Department paid $1.85 million in a jury award to a police officer who was forced out in retaliation for a sexual harassment complaint. Home Depot, again, in 2004 paid a $5.5 million settlement to an employee for hostile environment sexual harassment and retaliation.[252] Accordingly, Farrell's attempt to use a disarming definition of sexual harassment to undercut the grounds for its enforcement fails miserably to make contact with workplace realities and the legal debate over sexual harassment in the United States.[253]

Despite the inadequacies of his definitions, Farrell goes on to propose a remedy for dealing with the problem of sexual harassment in the workplace. He thinks the problem can be resolved if women were just to confront their harassers and tell them that they find their behavior offensive. As proof that this approach will work, Farrell cites a book by Amber Sumrall and Dena Taylor that he says contains the sexual harassment stories of a hundred women.[254] Farrell claims that every male harasser in these stories who was directly told that his behavior was offensive stopped immediately and apologized.[255] Unfortunately, this is not what the stories in the book show. The book actually contains seventy-six, not a hundred, stories, and in the thirty-one stories in which the male harassers were made to understand that their behavior was unwanted, only six of them apologized and stopped their behavior. Accordingly, the book provides evidence against, not for, the effectiveness of Farrell's remedy for the problem of sexual harassment.[256]

9. ARE WOMEN DOING TWO JOBS WHILE MEN DO ONE?

Throughout history, women have been workers as well as wives and mothers, but they did not necessarily occupy these roles at the same times of their lives. As a consequence of the Industrial Revolution with its separation of paid work from home life, many women, other than the very rich and the very poor, began to occupy work and family roles sequentially. Young unmarried rural girls went to the towns and cities in order to work in factories or as domestics. When they married, they left their jobs if it was at all financially possible. As wives and mothers, these women also contributed to the family finances when needed, but in ways that did not significantly conflict with their most important homemaking duties. They ran boarding houses, took in laundry and sewing, and engaged in a variety of home industries on a piecework basis.[257]

The twentieth century added another form of sequencing to these women's lives, as they gradually began returning to employment after their children were grown. In 1900, fewer than 1 in 10 married women worked for wages, but that number increased steadily, especially after 1940. From 1940 to 1970, married women increased their employment rate by 28 percent each decade. By 1990 over half (59.44 percent) of married mothers of preschoolers and over half (51.35 percent) of the mothers of infants (children under age one) were in the labor market. By 1998, 75 percent of women with children were in the workforce.[258]

To better estimate the work that women do, the United Nations (UN) issued a *Human Development Report* with a focus on women. The report came out just before the Fourth World Conference on Women that took place in Beijing in 1995. It estimated the value of such unpaid work as childcare, household labor, and farm labor to be $16 trillion for both sexes, of which $11 trillion worth was done by women. The total for paid work in the world economy was $23 trillion.[259] The report also found that 70 percent of the 1.3 billion people living in poverty were women and that worldwide only 14 percent of top managerial jobs, 10 percent of legislative seats, and 6 percent of government cabinet posts were held by women.[260] While past reports had ranked the world's countries according to an index based on such criteria as life expectancy, education, and income, this report included gender in its index. With gender included, the United States, which had been the second highest in the traditional human development ranking, after Canada, fell to fifth place. Sweden, Finland, Norway, and Denmark all moved to the top. When women's access to political and economic power was taken into account, the United States fell to eighth place.[261]

In order to better measure women and men's contributions, the report used time allocation data and included a graph entitled "Women Work More Hours Than Men." Warren Farrell strongly objects to this graph. He writes: "I would consider the graph deceptive—but not an absolute falsehood—if it had said, 'Countries in which women work more hours Than men.'" But it was titled as an absolute: "Women Work More Hours than Men" ...exclud[ing] every single country where men were found to work more than women."[262] The text of the report right next to the graph does, however, provide the appropriate qualification: "Women work longer hours than men in nearly every country."

Farrell also makes it appear that the UN found that there were quite a few countries where men worked more than women and that it was hiding this fact from us.[263] However, according to the report, there were only four countries where men worked more than women, and for each of these countries the difference was so small (between 0.2 percent and 2 percent) that it was within the margin of error of the UN study.[264] Given this further information, it looks like it is Farrell, not the UN, who is distorting the findings of the report.

Farrell goes on to claim that he checked into the sources for the UN report concerning the hours that men and women work and had difficulty getting from the UN a copy of the study on which its results were based—a study I was able to access from the Internet.[265] Farrell then sought out another UN publication, a Series K publication entitled the *World's Women 1995, Trends and Statistics*, and notes that in this study, women are reported to work fewer hours than men in the United States—about three hours less per week.[266] On this basis, Farrell raises the possibility that the UN was lying to us in its *Human Development Report.*[267]

Fortunately, there is another and better explanation here. The Series K publication that Farrell cites, although published in 1995, was reporting on a study done in 1986 that found that men did work more than women in the United States, although the United States was the only country in which that difference was reported.[268] The *Human Development Report*'s own results in this regard, however, were based on studies done some years later. So once we see that we are talking about earlier and later studies and that the *UN Human Development Report* is based on the later studies, Farrell's case for condemning the *UN Human Development Report* evaporates.

Like the UN in its *Human Development Report,* Arlie Hochschild, in her book *The Second Shift,* makes similar claims about the amount of work women were doing in the United States. Citing a study done by Alexander Szalai that used national data from 1965, Hochschild claims that at that time husbands' average time in housework averaged seventeen minutes per day and in childcare averaged twelve minutes, citing further data, she claims that husbands' time in housework and childcare did not increase between 1965 and 1975.[269] Farrell criticizes Hochschild's work, claiming that "she uses mostly 1960s data in a 1989 book to 'prove' that men weren't doing any more housework in 1989 than they were in the 1960s."[270]

Yet this is not what Hochschild did at all. Although she does cite the Sazalai study using 1965 data, in her original 1989 book she also cites a study done in 1981, which found a 30-hour-per-week leisure gap between men and women in the United States; another study done in 1983, which found no difference in the help around the house between men whose wives worked outside the home and men whose wives didn't work outside the home; and still another study done in 1985, in which married mothers averaged 85 hours a week working at a job, housekeeping, and childcare, while married fathers averaged 66 hours—a 19-hour weekly leisure gap.[271] In addition, in the new introduction to the 2003 edition of her book, Hochschild cites a 2001 study that shows a 12.9-hour weekly housework gap between men and women.[272]

Nevertheless, Farrell thinks that the biggest mistake that Hochschild makes—one that he claims is made by virtually every housework study—is not adequately measuring men's contributions to work around the home.[273] For Farrell, housework is any contribution made to the family, however infrequent. Using this notion of housework, he generates a list of fifty housework activities that men tend to do. His list includes activities that are most likely to break an arm, leg, or neck or to crack a skull, like climbing a ladder while painting a house. It also includes buying a car and putting up Christmas lights. Farrell admits that many of the male housework activities he lists are seasonal, maybe done once a year if that. As he puts it, they are done "as needed."

But what is the point of drawing up such a list? Most of the items included on the list are not "housework" as we usually understand it to be; that is, they are not tasks that have to be done over and over again usually on a daily or weekly basis. Farrell admits that we could construct a similar expanded list of housework activities that women tend to do. Farrell even claims that this has already been done by Marjorie Shaevitz in her book *The Superwomen Syndrome.*[274] But Shaevitz and Farrell have different reasons for constructing their respective lists. Shaevitz constructs hers, which distinguishes between the frequency with which various tasks are done, in order to provide a plan of action for getting these various tasks done. Farrell constructs his either to show that men work as much as women do or to show that, in fact, men work more than women do.

However, the issue here should not be about how many hours or minutes or seconds women and men work; rather, it should be one of whether women and men are equal in this domain, specifically whether they both have equal opportunity to work either at home or in the workplace. And the general pattern in the United States is that they do not. Rather, the pattern is that when heterosexual couples choose to have children the social expectation is primarily that the women, not their male partners, will adjust their employment outside the home to meet the childcare and housekeeping obligations that the couples have inside the home. This is not fair.

When it comes to having and caring for children, it is a challenge for couples in the United States to create for themselves an equal opportunity arrangement. It is really difficult to be fair. That is why they need those institutional supports mentioned in Section 8:

1. A maternity leave policy that provides employed mothers job security and publicly financed wage replacements at the time of childbirth or adoption.
2. An additional parental leave policy that provides both parents periods of paid leave during their children's youngest years.
3. Parents should also be entitled to time off in order to attend to short-term needs that occur throughout their children's lives, such as routine illness or a school-related emergency, without lost pay.
4. There should also be a policy that subsidizes the costs of child-care available to all families on a variable scale depending on family income, the number of children, and their ages.

All of these policies need to be funded appropriately at the state and federal level.

With such institutional supports, the general expectation will be that both parents will make acceptable progress in their careers or jobs while approximately equally sharing the childcare and housekeeping duties, supplemented by a desirable level of day care. This would allow them to develop themselves in a career or job outside the home and serve the best interests of their children. It is what equal opportunity between women and men requires. It is the only alternative that is fair to both women and men. So instead of trying to determine how many hours each parent is working inside and outside the home, we should be asking how we can best realize the feminist ideal of equality both inside and outside the home.

10. MARRIAGE, DIVORCE, AND CHILD CUSTODY

In the Declaration of Sentiments adopted at the first women's rights convention in 1848, Elizabeth Cady Stanton wrote:

> The history of mankind is a history of repeated injuries and usur-
> pations on the part of man toward woman....He has made her, if
> married, in the eyes of the law, civilly dead. He has taken from her all

right in property, even to the wages she earns....In the covenant of marriage...the law gives him power to deprive her of her liberty and to administer chastisement.[275]

Happily, even conservative defenders of marriage today do not want those provisions of marriage to which Stanton was objecting in 1848. Rather, they want to defend marriage roughly the way it is presently legally constituted.

Feminists, however, still object to the way that marriage is presently legally constituted. For example, in the United States, married women generally do not have a right to choose their own legal domicile. Their legal domicile is determined by that of their husbands. If her husband's domicile is different from her premarital domicile a woman must reregister to vote. She may also lose the right to attend a university in her home state as a resident student and thus have to pay higher tuition as an out-of-state student, and she may lose the right to run for public office in her home state.[276] In addition, in the United States, only twenty states as of 2006 have no marital exemption for rape. Others have some type of an exemption, such as that a husband may be immune from prosecution for raping a wife who is "mentally defective" or immune unless legally separated or living apart from his spouse.[277] Feminists are opposed to these and other provisions of the current U.S. law of marriage that undermine the equality between women and men in marriage.

Feminists are also opposed to the exclusion of same-sex partners from the legal benefits of marriage.[278] In 1995, NOW made official its support for same-sex marriage, stating that the choice of marriage is a fundamental constitutional right, protected under the Equal Protection Clause of the Fourteenth Amendment, and should not be denied because of sexual orientation.[279] The U.S. Supreme Court in *Lawrence v. Texas* (2003) held that a right to liberty under the Due Process Clause of the Fourteenth Amendment does give consenting adults the right to engage in private homosexual conduct without governmental interference, but the court did not rule on the issue of same-sex marriage.

Feminists today are probably most critical of marriage because of the consequences it has for women at divorce, and in the United States over 50 percent of marriages today do end in divorce. Women entering marriage as equals should emerge from marriage as equals.

But they don't. Women after divorce are usually at a significant economic disadvantage compared to their ex-husbands. In her much acclaimed book *The Divorce Revolution: The Unexpected Social and Economic Consequences for Women and Children in America*, published in 1985, Lenore Weitzman maintained that women and children after divorce suffer on average a 73 percent drop in their standard of living while men experience a 43 percent increase in their standard of living as a result of divorce.[280] Subsequently, Weitzman, in response to criticisms, admitted that she had miscalculated and adjusted her figures to a 27 percent drop in the standard of living of women and children and a 10 percent increase in the living standard of men after divorce.[281] A number of other studies have come up with similar results.[282]

Nevertheless, Warren Farrell still criticizes Weitzman for focusing on the economic consequences of the first year after divorce without attending to the second year, when some women have remarried, or to five years later, when more than half of divorced women have remarried and their income levels have returned to what they were before they were divorced.[283] Farrell compares a woman's first year after divorce to a year of training like the internship served by a doctor after medical school.[284] But this suggests that divorced women can turn their economic fortunes around quickly after divorce (other than by remarrying), and that goes against what Farrell himself insists are the consequences of absenting oneself from the workforce in order to care for one's children.[285] According to one study, if women drop out of the workforce just for a year, their economic penalty is 32 percent of total earnings for the next fifteen years, and it goes up to 46 and 56 percent if they take off two and three years, respectively.[286] Rarely is one year of training going to restore a woman to the "human capital" she would have had if she had not devoted herself to a greater share of childcare and housekeeping over the course of her marriage. By contrast, her husband's human capital typically would have increased through his marriage, aided by her willingness to take upon herself a greater share of their childcare and housekeeping responsibilities. If there is a divorce, however, there is need to rectify for this imbalance. If both husband and wife had continued with their jobs or careers and equally shared their childcare and housekeeping responsibilities, then, if they divorced, they would only have needed to continue to equally share caring for their children. When both have had an equal chance to develop their human capital during their marriage, if they divorce, there is no need for compensation in that regard. However, when one spouse, typically the mother, has taken on a greater share of the child-care and housekeeping responsibilities at the expense of continuing to develop that spouse's human capital, there is a need for compensation from the other spouse if they divorce.

The current no-fault divorce laws in place in the United States typically do not recognize the need for any type of compensation. Generally, tangible assets are divided between the parties on the basis of either common law (who has title) or community law (divided equally), depending on which type of law is enforced in the state in which the couple divorce.[287] Although more than half of women list pathological behaviors such as adultery, violence, substance abuse, and abandonment as the reasons why they divorced their husbands,[288] no-fault divorce does not attempt to establish blame. Alimony is only paid out in 8 percent of divorce cases.[289] There is no attempt to compensate a spouse, typically the wife, for the human capital she might have lost or failed to develop while taking on the lion's share of the childcare and housekeeping during marriage. The feminist ideal of equality, however, requires just this sort of compensation.

Farrell objects to providing this sort of compensation.[290] If an ex-husband is supposed to continue to make an economic contribution to his ex-wife, Farrell argues, why isn't his ex-wife required to continue to make a comparable contribution to him, given that he no longer benefits from her housekeeping services? The reason is that it is typically wives who have taken upon themselves more than an equal share of the housekeeping and childcare during the course of their marriages, thus enabling their husbands to develop more of their human capital than they would otherwise have been able to do under conditions of equality. When that is the case, it is the wives alone who deserve compensation following divorce.

Child Custody

Let's now turn to the problem of child custody. Historically, fathers had an absolute right to custody and control over their children, while others had no rights whatsoever, even as guardians in the event of the father's death. In fact, during the long reign of the patriarchal family, mothers were legally entitled to, in the words of the English jurist William Blackstone, "no power but only to reverence and respect."[291] By the beginning of the nineteenth century, this paternal right began to give way to an emphasis on the welfare of children.[292] By the mid-twentieth century, mothers were even said to have a presumption in their favor when they were seeking custody of children "of tender years." In the 1980s, in the United States and elsewhere, however, there was an attempt to render child custody law "gender neutral" so that custody following divorce or separation would be determined on the basis of the "best interests" of the child.[293]

Yet beginning in the 1980s, in the United States and elsewhere, and continuing to the present, advocates of men's rights groups have challenged the gender neutrality of child custody law. According to these advocates, the family law system favors women by a huge margin. In the United States, they claim, mothers are the sole custodians an overwhelming 82 percent of the time, and fathers only 11 percent of the time; both parents have joint custody just 7 percent of the time.[294] Worse yet, they claim that nearly 40 percent of noncustodial fathers have no legal visitation or custody rights at all and that the men who actually have court-ordered access to their children are traditionally limited to visits every other weekend, on alternate holidays, and for a couple of weeks in the summer.[295] Now while other estimates for the United States find a lower percentage of mothers with sole custody (67 percent) and a higher percentage of joint custody arrangements (20 percent) the general picture presented by the men's rights advocates does seem to be correct.[296]

Moreover, according to Farrell, there is a clear correlation between child support payments and visitation in the United States.

> Eighty-five percent of fathers with joint custody pay child support in full and on time. When mothers have custody, but do not discourage or deny fathers the opportunity to see their children, 79% of those fathers paid child support in full and on time. When seeing children is undermined or denied, only 56% of fathers paid child support.[297]

So there appear to be financial benefits from having fathers more involved in child custody.[298] Farrell also claims that having to pay child support while being denied time with a child is akin to taxation without representation.[299]

Do these data, then, show that the child custody system, in the United States and elsewhere, is biased in favor of women? Well, not surprisingly, some additional data need to be taken into account in assessing the data just presented.

The first thing to note is that a significant percentage of custody arrangements following divorce or separation are in fact made outside the court. Parents report that they had a court order or were in the process of obtaining one in only 48 percent of cases in Canada.[300] In the United States, 46 percent of cases are decided outside the court.[301] In addition court order figures include far more custody arrangements that were just rubber-stamped by a judge after they were negotiated by parents themselves. In the United States, for example, only 4 percent of divorces involving dependent children are finalized by contested hearings.[302] What this shows is that the overwhelming majority of custody arrangements are made voluntarily by the divorcing or separating parents themselves, not by the courts.

Moreover, when fathers do contest custody, there are many ways that mothers can still lose custody even when they have a history of caring for their children.[303] Those women who are viewed as departing from the standard of white, middle-class, heterosexual motherhood may encounter difficulty.[304] In addition, mothers' complaints of abuse suffered from their male partners are not always taken into account by the court when assessing their partners' suitability for custody.[305] Moreover, as we noted in Section 5 of this essay, violence by men against their female partners does not always stop at separation. In fact, women are at a higher risk of violence from former partners after separation. Abusive men after separation may also turn their focus to the control of their children as a way of continuing to inflict suffering and violence on their former partners.[306] The relative lack of financial resources of mothers because of their greater poverty and unequal earning power also means that they are less able or willing to engage in prolonged legal disputes.[307] Fathers, who usually have more money, have an advantage in using the legal system to obtain custody or even just to engage in legal harassment of their ex-spouses. Faced with these disadvantages, some mothers may give up custody or agree to more shared custody than they really want.[308] And in Canada when fathers do actively contest custody, they are successful about 50 percent of the time. In the United States, different studies show that fathers are successful

38 to 70 percent of the time, even though mothers tend to be the primary caretakers of the children.[309] Accordingly, when more of the relevant data concerning our current practice of child custody is taken into account, it cannot be judged overall as biased in favor of women. Rather, it remains to a significant degree biased against women.

Clearly, things could be done to correct for this bias. For example, we could, as some feminists have proposed, focus on which parent has been the primary caretaker of the child in the past, which is usually the mother, and unless other arrangements are mutually agreeable, that parent, whether mother or father, should be given primary custody of the child following divorce or separation.[310] Clearly, starting with this presumption seems to be more in line with the best interest of the child than starting with a presumption of joint custody, as men's rights advocates favor.[311] Unfortunately, even this primary caretaker presumption can be interpreted in ways that are biased against women, as when some judges assume that the only parents who are primary caretakers are those who do not work outside the home.[312]

Sometimes, the feminist endorsement of the primary caretaker presumption is challenged as being inconsistent with their longstanding endorsement of equal responsibility in families for childcare and housekeeping. Farrell makes this objection.[313] But there is no inconsistency here. In families in which men have accepted their equal responsibility for childcare and housekeeping, there is no primary caretaker, but rather two equal caretakers, and child custody, in the event of divorce or separation, should be assigned as equally as possible. But when there has been a primary caretaker, which is still usually a woman in the United States and elsewhere, then child custody should presumptively favor her.[314]

Further Arguments

Moreover, while everyone grants that we should recognize the important contribution that fathers make to families, Farrell goes further, citing evidence that children raised by single fathers do better than children raised by single mothers.[315] He even claims this difference remains even when socioeconomic variables are controlled for, although the gap is less.[316] Yet he also observes that one reason why children raised by single fathers do better is that the mothers are more likely to stay involved, maintaining conditions more like those in an intact family.[317] And when this factor, along with the presence or absence of conflict between divorcing or separating parents, is also controlled for, any differences between children raised by single dads and (the six times as many) children raised by single moms will surely disappear.[318] As further evidence of the importance of the absence of conflict between parents in this context, studies have shown that children who have lost a parent through death do not experience the same psychological problems and poorer academic performance that are experienced by other single-parent children.[319]

Farrell also goes further in advocating that men be more involved in abortion decisions, even when they are only casually involved with the pregnant women who are making these decisions. While not denying women a right to abortion, Farrell maintains that "if together [a man and women] produce a fetus, equality would dictate joint rights and joint responsibilities," and he wants these rights to be legal as well as moral.[320]

The U.S. Supreme Court, in fact, addressed this question with respect to married women and abortion in *Planned Parenthood v. Casey* (1992).[321] The court recognized that the vast majority of women do consult their husbands prior to deciding to terminate their pregnancy to have an abortion, and so a legal requirement in this regard would not restrict what these women want to do. In other cases, however, in which women are experiencing marital difficulties or domestic violence, a legal notification requirement could impose a serious obstacle to a woman's getting an abortion. Recognizing this, the court refused to add a legal requirement to the moral requirement the vast majority of women already recognize in this area. By contrast, Farrell would impose such a requirement in both marital and nonmarital cases, thus ignoring the significant burden this would place on women, especially when they are in relationships involving domestic violence.

Farrell goes on to consider an unusual adoption case in which a woman realized that she was pregnant after she terminated a fairly casual affair she had had with a man.[322] After the child was born she notified the man as required by law that she was going to put the child up for adoption.[323] Three months later, the man petitioned the court that he wanted custody of the child. The court decided that since the man had done little to establish himself as the "presumed father" either by offering to marry the mother or by seeking custody of the child immediately after he was notified of the child's birth, it was now in the best interests of the child to leave her with the adoptive parents. In cases like this, Farrell wants the woman to be legally required to notify the biological father within four or five days of when she becomes aware that she is pregnant, whatever the nature of their relationship.[324]

But although there may be moral reasons why a woman should give the man who got her pregnant more notification of her intention to bring her pregnancy to term and put the child up for adoption, just as in the case of decisions about abortion, legally requiring a woman to do so may result in undue pressure being placed upon her, for example, pressure to have an abortion rather than bring the fetus to term, and, therefore, such a requirement should not be imposed on women in these cases.

Farrell also portrays feminists as inconsistently supporting abortion rights on the grounds that a woman has a right to her own body while supporting custody or visitation rights for lesbian parents who have no biological tie to the children with respect to whom they are claiming those rights.[325] But there is no inconsistency here. Feminists are just asking that the same custody and visitation rights that are granted to nonbiological heterosexual parents on the basis of their past caring behavior also be granted to nonbiological homosexual parents on the same basis. By contrast, in cases of abortion, it is quite difficult to create any nonbiological grounds of "caring for the fetus" that would establish any rights that should legally be taken into account.

Finally, Farrell thinks that it is unfair that a man can be uncon-ditionally legally required to contribute support to a child for eighteen to twenty-one years because he got the child's mother pregnant.[326] But suppose the situation were reversed, and the man, but not the woman, wanted to raise the child borne of their casual relationship. Wouldn't she also be unconditionally legally required to contribute to the support of the child for eighteen to twenty-one years? The fact that men rarely choose to be the sole custodial parent of children borne of such casual relationships should not blind us to the fact that the legal requirements with respect to raising the children in such cases are perfectly symmetrical.

In sum, neither with respect to marriage, divorce, nor child custody do feminists discriminate against men. Rather, in each of these areas, it is sexual discrimination against women that still persists, and for which more correctives are needed.

11. POPULAR CULTURE AND THE MEDIA DISCRIMINATE AGAINST MEN?

It is commonplace in the United States that a pornographic view of women permeates popular culture, as is attested by the accompanying advertisements. Pornography is also a major industry in the United

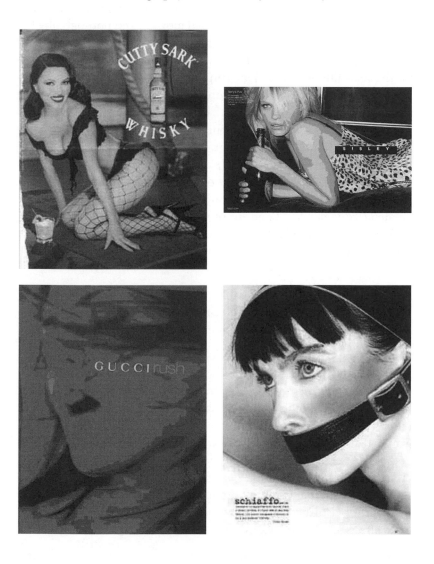

States. According to the trade publication *Adult Video News,* 1 in every 5 videocassettes in 1986 belonged in the adult category, and fifteen hundred new adult movies hit the market each year; between 1985 and 1992, the business expanded from $75 million to $490 million. Today 1 in 4 American adults admits to having seen an X-rated movie in the past year, and $4 billion a year is spent on video pornography in the United States—more than on football, baseball, or basketball. Americans rent upward of eight hundred million pornographic videos and DVDs per year (about 1 in 5 of all rented movies), and pornography far outpaces Hollywood's slate of four hundred feature films with eleven thousand pornos produced annually. Total annual revenues estimates for the adult film industry alone run from $5 billion to $10 billion.[327]

Not surprisingly, the pornography industry has grown right along with the expansion of the Internet. Type "XXX" into Google and 231 million pages arise, more than double what it was just one year ago. A 2004 study found that pornographic sites are visited three times more often than Google, Yahoo!, and MSN combined.[328] Another 2004 study found that 51 percent of all video files being shared on a peer-to-peer basis were pornographic.[329] Usenet groups on the Internet depicted violence 42 percent of the time.[330]

A standard pornographic website asks potential users to read and comply with the following conditions:

> I am at least 21 years of age.
> The sexually explicit material I am viewing is for my own personal use and I will not expose minors to the material.
> I desire to view sexually explicit material.

Compliance is signaled with the click of the mouse. One such website bills itself as "The Home of the Asshole Milkshake." It shows viewers a number of men anally penetrating a woman and then forcing her to drink the ejaculated semen extracted from her own anus. Another video on this website simulates vivid rape and murder scenes of women. According to Pamela Paul, author of *Pornified,* this website does not differ substantially in content or tone from vast numbers of other pornographic websites.[331]

The presentation and enjoyment of women in pornography (men frequently masturbate as they view pornography) are not without their effects in the real world. Some studies show that exposure to hard-core pornography increases discriminatory attitudes and be-havior in men toward women that take both violent and nonviolent forms.[332] Other studies reveal that in 68 percent of 2,380 sexual as-sault cases, the abuser beat or sexually abused the victim or someone else after looking at pornographic material and that 58 percent of these abusers pointed out pornographic pictures or articles to their victims as they were abusing them.[333]

Consider the following case, in which a woman describes her husband's increasing interest in pornography as their marriage pro-gressed.

> He told me if I loved him I would do this. And that, as I could see from the things that he read me in the magazines initially, a lot of times women didn't like it, but if I tried it enough I would probably like it and I would learn to like it. And he would read me stories where women learned to like it. [The husband then tried to initiate sex with a third person]...To prevent more of these group situations, which I found very humiliating and very destructive to my self-esteem and my feeling of self-worth as a person, to prevent these I agreed with him to act out in privacy a lot of those scenarios that he read to me. A lot of them depicting bondage and different sexual acts that I found very humiliating. About this time when things were getting really terrible and I was feeling suicidal and very worthless as a person, ... [h]e would read from pornography like a textbook, like a journal. In fact, when he asked me to be bound, when he finally convinced me to do it, he read in the magazine how to tie the knots and how to bind me in a way that I couldn't get out. And most of the scenes that we—most of the scenes where I had to dress up and go through different fantasies were the exact scenes he had read in the magazines. [After their divorce, her hus-band remarried.] And at the time I had seen him to finalize things on our divorce and get some of my last possessions, he showed me pictures of [his new wife] and said, "Do you want to see what she looks like?" They were pictures of her naked and in pornographic poses.[334]

Another case involved a woman and her boyfriend with whom she was having a sexual relationship.

> [My boyfriend] had gone to a stag party, this particular evening I was home alone in my apartment. He called me on the telephone and he

said that he had seen several short pornographic films and that he felt very horny.... So he asked if he could come over specifically to have sex with me. I said yes because at that time I felt obligated as a girlfriend to satisfy him.... When he arrived he informed me that the other men at the party were envious that he had a girlfriend to fuck. They wanted to fuck too after watching the pornography. He informed me of this as he was taking his coat off. He then took off the rest of his clothes and had me perform fellatio on him. I did not do this of my own volition. He put his genitals in my face and he said, "Take it all." Then he fucked me on the couch in the living room. All this took about five minutes. And when he finished, he dressed and went back to the party. I felt ashamed and numb and I also felt very used. This encounter differed from others previous. It was much quicker, it was somewhat rougher, and he was not aware of me as a person. There was no foreplay. It is my opinion that his viewing of the pornography served as foreplay for him.[335]

In a 2004 poll, 58 percent of women believed that pornography is demeaning to women.[336] According to Pamela Paul, the vast majority of women do not like it when men look at pornography.[337] According to Mark Schwartz, clinical director of the Masters and Johnson Clinic in St. Louis, a man who uses pornography may be making love to his wife while picturing someone else. Schwartz claims that men need to recognize that the more they focus on pornography the less satisfying they'll find their partners.[338] In a 2004 study, a third of women said they considered their partners' online sexual activities to be cheating, and 1 in 3 felt "betrayed."[339] In another study, 34 percent of women see men using pornography to be cheating in absolutely all cases.[340]

Warren Farrell, however, sees little to object to in (male) pornography. What he really finds objectionable is the man bashing that he finds in popular culture, exemplified by the Shoebox Division of Hallmark Greeting Cards. According to Farrell,

> [Hallmark's Shoebox Division] specializes in man bashing cards.... The Shoebox division calls itself "A Tiny Little Division of Hallmark." They were tiny when they started in 1986. But man bashing was so popular by 1998 the Shoebox division was Hallmark's largest selling division. Two hundred fifty million dollars a year cashing in mostly on women's anger toward men.[341]

But have you seen such man-bashing cards in the Shoebox section of your local card stores? I myself have searched stores in my area and elsewhere and have rarely ever been able to find even one card that could be described as man bashing. Recently, I searched the Shoebox Division online, and of the fifty-four paper cards being offered there, I have reproduced here the only card that could even remotely be called man bashing; even here the main message seems to be just that all the good men are taken—hardly a particularly man-hating theme.

Inside Message: Probably monsignor

Of course, it could be that man-bashing cards dominated Shoebox's offerings, as Farrell claims, from its founding in 1986 until the late 1990s and then they just lost their popularity and completely dropped out of sight. If so, this would be totally unlike the (male) pornography industry, which continues to grow rapidly, especially on the Internet, with its negative portrayals of women and the destructive consequences such portrayals have on women themselves and on their relationships with men.

We can also come to understand the significance that man-bashing cards have had for the history of Hallmark's Shoebox Division from a twentieth anniversary volume published by Hallmark just this year. This volume, *Shoebox, Greatest Hits and Misses,* contains over three hundred cards and card messages.[342] Of these, however, only two can be labeled man bashing, and one of the two is even reproduced along with a letter from the National Coalition of Free Men protesting its distribution. The response by the editors of the volume to the letter is that the card was created by "a man who could make a joke and take a joke."[343] It would seem, therefore, that the best conclusion we can draw here is that male bashing cards served a minor and now almost nonexistent role in the success of Hallmark's Shoebox Division.

Nevertheless, Farrell thinks that there are other centers of man-bashing in the publishing and Hollywood film industries.[344] He is particularly troubled by the publication of a book of cartoons entitled *No Good Men* by Simon & Schuster and by their unwillingness to publish a comparable volume entitled *No Good Women.* Turnaround here is Farrell's sign of fairness or nondiscrimination.[345]

Yet Farrell does not quite believe what he says about the fairness of turnaround. For example, he does not think we would be justified in publishing books of cartoons entitled *No Good Blacks* or *No Good Jews* as long as turnaround was satisfied.[346]

Why is that? Presumably because Farrell recognizes that we are not yet beyond discrimination against blacks and Jews in our society and that past discrimination against these groups is still vivid in many people's minds, making it difficult to be a subject of humor. But if Farrell grants that this is true with respect to blacks and Jews, why should he not think that it is similarly true of women? Surely, we are not beyond discrimination against women in the United States and elsewhere, and still past forms of discrimination against women are quite vivid in many people's minds. Why would this not similarly render it more difficult to make women as a group the subject of humor?

By contrast, if the general argument of my essay is correct, and men have enjoyed the benefits of discrimination against women in the past and still continue to do so, albeit to a lesser degree, in the present, then, making them the subject of humor, unlike in the case of women, is a tribute to their greater power. Men usually find it easier to be poked fun at knowing as they do that they are protected by their greater power.

Moreover, if you examine *No Good Men,* the book that Farrell was so offended by, you also see how tame the humor directed at men in this book really is. There is no great assault on the power of men here. The cartoons in the book criticize men for such things as leaving the caps off of toothpaste tubes, leaving their laundry knotted and inside out, and blowing their noses in their hands in the shower. Some of the cartoons, like those that follow, criticize men for opposing traits that suggest that the same criticisms could be made of women as well.

Men can read this book and enjoy it (almost) as much as women can. Its impact is nothing like the impact of (male) pornography on women. As Catherine MacKinnon points out, in pornography, women want to be raped, battered, and sexually harassed, and men want to do all these things to them. It is thus by conditioning men to

They're always late.

think that women want such things done to them that pornography seriously harms women.

Farrell also criticizes a number of films for man bashing. He singles out *Thelma & Louise,* in particular, because NOW featured the film at its twentieth-fifth national convention.[347] Farrell calls Thelma and Louise serial killers even though only one person is killed in the film, not counting Thelma's and Louise's dramatic suicides at the film's end.[348] Although Thelma and Louise are the main characters, two male characters are portrayed sympathetically—Hal, the Arkansas detective who initially hopes that Thelma and Louise will escape the reach of the law; and Jimmy, Louise's boyfriend, who shows up with a ring and provides Louise with over $6,000 of his own money to aid in her flight. This film is anything but anti-male.

In *First Wives Club,* Farrell claims that three ex-wives kill their husbands financially, destroy their reputations, and poison a dad's relationship with his child.[349] But the film actually starts out with the child in this case trying to convince her mother of what a scoundrel her father is. Further, while the three ex-wives do wrestle back control of their family finances from the ex-husbands, this is presented as perfectly justified by the machinations of these men during their marriages. And far from destroying the reputations of the ex-husbands, two of them actually have their reputations improved by the end of the film (one is even reconciled with his wife), and the third is left with much the same reputation he had at the beginning of the film.

Farrell also singles out a number of films such as *Ghost* with Patrick Swayze and *Defending Your Life* with Albert Brooks for showing men being improved by their deaths.[350] Yet it is not death that improves the male characters played by Swayze and Brooks. Rather, it is the transformation they undergo after they are dead. In substance, their improvement is no different from the one that the three wives undergo, in *First Wives Club,* albeit without dying first.

Media

In the 1970s, riding the wake of the second wave of feminism in the United States, women began filing complaints and lawsuits charging sex discriminating against major press organizations such as *Newsweek,* the *Washington Post,* and the *New York Times.* In 1970, female employees charged *Newsweek* with violating Title VII of the Civil Rights Act of 1964 by making the writing of news an almost exclusively male domain and the researching of news (which was given no byline) an almost exclusively female domain. In 1974, the EEOC found that the *Washington Post* had engaged in illegal employment practices.[351] In 1978, the *New York Times* settled a class-action lawsuit that had brought ninety charges of sexual discrimination against the paper.[352]

Almost thirty years later, in 2003, women constituted nearly 40 percent of all daily reporters, but only 32 percent of those working at the *Times,* and few of the women reporters working at the *Times* received prominent layout positioning for the stories they wrote. From Sunday, May 2, 2004, to Saturday, May 8, 2004, there were sixty-one bylines on the paper's front page, but just 12 percent of them belonged to women. On the Metro section's front page, 27 percent of the bylines belonged to women; on the sports section's front page, 10 percent. Moreover, although two of the three staff book reviewers for the daily paper were women, the Sunday book review section (where most reviewers are freelancers, not staff) featured primarily male reviewers, reviewing primarily books written by men. Nor at the *Times* does the presence of women in high places necessarily lead to more bylines by women. At the time, Gail Collins was editorial page

editor at the *Times,* but during the week of May 2 only 20 percent
of the op-eds and columns were by women. The only regular female
Times columnist is Maureen Dowd.[353] Nevertheless, Warren Farrell
claims that the *New York Times* is unequivocally profeminist.[354] But
the history of the paper and the current status of women working at
it belie this charge.[355] Nor is the *Times* alone in its neglect of women.
The largest newspapers in the United States also have the lowest percentage of women in their newsrooms.[356]

   Farrell criticizes the *Times* for supposedly polling "both sexes' point
of view, [when] they, in fact, poll[ed] women at more than a two
to one ratio to men."[357] The *Times's* justification was that it wanted
"enough women interviewed to provide statistically reliable comparisons among various subgroups of women."[358] Farrell complains that
in so doing the *Times* avoided the issue of subgroups of men.[359] However, the poll in question was taken for a series of articles with the
title "Women's Lives: A Scorecard of Change." The articles did not
purport to be equally about men and women; they were primarily
about women. Hence, using a larger sample of women, while at the
same time including a sufficiently large sample of men to ground the
fewer male/female comparisons the reporters wanted to make, was
perfectly justified, given that the articles in this series, as announced,
were primarily about women.[360]

   Looking at the media more generally, an Annenberg Public Policy
Center Report in 2003 found that women still are only 15 percent
of executive leaders and only 12 percent of board members in top
communication companies. Only 5 percent had "clout" titles (senior
vice president up through chief executive officer).[361] Turning to evening news programs on CBS, ABC, and NBC, there were, on average, 14 percent female protagonists in news stories in 2002.[362] Women
were consulted on top issues only 5 percent of the time on all three
networks. Clearly, these data do not accord with the picture that Farrell paints in *Women Can't Hear What Men Can't Say* of a media dominated by feminists.[363]

   In films, women make up only 31 percent of those working on
romantic dramas, 30 percent on romantic comedies, 22 percent on
documentaries, 17 percent on dramas, 16 percent on comedy/dramas,
16 percent on sci-fi features, 15 percent on animated features,
14 percent on comedies, 9 percent on action adventure features,

and 4 percent on horror features. Overall, female characters are younger than male characters. Women forty years old and older are only 12 percent of all characters, while men forty years old and older constitute 27 percent of all characters.[364] In a survey of 101 G-rated films from 1990–2004, only 28 percent of the speaking characters were female, fewer than 17 percent of the characters in crowd scenes were female, and 83 percent of the films narrators were male.[365] In video games, 38 percent of the female characters are scantily dressed, 23 percent are seen baring breasts or cleavage, 31 percent expose thighs, 31 percent reveal stomachs or midriff, and 15 percent show behinds. Moreover, teenage boys spend, on average, two hours a day playing these same video games. [366] According to Robin Gerber, "[Women] don't need Afghan-style burquas to disappear as women. [Women] disappear in reverse—by revamping and revealing [their] bodies to meet externally imposed vision of female beauty."[367] Farrell complains that women are overwhelming shown as victims in the media, but this is something that feminists complain about, too.[368]

So in the pornographic popular culture and the media in the United States, it is clearly women, not men, who are suffering from sexual discrimination. There is no second sexism here directed at men. Pornography turns women into willing sex objects that can be used and abused in any way men want, and women in the media are denied the better opportunities provided to men.

12. ARE SCHOOLS BIASED AGAINST WOMEN? OR MEN?

In the late nineteenth century, Edward Clarke, a well-known physician and professor at Harvard, argued that if women devoted the same effort to getting an education as men did, the energy that should go to developing their wombs would be diverted to developing their brains, thereby leaving them too feeble to produce healthy babies.[369] At the time, a pioneering group of women, later known as the American Association of University Women (AAUW), published a study refuting Clarke's view.[370] Over a hundred years later, in 1992, the AAUW published another study, *How Schools Shortchange Girls,* showing that girls experience a significantly greater loss of self-esteem than boys from grade school to high school and how, in other ways, girls were disadvantaged as well.[371] Like the AAUW's first report, this one provoked a torrent of criticism, much of it claiming that it is boys, not girls, who are at an educational disadvantage, a view that Warren Farrell endorses in *Women Can't Hear What Men Don't Say.*[372]

However, five years before Farrell's book and just three years after its 1992 report, the AAUW issued a follow-up report, *The Influence of School Climate on Gender Differences in the Achievement and Engagement of Young Adolescents,* in which it documented patterns of male underachievement in school, concluding that "inequity [in education] can (and does) work in both directions."[373] More recently, in 2000, the AAUW sponsored a symposium, "Beyond the Gender Wars: A Conversation About Girls, Boys and Education," which rejected the zero-sum logic of the so-called gender wars that followed its 1992 report.[374] According to William Pollack, one of the participants in the symposium, "what holds girls back is also what holds boys back," at least in some areas.[375] Moreover, the reluctance of boys to pursue certain fields, such as nursing, parallels the reluctance of girls to pursue other fields, such as engineering and the physical sciences. This suggests that the educational problems that girls and boys face are interconnected, so that the only way to really understand the problems girls face is to really understand the problems boys face and vice versa.

One of the statistics frequently cited to show that boys are faring less well than girls in school is the higher percentage of women that are now attending college in the United States.[376] About 9.9 million women (57.4 percent) and 7.4 million men (42.6 percent) were enrolled in colleges in 2003–04. Farrell also points to the existence of a *Directory of Financial Aids for Women* when there is no comparable *Directory of Financial Aids for Men* as further evidence of discrimination against men.[377] But the inferences to discrimination here are far too quick.

First, the *Directory of Financial Aids for Women* came into existence over thirty years ago in the United States when men had a clearly unfair advantage in receiving financial assistance to go to college. In those days, women had to work much harder to get the assistance they needed, and the directory served as a useful resource.[378] Even today, despite attempts to rid the PSAT and the SAT of bias, the tests still remain skewed in favor of men, and fellowships and scholarships that are tied to scores on these tests unfairly advantage men.[379] Second, if you examine the directory you quickly see that most, if not all, of the aid that is given requires additional racial, ethnic, or relational qualifications, like being an Italian or Greek American or the spouse of a member of the U.S. Air Force.[380] Some scholarships and fellowships in the directory don't even require that you be a woman. Furthermore, no one is prohibited from publishing a *Directory of Financial Aids for Men* that would provide comparable information for men.

Turning to the difference in college enrollment, first, it should be noted that the difference in the percentage of male and female high school graduates who immediately attend college is not that great—61 percent male high school graduates to 63 percent female high school graduates immediately entered college after high school in 2001. The greater percentage of women in college primarily derives from the greater numbers of women who return to college when they are twenty-five or older.[381] Second, it should be noted that most of the differences here between women and men are based on class and race or ethnic differences. There is no difference between the number of women and men attending college from the highest income bracket ($70,000 or more). As we move to lower income brackets, a difference between the number of women and men attending college begins to emerge among racial and ethnic groups, particularly African Americans and Latinos.[382] So whatever gender differences exist must be seen as having a distinctive class and race or ethnicity component. Third, it should be noted that this difference between the percentage of women and men attending college does not hold of Ivy League schools, except for Columbia and Brown. In most elite colleges and universities, men still outnumber women.[383] So if we want to explore differences in college enrollment between women and men, as we should, it will lead us into a discussion of class, race, and ethnicity. Opponents of feminism are usually not interested in discussing how class, race, and ethnicity interact with gender issues, but this is how the discussion must proceed here if we really want to understand what is going on.

According to Farrell, more men than women choose to major in engineering and the physical sciences because men are more likely to aspire to be primary breadwinners in their families. While this explanation ignores the discrimination and hostility that discourage women from entering male-dominated workplaces in engineering and the physical sciences, there is still something to it. Farrell's solution is to resocialize women and men so that both will be willing to take on either the primary breadwinner role or the primary homemaker/childcarer role in their families. Under this resocialization, women and men, at least initially, would have the same chance of occupying either the primary breadwinner role or the primary homemaker/childcarer role in their families. And this would have as a consequence that roughly the same number of women and men would take up careers in engineering and the physical sciences.

My solution, however, produces the same result as Farrell's— roughly the same number of women and men would take up careers in engineering and the physical sciences—without requiring the drastic resocialization that Farrell's requires. My solution requires resocializing women and men so that each will be willing to take on half the homemaking role and half the breadwinner role, other things being equal. They will also be assisted in this endeavor by state and federal institutions. In addition, my solution, unlike Farrell's, also allows both parents to be relatively equally involved in caring for their children, which even Farrell allows generally best promotes their children's well-being.[384] So why pursue equality between women and men the hard way, when there is a better and easier way to get there?

13. THE FUTURE OF FEMINISM AND MEN

If feminism had been used by its defenders to discriminate against men, the future of feminism and men would be bleak indeed. Fortunately, this was not the case. As I have argued in this essay, feminism has not discriminated against men. Recall the main points of my argument:

1. In the U.S. military, it is the male military elite who have kept the all-male draft and the combat exclusion of women in place for their own benefit and the benefit of other men.

2. In medical research, it is women, not men, who have been excluded from the testing of drugs that are then more often used on them. As far as the seven-year life expectancy gap between women and men, currently reduced to five years, feminism did not create that gap, but it has a strategy for getting rid of it.

3. With respect to domestic violence, the claim that men are equally battered was carefully examined and rejected. So the failure of feminists to endorse that claim does not provide evidence of discrimination against men.

4. With regard to rape, the attempt to show that feminists have discriminated against men by using an expanded notion of rape, advocating rape-shield laws, and ignoring the evidence of false allegations of rape is seen to fail.

5. The long history of discrimination against women in the U.S. criminal justice system has not reversed direction overnight. A number of purportedly recent examples of sexual discrimination against men in the criminal justice system are examined and rejected.

6. Although men do suffer from some discrimination in such fields as nursing and K–12 education, men are doing better overall in these same fields than women are. The attempt to show that the wage gap is the result of women's choices fails to recognize how women's choices in the workplace are socially constrained in ways that men's are not. While some men do suffer from sexual harassment in the workplace (more frequently at the hands of other men), overwhelming it is women, not men, who suffer from sexual discrimination there. Moreover, none of the discrimination that men suffer from in the workplace is because of feminism.

7. The claim that feminists have discriminated against men by failing to recognize that men work more hours than women relies upon an attack by Warren Farrell on a *UN Human Development Report* and on Arlie Hochschild's book *The Second Shift;* this attack is seen to fail. Here, the primary source of discrimination is the social expectation that women, not men, should adjust their employment outside the home to meet the obligations they both have inside the home.

8. While it is argued that child custody arrangements discriminate against men because of the high frequency with which women

are given sole custody following divorce, this argument fails once it is recognized that in the United States, for example, child custody is, for the most part, voluntarily arrived at, and in the 4 percent of cases in which it is contested in the U.S., fathers win about 38–70 percent of the time, even though mothers tend to be the primary caretakers of the children.

9. The pornographic culture in the United States and the current statistics about how women are employed and treated by the media in the United States undercut the claim that popular culture and the media are dominated by feminists who discriminate against men.

10. The issue of whether men are being discriminated against in schools in the United States turns out to be primarily a race and class issue rather than a gender issue, and it must be treated as such.

Given that feminism has not discriminated against men, the future of feminism and men looks very promising indeed, especially if men in sufficient numbers come around to endorse the feminist ideal of equality, so that it can be legally enforced.

For all too long, men have had a disproportionate amount of power in society, including control over their own lives. It is high time that the feminist ideal of equality, understood as an ideal of equal power or equal opportunity to acquire power in society, be better incorporated into the world in which we live. Once men recognize that feminism has not discriminated against them, they should be able to see that they face a stark choice: Either endorse the feminist ideal of equality or abandon that same morality that they endorse in so many other areas of their lives. We can only hope that a sufficient number of men will make the only morally right choice, and so do their part to help bring about the equality between women and men that will give both women and men equal control over their own lives.

Notes

1. Jane Rendell, *The Origins of Modern Feminism: Women in Britain, France, and the United States, 1780–1860* (New York: Schocken, 1984); Eleanor Flexner and Ellen Fitzpatrick, *A Century of Struggle* (Cambridge, MA: Harvard, 1996).

2. That provision of the Civil Rights Act was, in fact, a last minute amendment to the act as part of a failed attempt to defeat it. Opponents wrongly estimated that the act would not pass with such an amendment. See Caroline Bird, *Born Female* (New York: David McKay, 1970), pp. 1ff.

3. Judith Hole and Ellen Levine, *Rebirth of Feminism* (New York: Quadrangle, 1971); Lois Banner, *Women in Modern America* (New York: Harcourt Brace, 1995), pp. 239ff; and Virginia Sapiro, *Women in American Society,* 4th ed. (Mountain View, CA: Mayfield, 1994), Chapter 4.

4. Marilyn Frye, "Feminism over Three Decades," Symposium Paper, APA Central Division, April 29th, 2005, Chicago, fryem@msu.edu.

5. See http://www.now.org/issues/lgbi/marr-rep.html.

6. Frye, "Feminism."

7. For my attempt to face this challenge to affirmative action, see my contribution to James P. Sterba and Carl Cohen, *Affirmative Action and Racial Preference: A Debate* (New York: Oxford, 2003).

8. Here is a definition of sexual discrimination that I think both Farrell and I can accept: Sexual discrimination is treating people unfairly, and thereby usually disadvantaging them, on the basis of sex or some obviously inappropriate sex-based ideal. The second disjunct of the definition is needed to explicitly include as sexual discrimination, for example, the harassment Joseph Oncale suffered at the hands of other men where he worked. See *Oncale v. Sundowner Offshore Services, Inc.* (1998).

9. See Marilyn Boxer, *When Women Ask the Questions* (Baltimore: Johns Hopkins, 1998), p. xii. The National Women's Studies Association does not maintain records on the number of women's studies programs nationally. It only has records on its member institutions, which numbered 385 in 2005, according to Allison Kimmich, the organization's executive director.

10. James Doyle and Sam Femiano, "Reflections on the Early History of the American Men's Studies Association and the Evolution of the Field," http://mensstudies.org/history.htm.

11. NOMAS homepage, 2005 (http://www.nomas.org/sys-tmpl/door).

12. See, for example, the Introduction to Dale Spender, *Men's Studies Modified* (New York: Pergamon, 1981).

13. Warren Farrell, *The Myth of Male Power* (hereafter *MOMP*) (New York: Simon and Schuster, 1993), pp. 16–17.

14. Ibid.

15. For a discussion of these two ways of putting the ideal of equality, see my *How to Make People* (Lanham, MD: Roman & Littlefield, 1988), Chapter 9.

16. *MOMP*, p. 30; Warren Farrell, *The Myth of Male Power,* audiotapes (New York: Simon and Schuster,1993), Tape 1. Side I.

17. *MOMP*, p. 52.

18. Ibid., pp. 42–54.

19. Ibid., p. 52.

20. *MOMP*, audiotapes, Tape 1, Side 2. Moreover, some of the roles and responsibilities that people have are not so other-directed, for example, many of the *legal* roles and responsibilities that very wealthy people have. Accordingly, such roles and responsibilities, unless abused, can fairly easily be translated into control over one's own life.

21. Farrell also argues that influence power is not real power. He contends that executives who increase their responsibilities by moving up in their firms and taking on the supervision of more and more people do not thereby have more power any more than mothers would be increasing their power by just having more children for which they are then responsible, where the relevant sense of power is control over one's own life. However, in each case, I think we need to ask what the relevant costs and benefits are to the person involved from taking on additional responsibilities for others. I think that the results of such an assessment will show that frequently in the business context, less frequently in the procreation context, taking on such responsibilities does, in fact, contribute to greater control over one's own life. Surely, we cannot claim, as Farrell does, that so increasing one's responsibilities never thereby increases one's control over one's own life. Think again of the Bill Clinton example.

22. For a related real life discussion, see Timothy O'Brien, "Why Do So Few Women Reach the Top of Big Law Firms?" *New York Times,* March 19, 2006.

23. I am assuming here that Jill and Tom are equally capable overall with respect to their careers and family life.

24. Joan Jensen, "Native American Women and Agriculture: A Seneca Case Study," in Ellen DuBois and Vicki Ruiz, *Unequal Sisters* (New York: Routledge, 1990), pp. 51–65.

25. Farrell spends a lot of time talking about what is primarily the class-based oppression of garbage collectors.

26. Hilary Lips, *Women, Men and Power* (Mountain View, CA: Mayfield, 1991), p. 19. Interestingly, 25 percent of both males and females named their fathers as the most powerful individual they personally knew, and 91 percent of the males and 69 percent of the females named a man as the most powerful individual they personally knew.

27. There are some exceptions, such as Germany, Switzerland, Denmark, Norway, Venezuela, and Malaysia, that open up combat positions to both men and women. See http://encyclopedia.laborlawtalk.com/Conscription.

28. David Benatar, "The Second Sexism," *Social Theory and Practice* 29 (2003), pp. 177–210.

29. *MOMP* audiotapes, Tape 2, Side 1. See also his *MOMP,* Chapter 5.

30. See, for example, the position of NOW: http://www.now.org/issues/military/policies/tailhk.html.

31. See Judith Wagner DeCew, "The Combat Exclusion and the Role of Women in the Military," *Hypatia* 10 (1995) pp. 56–73; and Lucinda Peach, "Women at War—The Ethics of Women in Combat," *Minerva* 12, pp. 1–57.

32. Linda Bird Franke, *Ground Zero* (New York: Simon and Schuster, 1997), pp. 225–226. Similarly, when Barbara Winters became a finalist at the Acapulco cliff-diving championships, she was promptly disqualified from further jumping for "her own protection," she was told. The men had complained about having to compete against her. "This is death-defying activity," one male diver protested. "What would be the point if everyone saw that a woman could do the same." Collette Dowling, *The Frailty Myth* (New York: Random, 2000), p. 194.

33. Franke, *Ground Zero,* p. 236.

34. This fitness test is a measure of overall fitness, not of the ability to perform particular tasks, and there is no clear correlation between the two. Even so, the test is biased toward male capabilities. For instance, flexibility, a crucial part of overall fitness and an area in which women tend to score higher than men, is not included in the test. Moreover, if meeting this general standard is so important, why then is it age-normed so that those who stay in the military can satisfy lower standards? For further discussion, see Carol Cohon, "How Can She Claim Equal Rights When She Doesn't Have to Do as Many Push-Ups As I Do?" *Men and Masculinities* 3 (2000) pp. 131–151.

35. Ibid., p. 248.

36. Dowling, *Frailty Myth,* p. 54. It is worth noting that before puberty boys are neither taller nor heavier than girls (p. 64). Accordingly, one wonders whether, if girls were given the same opportunities for physical development as boys, then, as women, they would have more of the same physical accomplishments that men do.

37. Franke, *Ground Zero,* p. 16.

38. Ibid.

39. Ibid., p. 198.

40. Ibid., p. 16.

41. This is recognized in the U.S. military by the extension of the time permitted for women to attain promotions necessary to continued service. See *Rostker v. Goldberg 453 U.S. 57* (1981), p. 67.

42. Dowling, *Frailty Myth,* p. 12.

43. Sigal Benporath, "Feminism Under Fire" (unpublished).

44. Even in a patriarchal society that was classless and nonracist (which is hard to imagine), there would still be some men who do not benefit overall from the patriarchy of such a society because they are unlucky or because they just fail to adequately meet the masculinist ideals of that society.

45. Keeping the male-only draft in the United States at the moment just means keeping a male-only draft registration.

46. Les Aspin, Secretary of Defense, press briefing on the New Role of Women in Combat, January 13, 1994.

47. Franke, *Ground Zero*, p. 71.

48. See http://www.sss.gov/wmbkgr.htm.

49. Franke, *Ground Zero*, p. 187.

50. Ibid., p. 232.

51. Marysia Zalewski and Jane Parpart, *The "Man" Question in International Relations* (Boulder, CO: Westview, 1998), p. 1.

52. Franke, *Ground Zero*, p. 23.

53. Jeanne Holm, *Women in the Military* (Novato, CA: Presidio Press, 1992), p. 483.

54. Interestingly, it was the U.S. military elite in 1948, including Secretary of Defense James Forrestal; Generals Eisenhower and Bradley of the Army; Admirals Denfeld, Nimitz, and Radford of the Navy; Air Force Generals Spaatz, Vandenberg and Eaker; and Marine Corps General Vandegrift who overcame opposition in the ranks to get the act through Congress authorizing regular corps of women in each of the services. Opposition at the time centered on the general fear that women would command men. To quell this fear, language was inserted to give the service secretaries the prerogative of prescribing "the military authority which female persons...may exercise and the kind of military duty to which they may be assigned." See Holm, *Women in the Military*, Chapter 10.

55. It is, of course, possible for men to unintentionally discriminate against other men. However, this requires that these men somehow be acting negligently, and that if they were to view the situation properly, they would see that what they are doing is not for the overall benefit of men or that it unfairly discriminates against some particular group of men. But this does not appear to be the case with respect to those men who do support the male-only draft and the combat exclusion of women because in this case their support does seem to work to the overall benefit of men or at least to not discriminate against any particular group of men.

But what if they are wrong? What if the male-only draft and the combat exclusion of women don't really work for the overall benefit of men? Or what if these institutions do discriminate against some particular group of men? Put another way, what if both men and women would benefit here from a more egalitarian institution arrangement. In that case, in order for there to be any discrimination against men in this regard, those favoring those institutions would have to be negligent for failing to so recognize that they had these effects.

56. In other cases, however, a particular masculinist ideal can be so unrelated to benefiting men overall through the practices it engenders such that being treated badly for violating that ideal does constitute sexual discrimination. See *Oncale v. Sundowner Offshore Services, Inc.* (1998).

57. Sometimes, even when a particular masculinist ideal is inappropriately related to benefiting men overall through the military, men who are treated badly for violating that ideal may be wronged to some degree without being sexually discriminated against. In other cases, however, the particular masculinist ideal is so unrelated to benefiting men overall through the military that being treated badly for violating it does constitute sexual discrimination. Consider the "code red" order used for perceived slackers in the film, *A Few Good Men,* or if you want a real life example, consider the inappropriate male ideal that was imposed on Joseph Oncale in his workplace, which the U.S. Supreme Court judged to be sexual harassment in *Oncale v. Sundowner Offshore Services, Inc.* (1998).

58. Londa Schiebinger, *Has Feminism Changed Science* (Cambridge, MA: Harvard, 1999), pp. 113–125.

59. Ibid.

60. Ibid.

61. *MOMP,* pp. 188ff.

62. Schiebinger, *Has Feminism Changed Science.*

63. Londa Schiebinger, "Women's Health and Clinical Trials," *Journal of Clinical Investigations* 112 (2003) pp. 973–977.

64. Schiebinger, *Has Feminism Changed Science,* pp. 113–125.

65. Jo Ann Manson et al., "A Prospective Study of Aspirin Use and Primary Prevention of Cardiovascular Disease in Women," *Journal of the American Medical Association,* 266, no. 4 (1991), pp. 521–527.

66. Schiebinger, *Has Feminism Changed Science,* pp. 113–125.

67. Ibid.

68. Ibid.

69. Ibid.

70. Sue Rosser, *Women's Health—Missing from U.S. Medicine* (Bloomington: Indiana, University Press, 1994), p. 22.

71. Stella Hurtley and John Benditt, "Women's Health Research," *Science* 269 (August 1995), p. 777.

72. Rosser, *Women's Health*, Bureau of Health Professions, U.S. Department of Health and Human Services, p. 11.

73. Council on Graduate Medical Education, Women in Medicine: Summary of Fifth Report, May, 1998.

74. *MOMP*, p. 189.

75. Schiebinger, *Has Feminism Changed Science*, pp. 113–125; Council on Ethical and Judicial Affairs, "Gender Disparities in Clinical Decision Making, *JAMA* 266 (1991), pp. 559–562.

76. Gayle Feldman, "Women Are Different," *Self* (July 1997), pp. 105–108, 154.

77. Farrell argues that with respect to coronary bypass surgery when age and other factors are taken into account, men are not inappropriately favored over women in receiving this operation. Others contest this. According to Sue Rosser, "women were significantly less likely than men to undergo coronary angioplasty, angiography or surgery when admitted to the hospital with the diagnosis of myocardial, unstable angina, or chronic ischemic heart disease or chest pain. This significant difference remained even when variables such as race, age, economic status etc. were controlled for" *Women's Health*, p. 11. But even if Farrell were right about coronary bypass surgery, which doesn't seem to be the case, we still would have neglect in these other areas.

78. *MOMP*, pp. 190ff.

79. Ibid.

80. It also should be pointed out that neglect of research in these seventeen areas is nothing like the neglect of women's health that occurs when medications are tested on men and then prescribed for women with adverse, even fatal, results.

81. *MOMP*, pp. 30, 180–188.

82. It is interesting to note that the increased longevity of women and men from the 1920s to the present is due primarily to a huge reduction in infant mortality rates over the intervening period; see "Life Expectancy Profiles," http://www.bbc.co.uk/dna/h2g2/A3784854.

83. C. A. Nathanson, "Sex Differences in Mortality," *Annual Review of Sociology* (1984), 191–213.

84. Ibid.

85. Ibid.

86. *MOMP*, pp. 30, 182–184.

87. Stephan Harris, "Survey: Women Feel More Stress Than Men," August 4, 1999 (http://my.webmd.com/content/Article/107/108405.htm).

88. See Kate Zernike, "The Bell Tolls for the Future Merry Widow," *New York Times,* April 20, 2006.

89. Nancy Lemon, *Domestic Violence Law* (St. Paul, MN: West Group, 2001), p. 2.

90. Elizabeth Davis, *The First Sex* (New York: Putnam, 1971), pp. 252–255.

91. *Ibid.*

92. Cherubino da Siena, *Regole della vita matrimoniale* (Bologna, Italy, 1888).

93. William Mandel, *Soviet Women* (New York: Anchor, 1975), p. 12.

94. *Code Napoleon.* Literally translated from the original and official edition, published at Paris in 1804 by a barrister of the Inner Temple, Baton Rouge: Claitor's Book Store, 1960.

95. The Puritans in the Massachusetts Bay Colony enacted the first laws anywhere in the world against wife beating. See Elizabeth Pleck, *Domestic Violence* (New York: Oxford, 1987), p. 4.

96. Betsy Warrior and Lisa Leghorn, *Houseworker's Handbook,* 3rd expanded ed. (Cambridge, MA: Women's Center, 1995), p. 38.

97. Michael Atkus, "Ban on Wife Selling," *San Francisco Chronicle,* March 28, 1975.

98. "Zulu Queen's Custody Case," *San Francisco Chronicle,* May 5, 1975, p. 24.

99. Warrior and Leghorn, *Houseworker's Handbook,* p. 38; The Digger, "Flipside of the Japanese Miracle," *Alternative Press Digest* 3 (1975), p. 66.

100. Murray Straus, Richard Gelles, and Suzanne Steinmetz, *Behind Closed Doors* (New York: Anchor, 1980), p. 11.

101. Del Martin, *Battered Wives,* rev. ed. (Volcano, CA: Volcano Press, 1981), p. 275.

102. Ruth Shaughter, *While Ruth Was at Haven House* (Pasadena, CA: n.p., n.d.).

103. See the National Domestic Violence Hotline at http://www.ndvh.org/index.php.

104. Commonwealth Fund Survey 1998. Commonwealth Fund, 1 East 75th Street, New York, NY; Sheila Ruth, *Issues in Feminism,* 4th ed. (Mountain View, CA: Mayfield, 1997); Michael Rand, "Violence-Related Injuries Treated in Hospital Emergency Rooms," Bureau of Justice Report (1997) http://www.ojp.usdoj.gov/bjs/pub/pdf/vrithed.pdf.

105. For such an account, see Mary White Stewart, *Ordinary Violence* (Westport, CT: Bergin & Garvey, 2002). See also Donald Dutton, *The Batterer* (New York: Basic, 1995), pp. 69ff.

106. R. Emerson Dobash and Russell Dobash, *Violence Against Wives* (New York: Free Press, 1979), p. 24.

107. Warren Farrell, *Women Can't Hear What Men Don't Say,* hereafter *WCHW MDS* (New York: Jeremy P. Tarcher/Putnam, 2000), p. 129.

108. Ibid., p. 133.

109. See Farrell's annotated bibliography of such studies in ibid., pp. 323–329.

110. Another oddity of this charge of "equal battering" is that in every other area of social life overwhelming evidence shows that men are far more likely to use violence than women are.

111. *WCHWMDS*, pp. 131ff.

112. See the arguments of Carl Cohen in *Affirmative Action and Racial Preference: A Debate.*

113. See Murray Straus and Richard Gelles, "Societal Change and Change in Family Violence from 1975 to 1985 as Revealed by Two National Surveys," *Journal of Marriage and the Family* 18 (1986), pp. 465–479.

114. Of course, women may have been engaging in "equal battering" even when the law gave men, and not women, the right to batter, but this too is very unlikely to have been the case.

115. Callie Rennison and Sarah Welchans, "Intimate Partner Violence" (Washington, DC: U.S. Department of Justice, rev. 2002).

116. Murray Straus, "Physical Assaults by Women Partners: A Major Social Problem" in M. R. Walsh, ed., *Women, Men and Gender: Ongoing Debates* (New Haven, CT: Yale, 1997), p. 216.

117. Murray Straus et al., "The Revised Conflict Tactics Scales (CTS-2)," *Journal of Family Issues* 17 (May 1996), p. 285.

118. Not all uses of CTS, however, are similarly tainted. The scales can be used in very restricted contexts and so modified that they are not distorting. I owe this point to Sonya Kourany Sterba, Ph.D. candidate in quantitative psychology at the University of North Carolina.

119. Murray Straus, "Measuring Intrafamily Conflict and Violence: The Conflict Tactics Scales," in Murray Straus and Richard Gelles, eds., *Physical Violence in American Families* (New Brunswick, NJ: Transation, 1990), p. 33.

120. P. Tjadens and N. Thoennes," Prevalence and Consequences of Male-to-Female and Female-to-Male Intimate Partner Violence as Measured by the National Violence Against Women Survey," *Violence Against Women* 6 (2001), pp. 142–161; and Lisa Birningham, "Closing the Loophole: Vermont's Legislative Response to Stalking," *Vermont Law Review* 18 (1994), p. 478.

121. Statistics Canada, *Family Violence in Canada* (Ottawa: National Clearinghouse on Family Violence, 2001).

122. R. Bachman and L. Saltzman, *Violence Against Women* (Washington, DC: U.S. Department of Justice, Bureau of Justice Statistics, 2001).

123. Murray Straus, The Controversy over Domestic Violence by Women," in X. Arriage and S. Oskamp eds., *Violence and Intimate Relationships* (Thousand Oaks, CA: Sage, 1999), p. 29.

124. Daniel Saunders, "Are Physical Assaults by Wives and Girlfriends a Major Social Problem? A Review of the Literature," *Violence Against Women* 8 (2002), pp. 1429ff.

125. J. Makepeace, "Gender Differences in Courtship Violence Victimization," *Family Relations* 35 (1986), pp. 383–388; C. Molidor, "Gender and Contextual Factors in Adolescent Dating Violence," *Violence Against Women* 4 (1998), pp. 180–194; P. Tjadens and N. Thoennes, *Full Report of the Prevalence, Incidence and Consequences of Violence Against Women* (Washington, DC: National Institute of Justice and Centers for Disease Prevention, 2000).

126. Straus et al., "Revised Conflict Tactics Scales," pp. 283–316.

127. Jack Straton, "The Myth of the "Battered Husband Syndrome," *Brother* 20 (2001–2002), pp. 8–9.

128. Saunders, "Physical Assaults," p. 1431.

129. Ibid.

130. K. Stout and P. Brown, "Legal and Social Differences Between Men and Women Who Kill Intimate Partners, *Affilia* 10 (1995), pp. 194–205.

131. Saunders, "Physical Assaults," p. 1432.

132. J. Campbell, "Misogyny and Homicide of Women," *Advances in Nursing Science/Women's Health* 3 (1981), pp. 67–85.

133. Murray Straus, "Physical Assaults by Wives," in Mary Roth Walsh, ed. *Women, Men and Gender* (New Haven, CT: Yale, 1997), pp. 67–87.

134. Murray Straus, Richard Gelles, and Suzanne Steinmetz, *Behind Closed Doors* (New York: Anchor, 1980).

135. J. Stets and Murray Straus, "Gender Differences in Reporting Marital Violence and Its Medical and Psychological Consequences," in Murray Strauss and Richard Gelles, eds., *Physical Violence in American Families* (New Brunswick, NJ: Transaction, 1990).

136. R. Emerson Dobash and Russell Dobash, "Women's Violence to Men in Intimate Relationships, *British Journal of Criminology* 44 (2004), p. 340.

137. Martin Fiebert and Denise Gonzalez, "College Women Who Initiate Assaults on Their Male Partners and the Reasons Offered for Such Behavior," *Psychological Reports* 80 (1997), pp. 383–390.

138. Murray Straus, "Physical Assaults by Women Partners," p. 211.

139. See *WCHWMDS*, pp. 146–147.

140. National Coalition of Anti-Violence Programs Report, April 26, 2005, http://www.ncavp.org/media/MediaReleaseDetail.aspx?p=1420&d=1492.

141. In other cultural environments, for example, in classical Greek culture, social expectations were different. See Thomas Scalon, *Eros and Greek Athletics* (New York: Oxford, 2002).

142. See James P. Sterba and Linda Lemoncheck, *Sexual Harrassment: Issues and Answers* (New York: Oxford, 2001).

143. Saunders, "Physical Assaults," p. 1425.

144. Charlene Muehlenhard and Leigh Ann Kimes, "Social Construction of Violence: The Case of Sexual and Domestic Violence," *Personality & Social Psychology* 3 (1999), pp. 234ff.

145. Ibid. Nothing like this happened when women's shelters were opened up across the United States with or without governmental assistance. This is just another indication that the domestic violence studies that use Straus's CTS are not measuring the actual pattern of violence among domestic partners.

146. These false claims of equal battering may also be leading police to think that they should be arresting women for domestic violence as frequently as they are arresting men. In any case, we are seeing an increasing number of women being arrested in cases of domestic violence. See S. Miller, "The Paradox of Women Arrested for Domestic Violence," *Violence Against Women* 7 (2001), pp. 1339–1376. However, Kris Henning and Lynette Feder argue that the females who are arrested do not share the same violent background profile of the males who are arrested. See their "A Comparison of Men and Women Arrested for Domestic Violence," *Journal of Family Violence* 19 (2004), pp. 69–80.

147. M. E. J. Richardson, *Hammurabi's Laws: Text, Translation and Glossary* (Sheffield, UK: Sheffield Academic, 2000), p. 83.

148. Deuteronomy, 22: 22–29.

149. Susan Brownmiller, *Against Our Will* (New York: Simon & Schuster, 1975), p. 24.

150. Ibid., p. 29.

151. Sir Matthew Hale, *The History of the Pleas of the Crown* (Philadelphia: R.H. Small, 1847), p. 628ff.

152. Ibid.

153. Julie Allison and Lawrence Wrightman, *Rape: The Misunderstood Crime* (London: Sage, 1993), Chapters 9 and 10.

154. Robin Warshaw, *I Never Called It Rape* (New York: Harper and Row, 1988), Introduction.

155. *MOMP*, p. 316.

156. Mary Koss, et al., "The Scope of Rape: Incidence and Prevalence of Sexual Aggression and Victimization in a National Sample of Higher Education Students," *Journal of Counseling and Clinical Psychology* 55, no. 2 (1987) pp. 162–170.

157. Charlene Muehlenhard and Stephen Cook, "Men's Self Reports of Unwanted Sexual Activity," *Journal of Sex Research* 24 (1988), pp. 68–72.

158. "Rape: The Making of an Epidemic," *The Blade,* Special Report, October 10–12, 1993.

159. Office of Sexual Assault Prevention and Response, *Rape on Campus* (Cambridge, MA: Harvard University).

160. Heather Karjane, Bonnie Fisher, and Francis Cullen, "Campus Sexual Assault: How America's Institutions of Higher Education Respond," http://www.securityoncampus.org/schools/research/csasummary.html.

161. Michelle Anderson, "From Chastity Requirement to Sexually Licensed Sexual Conduct and a New Rape Shield Law," *George Washington Law Review* 70 (2002), p. 51ff.

162. See *MOMP,* p. 332. For an even more direct endorsement of this view, see his *MOMP* audiotapes, Tape 2, Side 2.

163. Bureau of Justice Statistics, *Criminal Victimization, 2004* (Washington, DC: U.S. Department of Justice, September 2005), p. 3.

164. Patricia Rozee, "Rape Resistance," in Andrea Barnes, ed., *The Handbook of Women, Psychology and the Law* (San Francisco: John Wiley, 2005), p. 269.

165. Julie Allison and Lawrence Wrightman, *Rape,* p. 195. Farrell claims that when a charge of rape is made, the purported victim of rape is generally believed. This claim is clearly undercut by the very low conviction rate for reported rape and the kind of treatment purported victims of rape frequently report receiving from the legal system. In addition, 21 percent of convicted rapists are never sentenced to jail or prison time, and 24 percent receive time in local jail, which means that they spend an average of less than eleven months in jail. See the Majority Staff of the Senate Judiciary Committee, "The Response to Rape: Detours on the Road to Equal Justice" (Washington, DC: U.S. Congress Report, 1993).

166. Unfortunately, rape-shield laws, as they are presently constituted, do not usually achieve these goals. But there are viable suggestions for how to improve them. See Michelle Anderson, "Chastity Requirements," and Nancy Snow, "Evaluating Rape-Shield Laws: Why the Law Continues to Fail Rape Victims," in *A Most Detestable Crime,* Keith Burgess-Jackson, ed. (New York: Oxford, 1999), pp. 245–266.

167. *MOMP,* pp. 322ff.

168. See *MOMP* audiotapes, Tape 2, Side 2.

169. *MOMP,* p. 322ff.

170. See www.fbi.gov/ucr/Cius_97/96CRIME/96crime2.pdf.

171. Stephen Buckley, "Unfounded Reports of Rape Confound Area Police Investigations," *Washington Post,* June 27, 1992.

172. Sally Gold and Martha Wyatt, "The Rape System: Old Roles and New Times," *Catholic University Law Review* 27 (1978), pp. 709–710.

173. Lynn Schefran, "Writing and Reading About Rape," *St. John's Law Review* 66 (1992), pp. 1010–1012.

174. Ibid.

175. Charles McDowell, "False Allegations," *Forensic Science Digest* 11 (December 1985), pp. 57–75.

176. Ibid.

177. See *MOMP,* pp. 332ff, and McDowell, "False Allegations," p. 64.

178. Editorial, "Air Force in the Cross Hairs," *Milwaukee Journal Sentinel,* September 26, 2003.

179. Ibid.

180. Michael Janofsky, "Air Force Begins an Inquiry of Ex-Cadets' Rape Charges," *New York Times,* February 26, 2003, p. 18.

181. Ibid.

182. Diana Schemo, "Top Officers at Air Force Academy Replaced in Wake of Rape Scandal," *New York Times,* March 26, 2003, p. 10; Diana Schemo and Michael Moss, "Criminal Charges Possible in Air Force Rape Scandal," *New York Times,* March 27, 2003; Diana Schemo, "Air Force Secretary Says Academy Leaders Could Be Punished in Rape Scandal," *New York Times,* April 2, 2003, p.18.

183. Michael Janofsky with Diana Schemo, "Women Recount Life as Cadets: Forced Sex, Fear, and Silent Rage," *New York Times,* March 16, 2003, p. 1; and Michael Moss, "Air Force Academy Did Act on Complaints, Panel Finds," *New York Times,* June 20, 2003, p. 14.

184. Actually, the contrast is even greater. In a very short interview given to the *Chicago Lawyer* in 1985, McDowell claims to have investigated, not 556, but 1,218 cases of alleged rape. This would mean that there were more than twenty times more cases of alleged rapes and other sexual assaults investigated in the nine years covered by the McDowell study—when fewer women were at the Air Force Academy—than in the ten years covered by the more recent investigations! See http://christianparty. net/mcdowell.htm.

185. *MOMP* audiotapes, Tape 2, Side 2.

186. In the current legal environment, a woman's forwardness also dramatically undermines her ability to prosecute any rape she claims occurred.

187. Bureau of Justice Statistics, *Criminal Victimization, 2004* (Washington, DC: U.S. Department of Justice, August 2003), p. 10.

188. Mary Koss, et al., "Stranger and Acquaintance Rape," *Psychology of Women Quarterly* 12 (1988), pp. 1–24.

189. For the details of this proposal, see Ian Ayres and Katherine Baker, "A Separate Crime of Reckless Sex, *University of Chicago Law Review* 22 (2005), pp. 599ff.

190. Ibid.

191. Ibid.

192. Michael Kimmel, *The Gendered Society,* 2nd ed. (New York: Oxford, 2004), p. 112.

193. See Snow, "Evaluating Rape-Shield Laws," for a defense of this proposal.

194. L. Mara Dodge, *Whores and Thieves of the Worst Kind* (Dekalb: Northern Illinois University, 2002), p. 14.

195. Estelle Freedman, *Their Sisters' Keepers* (Ann Arbor: University of Michigan Press, 1981), p. 60.

196. Ibid.

197. *MOMP*, p. 241.

198. Such facts as the more extensive criminal histories or higher prevalence of convictions for violence in the backgrounds of the men would be relevant. In addition, there was also a relatively early case in which the lesser sentence for a female codefendant was found to violate her male codefendant's right to equal protection, see *U.S. v. Maples* (1974). This shows that there is a clear recognition in the criminal law that a person's sex cannot be a basis for the sentence the person receives.

199. Women's Economic Agenda Project, "Women in Prison," http://www.prisonactivist.org/women/women-in-prison.html.

200. *MOMP*, p. 265.

201. Status Report on Female Offenders (October 2001). In fact, women charged with homicide have the least extensive prior criminal records of any people convicted of crimes; see Freebatteredwomen.org.

202. Farrell also cites the case of Lynn Massip. While suffering from postpartum depression, she killed her six-month-old baby boy by driving her car over him and was sentenced to treatment alone. Farrell objects to this sentence because men are not treated similarly. But in the reference Farrell cites for this case, the judge justified his decision on the grounds that a man who had acted similarly, being temporarily insane, had been sentenced to treatment alone. So the judge justified sentencing Massip in the way he had because a man in similar circumstances had been treated exactly the same way. How then could Farrell think that Massip's sentence was an example of sexual discrimination favoring women over men? See *MOMP,* p. 270, and Andrea Ford, "Woman Who Killed Infant Son Allowed to Get Mental Help on Outpatient Basis," *Los Angeles Times,* March 11, 1989.

203. *MOMP*, p. 243.

204. Ibid., p. 249.

205. For the data on the McMartin preschool case, which can also be found in earlier newspaper articles, see Paul and Shirley Eberle, *The Abuse of Innocence* (Buffalo, NY: Prometheus, 1993), Chapter 1.

206. Charles Shepard, *Forgiven* (New York: Atlantic Monthly Press, 1989); Ken Garfield, "Bakkers, PTL's First Couple Divorcing She Writes to Church Members: It's All Over," *Charlotte Observer,* March 13, 1992, A1; Charles Shepard, "Bakker Portrayed as Victim," *Charlotte Observer,* August 29, 1989, A1.

207. Shelly Bannister, "Battered Women Who Kill Their Abusers," in *It's A Crime: Women and Justice,* Roslyn Muraskin and Ted Alleman, eds., (Englewood Cliffs: Prentice Hall, 1993), p. 326.

208. Sarah Leivick, "Use of Battered Woman Syndrome to Defend the Abused and Prosecute the Abuser," *Georgetown Journal of Gender and Law* 6 (2005), p. 391.

209. Ibid.

210. As many as 8 out of 10 battered women charged with killing their abusers are convicted or plead guilty to some charge. Many are sentenced to long prison terms. See Patricia Gagne, *Battered Women's Justice* (New York: Twayne, 1998), p. 41.

211. *MOMP,* p. 262.

212. See the one article Farrell cites for this case by Tom Gorman, "Court Told How Son Was Driven to Kill Spiteful Mother," *Los Angeles Times,* December 29, 1989.

213. Ibid.

214. Farrell does cite another case in which a man shot his wife as she was drawing her gun out of her purse to shoot him, but this case was properly resolved as one of justified self-defense without any need to have recourse to battered men's syndrome. See *MOMP,* p. 269.

215. For a discussion of this issue, see my book *Justice for Here and Now* (New York: Cambridge, 1998).

216. Jean-Marie Navetta, "Gains in Learning, Gaps in Earning," *AAUW Outlook* (Spring 2005), p. 12.

217. Joan Williams, *Unbending Gender: Why Family and Work Conflict and What to Do About It* (New York: Oxford, 2000), p. 274.

218. Warren Farrell, *Why Men Earn More,* hereafter *WMEM* (New York: AMACOM, 2005).

219. Ibid, p. xxi. Both groups are of men and women who are forty-five to fifty-four years old. See his note 14, p. 238.

220. Ibid.

221. Ibid., p. 220.

222. For research that controls for some of these factors, see U.S. General Accounting Office, "Women's Earnings Work Patterns Partially Explain Difference Between Men's and Women's Earnings" (October 2003), pp. 1–17, especially p. 29.

223. Ibid., pp. 12–13.

224. Bureau of Labor Statistics, Table A-26, "Usual Weekly Earnings of Employed Full-Time Wage and Salary Workers by Detailed Occupation and Sex, Annual Averages, 2003" (unpublished). Farrell's thirty-nine fields are virtually all fields with fewer than fifty thousand workers and so were only included in the raw data and not in the published version of the study. The one field that was included in the published version (education, training, and library occupations) is misclassified by Farrell because it too is a field in which men earn more. Two other of his thirty-nine fields (automotive body and related repairs and rolling machine setters, etc.) are also misclassified as fields in which women earn more. Farrell also mentions about forty other fields where women do earn more, but there are either fewer than six thousand workers in these fields or the difference between men's and women's salaries is not statistically significant. See *WMEM*, p. 11.

225. *WMEM*, p. 205.

226. *MOMP*, p. 53.

227. *WMEM*, Chapter 4.

228. There is also evidence that in the real world men are reluctant to marry up, although women are not as reluctant to marry down, as shown in a recent U.S study. See John Schwartz, "Glass Ceiling at Altar as Well as Boardroom," *New York Times*, December 14, 2004.

229. Pepper Schwartz, *Peer Marriage* (New York: Free Press, 1994), p. 4.

230. Ibid., p. 12.

231. The elements of this feminist plan are supported by Williams, *Unbending Gender*; Ann Crittenden, *The Price of Motherhood* (New York: Henry Holt, 2001); Janet Gornick and Marcia Meyers, *Families That Work* (New York: Russell Sage, 2003); and Neil Gilbert, *The Transformation of the Welfare State* (New York: Oxford, 2002).

232. See Gornick and Meyers, *Families That Work*.

233. Diana Furchtgott-Roth and Christine Stolba, *The Feminist Dilemma* (Washington, DC: AEI Press, 2001), pp. 127–8. *WMEM*, p. xxx.

234. Williams, *Unbending Gender*, p. 88.

235. Ibid., p. 92ff.

236. Ibid.

237. There is also the competitive advantage foreign businesses can have when their family-friendly support services for their employees, such as parental leaves and day care, are funded, in part or in whole, by their governments.

238. For further discussion, see Gornick and Meyers, *Families That Work*.

239. What is primarily at issue here is the unfairness of imposing these burdens and restrictions on women when no comparable burdens and restrictions are imposed on men.

240. All of these cases are cited by Evelyn Murphy with E. J. Graff in *Getting Even* (New York: Simon & Schuster, 2005), pp. 66–79.

241. See *WMEM*, Chapters 10 and 11.

242. Andrea Warren, "In Praise of Nurturing Men," in Kathleen Gilbert, ed., *The Family 05/06* (Dubuque, IA: McGraw-Hill/Dushkin, 2005), pp. 19–20; Charles Williams, "The Glass Escalator: Hidden Advantages for Men in the Female Professions," *Social Problems* 39 (1992), pp. 253–267, Christine Williams, *Still a Man's World* (Berkeley: University of California Press, 1995).

243. Why is it relevant that most of the discrimination that men suffer in the workplace is at the hands of other men, not women, when we don't think it is similarly relevant that most of the violence blacks suffer is at the hands of other blacks? In the first place, it is relevant that most of the violence blacks suffer is at the hands of other blacks because that is one aspect of the problem. But it is not similarly relevant because blacks who commit crimes against other blacks usually grow up in poor environments with very few opportunities. We know that if we change that environment for blacks, or any group that belongs to the underclass, the frequency of the crimes they commit goes way down. So while we still hold blacks responsible for the crimes they commit, we also know, or should know, that their responsibility is mitigated because of the conditions under which they live, and that their behavior can best be remedied by changing those conditions. By contrast, typically nothing similar holds of men who have sexually harassed other men in the workplace. There are rarely any comparable mitigating factors operating in such cases. What would be interestingly comparable here would be if a significant percentage of the sexual discrimination suffered by women was suffered at the hands of other women. But, of course, nothing of this sort obtains. Apropos to this issue, see *MOMP*, p. 215.

244. Cherly Gomez-Preston *When No Means No* (New York: Carol Publishing, 1993), pp. 35–36. Ellen Bravo and Ellen Cassedy, *The 9–5 Guide to Combating Sexual Harassment* (New York: John Wiley, 1992), pp. 4–5. The problem is international as well as national. A three-year study of women in Estonia, Finland, Sweden, and the then Soviet Union showed that nearly 50 percent of all working women experience sexual harassment. A survey released in 1991 by the Santama Group to Consider Sexual Harassment at Work showed that about 70 percent of Japanese women say they have experienced some type of sexual harassment on the job. See Teresa Webb, *Step Forward* (New York: Master Media, 1991), pp. xiv, xvii.

245. U.S. Department of Defense, *1995 Sexual Harassment Survey* (Arlington, VA: Defense Manpower Data Center, December 1996); Eric Schmitt, "Top Enlisted Man in the Army Stands Accused of Sex Assault," *New York Times*, February 4, 1997, A1.

246. Franke, *Ground Zero*, 157.

247. Ibid., p. 191; Diana Schemo, "Rate of Rape at Academy Is Put at 12 Percent in Survey," *New York Times*, August 29, 2003.

248. U.S. Department of Defense, "Armed Forces Survey 2002 Sexual Harassment Survey" (Ft. Belfort, VA: Defense Technical Information Center). Over 60 percent is the figure that would have resulted if the Defense Department had calibrated both surveys the way it had done the 1995 survey. But in 2002 the Department of Defense excluded "unwanted sexual behavior" as part of the measure for sexual harassment and in this way reduced the frequency of sexual harassment in 1995 to 45 percent and to 24 percent in 2002. But why was unwanted sexual behavior removed from the measure of sexual harassment? The 2002 survey provides no explanation for this change. Could it have been done just to reduce the overall figure for sexual harassment?

249. Stephanie Armour, "More Men Say They Are Sexually Harassed at Work," *USA Today*, September 17, 2004.

250. *MOMP*, p. 293. Farrell also characterizes sexual harassment as sexual initiatives in which men persist too much. See Farrell, *The Sex Tapes*, audiotape 2, Side 1. Published and distributed by the author at warren@warrenfarrell.com.

251. Warren Farrell, *Why Men Are The Way They Are*, audiotapes (Auborn CA: Audio Partners, 1992), Tape 2, Side 1. In *The Sex Tapes*, Tape 2, Side 1, Farrell grants that in 98–99 percent of sexual harassment lawsuits, it is men that persist and persist too much. So he seems to be admitting that these cases are justifiably brought against the men. Then he says that it only takes one time for this not to be true in order for the man's career to be messed up, and here he clearly thinks (rightly) that going forward with such a case (in which a man did not persist or persist too much) would not be justified. However, if Farrell really believes what he says here, I don't see what his complaint can be against existing sexual harassment law. This is because everyone recognizes that even the most perfectly just laws are unjustly applied now and then, without thereby thinking that this undercuts the justification we have for still following those laws, all things being equal.

252. Murphy with Graff, *Getting Even*, pp. 90–91.

253. Elsewhere, I have argued that the courts are using a far too stringent definition of sexual harassment, but the alternative definition I propose and defend bears no resemblance to any of the definitions that Farrell has suggested. See my "Understanding, Explaining and Eliminating Sexual Harassment," in *Sexual Harassment: Issues and Answers*, pp. 231–244.

254. Amber Sumrall and Dena Taylor, *Sexual Harassment: Women Speak Out* (Freedom, CA: The Crossing Press, 1992).

255. *MOMP,* p. 306.

256. For a possible remedy, see my "Understanding, Explaining and Eliminating Sexual Harassment."

257. Lynn Weiner, *From Working Girl to Working Mother* (Chapel Hill: University of North Carolina Press, 1985); Karen Anderson, "A History of Women's Work in the United States," in Ann Helston Stromberg and Shirley Harkess, eds., *Working Women,* 2nd ed. (Mountain View, CA: Mayfield Publishing, 1988), pp. 25–41; Phyllis Moen, *Women's Two Roles* (New York: Auburn House, 1992).

258. Weiner, *From Working Girl to Working Mother,* Moen, *Women's Two Roles.*

259. United Nations Development Programme, *Human Development Report* (New York: Oxford, 1995), pp. 4–6.

260. Barbara Crossette, "UN Documents Inequalities for Women as World Forum Nears," *New York Times,* August 18, 1995, A3.

261. Ibid.

262. *WCHWMDS,* p. 88, and *WCHWMDS* audiotape, Tape 2, Side 2. Farrell also claims that the UNs press release made a similar claim, but I haven't been able to see a copy of it. In any case, the press releases on the report from the *Women's International Network News* did not make this claim. See *Women's International Network News* 21, no. 4 (Autumn 1995), p. 32.

263. See the earlier quote.

264. *Human Development Report,* pp. 93–94.

265. Farrell claims that there was only this one study cited by the *UN Report,* when, in fact, there were six studies cited. See *WCHWMDS,* p. 89, and the *Human Development Report,* p. 88.

266. *WCHWMDS,* p. 89.

267. Ibid.

268. United Nations Department for Economic and Social Information and Policy Analysis, *UN Publication Series K* (New York: United Nations, 1995), pp. 105–106.

269. Arlie Hochschild, *Second Shift,* updated ed. (New York: Penguin, 2003), p. 3.

270. *WCHWMDS,* p. 95.

271. Arlie Hochschild, *Second Shift,* original ed. (New York: Viking, 1989), p. 272.

272. Hochschild, *Second Shift,* updated ed., p. xxvii.

273. *WCHWMDS,* p. 95.

274. Marjorie Shaevitz, *The Superwoman Syndrome* (New York; Warner, 1984), Appendix B.

275. Elizabeth Cady Stanton and Committee, *Declaration of Sentiments,* http://www.pinn.net/~sunshine/book-sum/seneca3.html.

276. Herma Hill Kay, *Sex-Based Discrimination,* 3rd ed. (St. Paul, MN: West Publishing, 1988), pp. 191–207.

277. Raquel Kennedy and Elizabeth Barnhill, Martial Rape: New Research and Directions (February 006) http://www.vawnet.org/DomesticViolence/Research/VAW netDocs/AR_MaritalRapeRevised.pdf. Michelle Anderson, "Marital Immunity, Intimate Relationships and Improper Inferences, *Hastings Law Journal* 54 (2003), p. 1465.

278. There are over a thousand legal benefits to marriage. Some of the most important ones are the right to receive a portion of the estate of a spouse who dies intestate, preference in being appointed as the personal representative of the spouse who dies intestate, the right to spousal benefits statutorily guaranteed to public employees, the opportunities to be covered as a spouse under group life insurance policies issued to an employee, the presumption of joint ownership, and hospital visitation and other rights incident to the medical treatment of a family member.

279. NOW, "Same-Sex Marriage Is a Feminist Issue," http://www.now.org/issues/lgbi/marr-rep.html.

280. Lenore Weitzman, *Divorce Revolution* (New York: Free Press, 1985).

281. Lenora Weitzman, "The Economic Consequences of Divorce Are Still Unequal," *American Sociological Review* 61 (1996), pp. 537–538.

282. See R. R. Peterson, " A Re-evaluation of the Economic Consequences of Divorce," *American Sociological Review* 61 (1996), pp. 528–536; and G. J. Duncan and S. D. Hoffman, "Economic Consequences of Marital Instability," in M. David and T. Smeeding, eds., *Horizonal Equity, Uncertainty and Economic Well-Being* (Chicago: University of Chicago Press, 1985), pp. 427–471.

283. Warren Farrell, *Father and Child Reunion,* hereafter *FACR* (New York: Jeremy Tarcher Putnam, 2001), pp. 162–163.

284. Ibid., p. 163.

285. *WMEM*, p. 88.

286. Martha Burk, *Cult of Power* (New York: Shribner, 2005), pp. 152–153.

287. Shapiro, *Women in American Society,* Chapter 11.

288. Demie Kurz, *For Richer, For Poorer: Confront Divorce* (New York: Routledge, 1995), Chapter 3.

289. Williams, *Still a Man's World,* p. 122.

290. *FACR,* p. 165.

291. William Blackstone, *Commentaries on the Law of England, ed.* T. Coeley (1884), p. 453.

292. Joel Brandes, "Child Custody: History, Definitions, New York Law," *New York Law Journal* (November 28, 2000).

293. Susan Boyd, *Child Custody Law, and Women's Work* (New York: Oxford, 2003), p. 2.

294. Ross Parke and Armin Brott, *Throwaway Dads* (Boston: Houghton Mifflin, 1999), p. 120.

295. Armin Brott, "Include Dad, Don't Just Send Him a Bill," http://mensight magazine.com/Library/includedads.htm.

296. Webster Watnik, *Child Custody Made Simple* (Claremont, CA: Single Parent Press, 2003), p. 36.

297. *FACR*, p. 61.

298. Actually, child support payments tend to be lower the more time fathers spend with their children after divorce or separation. Farrell admits as much. See *FACR*, pp. 125, 192; and Warren Farrell, *The Importance of Fathers,* audiotapes produced and distributed by the author, Side 1.

299. *FACR*, p. 193.

300. Nicole Marcil-Gratton and Celine Le Bourdais, "Custody, Access and Child Support" (Ottawa: Department of Justice, 1999), p. 13.

301. U.S. Census Bureau, "Custodial Mothers and Fathers and Their Child Support" (Washington, DC: U.S. Department of Commerce, 2001).

302. Watnik, *Child Custody*, p. 31.

303. Boyd, *Child Custody Law*, p. 8.

304. Ibid., p. 9.

305. Ibid.

306. Joan Zorza, "How Abused Women Can Use the Law to Help Protect Their Children," in Einat Peled et al., eds. *Ending the Cycle of Violence* (Thousand Oaks, CA: Sage, 1995), pp. 147–169.

307. Having recourse to lawyers in this area has pitfalls for women all by itself. See Karen Winner, *Divorced from Justice* (New York: Harper-Collins, 1996).

308. See Susan Crean, "Anna Karenina, Scarlett O'Hara, and Gail Besaire: Child Custody and Family Law Reform," in Anne Minas, ed., *Gender Basics* (Belmont, CA: Wadsworth, 1993), pp. 508–513.

309. Boyd, *Child Custody Law*, p. 8; Gender Bias Study Committee, "Gender Bias Study of the Court System in Massachusetts," *New England Law Review* 24 (1990), p. 745ff.; and Nancy Polikoff, "Why Are Mothers Losing," *Women's Rights Law Review* 7 (1982), pp. 2–10. Farrell cites two studies that purportedly show that women win 92 percent of the time in contested cases, one based simply on court records from Polk County, Iowa, in 1988, the other done by Michael

Geonoulis for the New Hampshire Department of Health and Human Services in 1991. In his tape *The Future of the Men's Movement,* produced and distributed by the author in 1991, Side 1, Farrell makes an unqualifiedly general claim that women win "over 90 percent" of contested custody cases, as though it holds across the United States, while citing no new evidence. But the evidence I have on this issue drawn from a number of studies gives a quite different picture—fathers win in contested custody cases 38 to 70 percent of the time, even though mothers tend to be the primary caretakers of the children. In addition, there is no record of the Polk County Study on file at Drake University Law School where Farrell claims it was done, and the state of Iowa keeps no comparable data. The other study Farrell cites was not done for the New Hampshire Department of Health and Human Services (NHDHHS) in 1991, as Farrell claims, but for Fathers United For Equal Justice of New Hampshire in 1988. However, that study does claim to be citing data from NHDHHS for 1985 that shows that fathers receive custody in less than 10 percent of contested cases. But this is just not the case. Data for 1985 show that in 22 percent of contested cases, fathers received either sole, joint, or split custody; see *New Hampshire Vital Statistics 1985* (Concord: State Center for Health Statistics, 1985). For 1997, the figure was about 30 percent; see *New Hampshire Vital Statistics 1997* (Concord: State Center for Health Statistics, 1997). Moreover, these percentages are not really low once you take into account that mothers tend to be the primary caretakers of the children.

310. Boyd, *Child Custody Law,* Chapter 7.

311. Some fathers' rights advocates propose interpreting "primary caretaking" to include being the breadwinner, the role men standardly occupy in families, but the sense of caretaking here has to be that of directly ministering to the needs of children. See Cathy Young, *Ceasefire* (New York: Free Press, 1999), p. 216.

312. Boyd, *Child Custody Law,* Chapter 7.

313. *FACR,* p. 126.

314. Farrell argues against using the primary caretaker presumption on the grounds that parity of reasoning would imply that we should also use the prime breadwinner presumption after separation and divorce. Although most women would probably not object to having their ex-husband's continuing financial support added to their personal earnings, the justification for the primary caretaker presumption is not to do whatever happened to have been done before in the marriage. Rather, the presumption is justified on the grounds that it would best serve the interest of any children who have resulted from the marriage. See *FACR,* p. 167.

315. *FACR,* p. 7.

316. Ibid., p. 42.

317. Ibid., p. 48.

318. U.S. Census Bureau, *Living Arrangements of Children, 2001* (Washington, DC: U.S. Department of Commerce, Economics and Statistics Administration, issued July 2005), p. 2.

319. Susan Golombok, *Parenting: What Really Counts?* (London: Routledge, 200), p. 6. Golombok also points out that while some studies indicate the special role of fathers in playing, particularly boisterously, with their children, in Sweden and Israel, where parents have less traditional family roles, no differences between mothers and fathers in the amount or type of play they engage in have been noted p.7.

320. *FACR*, p. 132.

321. Supreme Court of the United States, *Planned Parenthood v. Casey*, 505 U.S. 833 (1992).

322. *FACR*, p. 149.

323. Supreme Court of the United States, *Edward McNamara v. County of San Diego Department of Adoptions*, U.S. Trans Lexis 28 (1988).

324. *FACR*, p. 151.

325. Ibid., p. 135.

326. Ibid., p. 128ff.

327. Pamela Paul, *Pornified* (New York: Henry Holt, 2005), p. 54.

328. Ibid., p. 50.

329. Ibid.

330. Ibid., p. 58.

331. Ibid., pp. 239–240.

332. Catharine MacKinnon, *Feminism Unmodified* (Cambridge, MA: Harvard University, 1987), Chapter 14. See also Gloria Cowan, "Pornography: Conflict Among Feminists," in Jo Freeman, ed., *Women*, 5th ed. (Mountain View, CA: Mayfield Publishing, 1995), pp. 347–364; and Diana Russell, ed., *Making Violence Sexy* (New York: Teachers College Press, 1993). After studies with college students showing that exposure to pornography increases discriminatory attitudes and behavior in men toward women, it has been difficult to get new studies past academic boards monitoring the use of human subjects. If a study's effects are known to be detrimental and there is no proof the damage can be permanently reversed, ethics boards will refuse to allow a similar study to go forward; see Paul *Pornified*, p. 90.

333. Franklin Mark Osanka and Sara Lee Johann, *Sourcebook on Pornography* (New York: Lexington Books, 1989), p. 81.

334. Robert Jensen, "Using Pornography," in Estelle Disch, ed., *Reconstructing Gender*, 3rd ed. (Boston: McGraw-Hill, 2003), pp. 272–273.

335. Ibid., p. 273.

336. Paul *Pornified,* p. 80.

337. Ibid., p. 147.

338. Ibid., p. 105.

339. Ibid., p. 163.

340. Ibid.

341. *WCHWMDS,* p. 176.

342. Dan Taylor and other Shoebox writers, *Shoebox, Greatest Hits and Misses* (China: Hallmark, Licensing Inc., 2006).

343. Ibid., p. 198.

344. *WCHWMDS,* Chapter 7.

345. Ibid., p. 166.

346. Ibid., pp.188–189.

347. *WCHWMDS,* p. 181.

348. Ibid.

349. Ibid., p. 180ff.

350. Ibid., p. 180.

351. Sapiro, *Women in American Society,* p. 248.

352. Ibid.; and Nan Robertson, *The Girls in the Balcony* (New York: Random, 1992), Chapter 10.

353. Pat Arnow, "New York Times Bylines Sideline Women," *Extra!* (July/August 2004).

354. *WCHWMDS,* pp. 266–280.

355. For a recent example, of anti-feminism at the *Times,* see Katha Pollitt, "Desperate Housewives of the Ivy League?" *The Nation* (October 17, 2005).

356. Arnow, *Extra!* p. 14.

357. *WCHWMDS,* pp. 257–258.

358. National Desk, "*New York Times* Poll," *New York Times,* August 20, 1989.

359. *WCHWMDS,* p. 257.

360. Farrell also criticizes Anna Quindlen for saying, "Some of my best friends are men. It is simply that I think women are superior to men." However, Farrell fails to convey the larger context in which Quindlen makes this claim where she recounts the struggles of two women in New York to break down the barriers to their being hired as garbage collectors in the city. Quindlen's piece is serious, but it has that tongue-in-cheek quality that characterizes much of her work. Farrell's quotation out of context ignores all this. See Anna Quindlen, "Life in the 30's," *New York Times,* September 10, 1986.

361. Sheila Gibbons, "Inequalities Persist for Women in Media," *Women's News,* January 21, 2004.

362. Media Tenor Study, "U.S. Television News Ignores Women," *Media Report to Women* (Spring 2003).

363. *WCHWMDS*, pp. 256–322.

364. Martha Lausen's 2005 Celluloid Ceiling Report, http//www.film42.com/feature/Lauzen-2005.esp; and Martha Lauzen, "Women's Portrayal in Television Entertainment," *Media Report to Women* (December 2005).

365. Joe Kelly et al., "Where the Girls Aren't," Seejane.org (February 2006).

366. Media Use Statistics, "Video Game Users," http://medialit.med.sc.edu/mediause.htm.

367. Media Awareness, "Beauty and Body Image in the Media," http://www.media awareness.ca/english/issues/stereotyping/women_and_girls/women_beauty.cfm.

368. See Claire Renzetti and Daniel Curren, *Women, Men and Society*, 3rd ed. (Boston: Allyn and Bacon, 1995), Chapter 6.

369. Edward Clarke, *Sex and Education* (Boston: James R. Osgood and Co., 1873).

370. Gabrielle Lange, "The Gender Bias Debate," *AAUW Outlook* (Spring 1997), p. 14.

371. Wellesley College Center for Research on Women, *How Schools Shortchange Girls*, (New York: Marlowe, 1992).

372. *WCHWMDS*, pp. 250ff.

373. Valerie Lee et al., *The Influence of School Climate on Gender Differences in the Achievement and Engagement of Young Adolescents* (Washington, DC: AAUW Educational Foundation, 1996).

374. AAUW Educational Foundation, *Beyond the Gender Wars* (Washington, DC: AAUW, 2001), p. vi–vii.

375. Ibid., p. 19.

376. Christina Hoff Sommers, *The War Against Boys* (New York: Simon and Schuster, 2000), p. 14, and *WCHWMDS*, p. 255.

377. *WCHWMDS*, p. 234.

378. *Directory of Financial Aids for Women* (El Dorado Hill, CA: Reference Service Press, 2001).

379. Fair Test, "Gender Bias in NCAA Eligibility Requirements," http://www. fairtest.org/. In the early days of the SAT, ETS manipulated test content to improve the average reading scores of men compared to women, but today it refuses to do the same for women—manipulate test content to improve the average mathematical scores of women compared to men. According to one study, the bias in the SAT leads to the yearly exclusion of twelve thousand women from large, competitive flagship

state universities. See D. Leonard and J. Jiang, "Gender Bias and College Predictions of the SATs," *Research in Higher Education* 40 (June 1999).

380. There is also a *Directory of Financial Aids for Minorities* put out by the same publisher, which lists many of these same sources of aid.

381. National Center for Educational Statistics, "Trends in Educational Equity of Girls and Women 2004," http://nces.ed.gov.

382. Phyllis Rosser, "Too Many Women in College?" *Ms.* (Fall 2005), pp. 42–45.

383. Ibid.

384. *FACR.*

SELECTED BIBLIOGRAPHY

AAUW Educational Foundation, *Beyond the Gender Wars.* Washington, DC: AAUW, 2001.

Ayres, Ian and Katherine Baker, "A Separate Crime of Reckless Sex." *University of Chicago Law Review* 22 (2005): 599–666.

Bachman, R., and L. Saltzman. *Violence Against Women.* Washington, DC: U.S. Department of Justice, Bureau of Justice Statistics, 2001.

Benatar, David. "The Second Sexism," *Social Theory and Practice* 29 (2003): 177–210.

Bolles, Richard. *What Color Is Your Parachute?* Berkeley, CA: Ten Speed Press, 2006.

Boyd, Susan. *Child Custody Law, and Women's Work.* New York: Oxford, 2003.

Branden, Nathaniel. *The Six Pillars of Self-Esteem.* New York: Bantam Books, 1994.

Braver, Sanford L., and Diane O'Connell. *Divorced Dads.* New York: Putnam/Berkley, 1999.

Bruce, Tammy. *The New Thought Police.* New York: Crown, 2003.

Bureau of Labor Statistics, Table A-26. "Usual Weekly Earnings of Employed Full-Time Wage and Salary Workers by Detailed Occupation and Sex, Annual Averages, 2003" (unpublished table).

DeCew, Judith Wagner. "The Combat Exclusion and the Role of Women in the Military." *Hypatia* 10 (1995): 56–73.

Dobash, R. Emerson, and Russell Dobash. "Women's Violence to Men in Intimate Relationships." *British Journal of Criminology* 44 (2004): 324–349.

Dutton, Donald, *The Batterer.* New York: Basic, 1995.

Farrell, Warren. *Why Men Are the Way They Are.* New York: Putnam/Berkley, 1988. Also available as a CD and audiotape.

———. *The Myth of Male Power.* New York: Putnam/Berkley, 1994. Also available as a CD and audiotape.

———. *Women Can't Hear What Men Don't Say.* New York: Putnam/Berkley, 1999. Also available as a CD and audiotape.

———. *Father and Child Reunion.* New York: Putnam/Berkley, 2001.

Farrell, Warren. *Why Men Earn More.* DVD. New York: Amacom, 2005.

———. *The Best Interests of the Child.* DVD. 2006.

Fekete, John. *Moral Panic.* Montreal: Robert Davies Publishing, 1994.

Franke, Linda Bird. *Ground Zero.* New York: Simon & Schuster, 1997.

Gelles, Richard J., and Murray A. Straus. *Intimate Violence.* (New York: Simon & Schuster, 1988).

Gilder, George. *Men and Marriage.* Gretna, LA: Pelican, 1987.

Goldberg, Bernard. *Bias.* Washington, DC: Regnery, 2002.

Gomez-Preston, Cherly. *When No Means No.* New York: Carol Publishing, 1993.

Gornick, Janet, and Marcia Meyers. *Families That Work.* New York: Russell Sage, 2003.

Gurian, Michael, and Stevens, Kathy. *The Minds of Boys.* San Francisco, CA: Jossey-Bass, 2005.

Hochschild, Arlie. *Second Shift.* New York: Penguin, 2003. First published 1989 by Viking Press.

Jeffers, Susan. *Feel the Fear and Do It Anyway.* New York: Ballantine Books, 1987.

Jensen, Joan. "Native American Women and Agriculture: A Seneca Case Study." In *Unequal Sisters,* edited by Ellen DuBois and Vicki Ruiz, pp. 51–65. New York: Routledge, 1990.

Koss, Mary, et al. "The Scope of Rape: Incidence and Prevalence of Sexual Aggression and Victimization in a National Sample of Higher Education Students," *Journal of Counseling and Clinical Psychology* 55, no. 2 (1987): 162–170.

LaFramboise, Donna. *The Princess at the Window.* Toronto: Penguin Books, 1996.

Lee, Valerie, et al. *The Influence of School Climate on Gender Differences in the Achievement and Engagement of Young Adolescents.* Washington, DC: AAUW Educational Foundation, 1996.

Leivick, Sarah. "Use of Battered Woman Syndrome to Defend the Abused and Prosecute the Abuser." *Georgetown Journal of Gender and Law* 6 (2005): 391–404.

Lips, Hilary. *Women, Men, and Power.* Mountain View, CA: Mayfield, 1991.

Lynch, Frederick R. *The Diversity Machine.* New York: Simon & Schuster, 1997.

McDowell, Charles. "False Allegations." *Forensic Science Digest* 11 (December 1985): 57–75.

Nathanson, Paul, and Katherine Young. *Legalizing Misandry.* Montreal: McGill University Press, 2006.

Nielsen, Linda. *Embracing Your Father.* New York: McGraw Hill, 2004.

Patai, Daphne. *Professing Feminism.* New York: Lexington Books, 2003.

Paul, Pamela. *Pornified: How Pornography Is Transforming Our Lives, Our Relationships, and Our Families.* New York: Henry Holt, 2005.

Peterson, R. R. "A Re-evaluation of the Economic Consequences of Divorce." *American Sociological Review* 61 (1996): 528–536.

Philpot, Carol L., et al. *Bridging Separate Gender Worlds.* Washington, DC: American Psychological Association, 1997.

Renzetti, Claire, and Daniel Curren. *Women, Men and Society.* 3rd ed. Boston: Allyn and Bacon, 1995.

Robertson, Nan. *Girls in the Balcony.* New York: Random, 1992.

Rooser, Sue. *Women's Health—Missing from U.S. Medicine.* Bloomington, IN: Indiana University Press, 1994.

Rosser, Phyllis. "Too Many Women in College?" *Ms.,* Fall 2005, 42–45.

Saunders, Daniel. "Are Physical Assaults by Wives and Girlfriends a Major Social Problem? A Review of the Literature." *Violence Against Women* 8 (2002): 1424–1448.

Schiebinger, Londa. *Has Feminism Changed Science?* Cambridge: Harvard University Press, 1999.

Sommers, Christina Hoff. *Who Stole Feminism?* New York: Simon & Schuster, 1994.

Sterba, James P. *How to Make People Just.* Lanham: Roman & Littlefield, 1988.

———. *Three Challenges to Ethics.* New York: Oxford University Press, 2001.

Sterba, James P., and Linda Lemoncheck. *Sexual Harrassment: Issues and Answers.* New York: Oxford University Press, 2001.

Stewart, Mary White. *Ordinary Violence.* Westport, CT: Bergin & Garvey, 2002.

Straus, Murray, Richard Gelles, and Suzanne Steinmetz. *Behind Closed Doors.* New York: Anchor, 1980.

Straus, Murray. "Physical Assaults by Wives: A Major Social Problem" In *Women, Men and Gender: Ongoing Debates,* edited by M.R. Walsh, pp. 67–87. New Haven, CT: Yale University Press, 1997, 67–87.

———. "The Controversy Over Domestic Violence by Women." In *Violence and Intimate Relationships,* edited by Arriage and S. Oskamp, 283–317. Thousand Oaks: Sage, 1999.

Straus, Murray, et al. "The Revised Conflict Tactics Scales (CTS2)." *Journal of Family Issues* 17 (May 1996): 283–317.

Sukiennik, Diane, et al. *The Career Fitness Program.* New York: Prentice Hall, 2003.

Sumrall, Amber, and Dena Taylor, *Sexual Harassment: Women Speak Out.* Freedom, CA: The Crossing Press, 1992.

Tjadens, P., and N. Thoennes. *Full Report of the Prevalence, Incidence and Consequences of Violence Against Women.* Washington, DC: National Institute of Justice and Centers for Disease Prevention, 2000.

United Nations Development Programme, *Human Development Report.* New York: Oxford University Press, 1995.

Warshaw, Robin. *I Never Called It Rape.* New York: Harper and Row, 1988.

Weitzman, Lenore. *Divorce Revolution.* New York: Free Press, 1985.

Wellesley College Center for Research on Women, *How Schools Shortchange Girls.* New York: Marlowe, 1992.

INDEX

Bold numbers indicate material in graphs, photographs, and tables.